JOHN UNTERECKER

Foreword

Some poets find an immediate audience. Others wait years to
be discovered. Hart Crane is in neither category. For his
poetry, which was initially championed in the twenties by a
small but very vocal group of admirers, has steadily grown in
popularity. Thirty-five years after his suicide and only sixty-
eight years after his birth, his poetry was available either in
the original or in translation in every civilized country on
earth. Crane himself, in the words of the literary historian
R. W. B. Lewis, was in the mid-sixties properly acknowledged
to be "one of the finest modern poets in our language, and one
of the dozen-odd major poets in American history."

During his lifetime, his poetry had been treated as an odd
amalgam of nineteenth-century American themes, French Symbolist literary techniques, and English Metaphysical rhetoric.
Just after his death, critics had a field day locating the authors
and the philosophical systems that had influenced him, in the
process often devoting a great deal of their energy to debates
concerning the relative "success" or "failure" of his long poem
The Bridge.

Now that that initial hullabaloo has ended and we have

grown less strident in qualitative battles, a clear picture of the man and his work is beginning to emerge. Instead of being seen as a person influenced by other men and their ideas, Crane is now recognized to be a great synthesizer: a man consciously welding disparate materials into coherent and aesthetically satisfying poems. Eloquent and witty, he is credited —like Eliot and Hopkins, both of whom he admired—with being a remarkable technician, one of the finest literary craftsmen of recent times.

But craftsmanship is only a machine for turning human emotion into art. What we admire in Crane's work and finally, I think, what we admire in any great poet is neither theme nor craft but rather the subtlety of feeling that has been forced into still more subtle form. Such disciplined emotion can work not only on us but for us—offering us "expression" of that for which otherwise we have no adequate speech.

Manipulating passion into poems, Crane is a major poet because for each of us he speaks private truth—the absolute, untranslatable, unique truth that is the core of what we choose to call the self.

HART CRANE

HART CRANE

AN INTRODUCTION

TO THE POETRY

HERBERT A. LEIBOWITZ

COLUMBIA UNIVERSITY PRESS

NEW YORK & LONDON

1968

Herbert A. Leibowitz is Assistant Professor
of English at Columbia University.

To my Father and Mother

Copyright © 1968 Columbia University Press
Library of Congress Catalog Card Number: 68–13559
Printed in the United States of America

Acknowledgments

In the course of writing this book I have incurred many debts which I am pleased to repay now. Professors John Unterecker and F. W. Dupee of Columbia University supervised the dissertation which formed the nucleus of this book, and, besides sharing their wide knowledge of modern poetry and of Hart Crane, kept me to a high standard of prose. Professor Robert Austerlitz' meticulous reading and suggestions on organization and terminology helped greatly in improving the final manuscript. My colleague and friend, George Stade, not only read the work with an exacting critical eye, but also gave of his time for many lively and stimulating conversations about particular Crane poems and general problems of poetic theory and style. The many valuable suggestions of my friends Dudley Flanm and Nathan Lyons enabled me to tighten the argument and clarify the presentation. I should also like to thank the following: Mrs. Dedee Rigg and Mrs. Gladys Mizumo Weintraub for typing an often illegible manuscript on short notice; and Cody Barnard, my editor, who patiently withstood scores of questions. I am particularly grateful to Carol Berkin who undertook a host of important editorial chores. Finally, I would like to thank Irene Skolnick, the "unfettered leewardings" of whose mind was a source of unfailing support during the writing of this book. Needless to say, whatever faults remain are mine, not theirs.

Permission to quote from the following is gratefully acknowledged: *White Buildings*, manuscript, Hart Crane Collection; by permission of the Columbia University Libraries. The list of words on pp. 108–9 from *Concordance to the Poems of Hart Crane*, manuscript, prepared by Professors Maurice Kramer of Brooklyn College and Hilton Landry of Kent State University. *The Letters of Hart Crane, 1916–1932*, edited by Brom Weber; by permission of Brom Weber. Published by the University of California Press, 1965. *The Complete Poems and Selected Letters and Prose of Hart Crane*, by Hart Crane, Black and Gold Library $5.95; by permission of Liveright Publishers, N.Y. © 1966 copyright 1933 Liveright Publishing Corp.

Herbert A. Leibowitz

Columbia University
March, 1968

Contents

HART CRANE

Poetry is a purging of the world's poverty and change and evil and death. It is a present perfecting, a satisfaction in the irremediable poverty of life.

WALLACE STEVENS, *Adagia*

It may be foreseen in like manner that poets living in democratic times will prefer the delineation of passions and ideas to that of persons and achievements. The language, the dress, and the daily actions of men in democracies are repugnant to conceptions of the ideal. . . . This forces the poet constantly to search below the external surface which is palpable to the senses, in order to read the inner soul; and nothing lends itself more to the delineation of the ideal than the scrutiny of the hidden depths in the immaterial nature of man. . . . The destinies of mankind, man himself taken aloof from his country and his age, and standing in the presence of Nature and of God, with his passions, his doubts, his rare prosperities and inconceivable wretchedness, will become the chief, if not the sole, theme of poetry.

ALEXIS DE TOCQUEVILLE, *Democracy in America*

> —O Choir, translating time
> Into what multitudinous Verb the suns
> And synergy of waters ever fuse, recast
> In myriad syllables,—Psalm of Cathay!
> O Love, thy white, pervasive Paradigm . . . !
>
> HART CRANE, *Atlantis*

CHAPTER 1

Life and Criticism

A strong temptation arises to read into Hart Crane's life an emblematic symmetry and to interpret it as yet another version of the *poète maudit* driven to suicide by his own compulsive nature and by American philistinism. Crane was born at the turn of the century, in Garretsville, Ohio, one of those small towns that interrupted the vast stretch of the prairies across the middle of America. The family moved, first, to Warren, Ohio, a more prosperous, bustling town than Garretsville, and then to Cleveland. Crane's childhood and early manhood were thus spent in that inauspicious atmosphere in which the religion of business (the rubber and automobile factories were its Temple) and the older evangelical creeds together held the allegiance of the majority of citizens. The Middle West was, for Crane, as for many writers, a cultural desert, despite a few oases—Ernest Bloch, for example, taught at the Cleveland Conservatory of Music, and Crane formed friendships with the few people (musicians, writers, and painters like William Sommer and Ernest Nelson, the latter a European emigré), who had a lively and wide knowledge of all the arts and exchanged ideas about the experiments of modernism. It was a place from which as an adolescent Crane plotted his escape and to which he always returned with great reluctance. He refused to become the misfit poet of Winesburg, Ohio, isolated and broken by provincial stupidity. When he was forced to live in exile in Akron and Cleveland, he subsisted on news of the New York scene that his friends sent him.

His family life was equally distressing. His father, Clarence Crane, a fairly successful candy manufacturer who thought that writing poetry was an impractical and effeminate pursuit, preached the businessman's gospel that his son should put his mind to a career that would earn a good living. Crane resented this attitude, considering it a censure not only of his hopes to write poetry but of his very being. Consequently, most of his life, in spite of occasional periods of amity, Crane could not overcome his hatred of his father whom he also blamed, somewhat unfairly, for mistreating his mother.

Grace Crane was a high-strung, unhappy, demanding woman, who made her impressionable son confidant and partner in the chronic quarrels, separations, and reconciliations of her marriage. Not surprisingly, as his friend Solomon Grunberg recounts,[1] Crane once dreamed that he was searching through his mother's entrails, like a Greek diviner, for the secret of his life. He never gained the definitive knowledge he sought. At nineteen, with unusual precocity, he rebuked his mother with the charge that "for the last eight years my youth has been a rather bloody battleground for yours and for father's sex life and troubles."[2] That sexual disturbance divided and haunted him to the end of his days. As he later put it in "Quaker Hill," he was forced to "shoulder the curse of sundered parentage."

This "sundered parentage" became the troubled heart of his poetic struggles, too, for the masculine and feminine parts of his sensibility did not always fuse and work smoothly. Crane was a homosexual, and this fact and the consequences of it burdened him until death.

Poetic imagination, as Crane often insisted, requires both a surrender to sensation and experience and an intellectual shaping of those materials into significant form. This balance is necessary for the poet to discriminate true from false vision, to resist the allure of appearances and counterfeit images. A tentative solution to the problem is given in "The Wine Menagerie":

> New thresholds, new anatomies! Wine talons
> Build freedom up about me and distill
> This competence—to travel in a tear
> Sparkling alone, within another's will.

Through the release afforded by wine, the poet attains a temporary concord. Like Whitman boldly announcing in *Song of Myself*, "Unscrew the locks from the doors!/Unscrew the doors from their jambs!" Crane proclaims that barriers have been thrown down and he can now see unimpeded into the essence of things. The wine is claw-like, endowing him with the strength to grasp onto the "new thresholds"—the talons belong perhaps to the "leopard ranging always in the brow" that "Asserts a vision in the slumbering gaze."

The imagination is active, masculine, constructive, like a cutting tool; it builds freedom and distills poetic competence. It uses its power not to prey on the world but to cut away whatever veils perception. The imagination escapes the solipsistic trap, traveling outside itself and coupling, so to speak, with the world, "another's will." This requires a prior openness: his "blood dreams a receptive smile/Wherein new purities are snared." (The sexual imagery is explicitly feminine, and Crane frequently associates susceptibility with tenderness.) That this atmosphere of visionary love does not last long is unimportant. What matters is that he can endure the loneliness of the journey because the tear—a drop of wine, empathy, Blake's "Intellectual Thing"—sparkles in the light of his excited discoveries of the peaceful unity of self and other. He has passed beyond the "spiritual gates" that were shut to him in "Emblems of Conduct."

This reciprocal process of submission and creation is parodied by Crane earlier in the poem. In stanza three, which is set in a bar, the urchin (the young Crane) watches fascinatedly the hostile sexual byplay of a man and a woman (his parents): "Regard the forceps of the smile that takes her./ Percussive sweat is spreading to his hair. Mallets,/Her eyes, unmake an instant of the world." There is a confusion or usurping of roles here which deters proper vision. When the feminine side becomes aggressive, brutal, and destructive, the eyes "unmake" the world instead of wreathing or building it; the threshold is made of "imitation onyx wainscoting"; the smile is a surgical claw that anatomizes in the way lust anatomizes Regan's heart in *King Lear,* and sweat, not tears, is distilled by the pounding of their mutual enmity. Where love is missing vision cannot sustain itself.

Because he is on guard against self-pity, Crane is generally reticent about dredging up memories of his childhood when he was hostage to his parents' emotional battles, but he cannot wholly unburden himself of disagreeable recollections or cease taking a kind of spiritual inventory. "I was promised an improved infancy," he exclaims bitterly in "Passage," a crucial autobiographical poem written in 1925. Is his imagination strong enough to convert his passage from childhood to adulthood into the stuff of poetry, Crane asks himself? He is at first hopeful, but memory turns out to be the "casual louse" that blights his poems, for although he had joined the "entrainments of the wind," that is, was buoyed by the prospect of ransoming his past, the wind, creative inspiration, dies down: "Memory, committed to the page, had broke." "The dozen particular decimals of time" remain fractional experiences. The question of memory lingers as the central debate of Crane's last great poem, "The Broken Tower."

The second act of Crane's tragically exemplary life roughly corresponds with the heady days of the literary renaissance that began about 1917 and continued through the twenties. A sensualist who enjoyed staging bizarre scenes, a spendthrift of the emotions—like F. Scott Fitzgerald, there was little in his nature that was fussy, prudent, or self-protective—he best typifies the period's euphoria and brashness, its pleasure sprees and serious ambitions, its failure to transform American life as it had promised—and its final collapse. The mania, the coruscating brilliance, the desperate, homeless, voyaging spirit, all these are more than mere presences or random episodes in his poetry: they are its animating principle.

Crane died while America was in the throes of the Depression. Like Dreiser and Sherwood Anderson, he flirted with communism, but his consciousness was not political or theoretic. He could not endure the ideological disputes or the tedious practical duties the party required. He was not disciplined enough. And he thought too highly of poetry to prostitute it by writing propaganda in verse. Atlantis, his wondrous kingdom of the spirit, was sinking in the sea, as he well knew, and he needed to clutch at any illusion. The paralysis of American institutions, the country's failure to realize its spiritual mission, demoralized Crane because it was bound up in his own mind with his own galling failure to write the epic poem of the United States.

The link between Crane's life, poetry, and times is an undeniably close one. If, at times, like Donne, he spoke of his poetry as "my art, map of my misery," he also felt a devotion to it that represented, most movingly, his deepest piety toward life. Like Dylan Thomas, in his rash, impecunious way, he held himself accountable to nothing but his talent. And that, he felt at the end of his life, he had betrayed and wasted. As a man, Crane was heedless of consequences, imbalanced, vulnerable, an Ishmael whose suicidal urges were finally acted out in the mild waters of the Gulf of Mexico. The poetry is faithful to the life and the death: to the intensely human yearning for supreme beauty, to the almost heroic pushing back of violence from within and without. Art, his harshly beneficent deity, was what made life worth living. "The imagination is the only thing worth a damn," [3] he once wrote to Gorham Munson.

What kind of man was Crane? Elizabeth Hardwick has suggested that he was essentially a *happy* man, that he profited from his temperamental inability to withhold himself from any activity, be it listening to music, talking, dancing, falling in love, or writing verse.[4] This is too easy. Miss Hardwick correctly notes Crane's Nietzschean gaiety, but she neglects the grievous suffering, the sudden seizures of black melancholy, and the depth, degradation, and tragic buffoonery that make him such a Dostoyevskian figure. Ravaged equally by his debauches and spirituality, he appears like a St. Sebastian in Renaissance paintings. Certainly he was not an unprivileged man, and his marginal life was not unexamined—he had no shallow myth of the doomed and dissolute poet—he simply could not solve the contradictions of his nature and upbringing, or decide the rival claims of the sensuous and spiritual worlds. He knew that, like Columbus, "few evade full measure of their fate," and to the end strove for an equilibrium that might allow him to write. That balance eluded him, mainly because there was so *much* in the man to be expressed.

In this and other traits Crane is an American Keats. Both matured rapidly as poets; both were extraordinary letter writers; both were endowed with a genial, raffish nature; both were self-educated; both worshipped the genius of the Elizabethan poets; both were delightful companions, though Crane, when drunk, became bumptious and overbearing; both were beset by family and money problems; and both died prematurely. In the busy and careless life of the twenties, Crane's excesses were casually indulged and forgiven by his friends. Believing in his talent and understanding that he was hounded by Furies he could not appease, his friends did not condemn his conduct. They bailed him out of jail, rescued him from a waterfront bar where he had been beaten by sailors he tried to pick up, lent him money, got him jobs, and listened to his harangues, jokes, tireless plans, and literary comments about their work.[5]

In a letter to his mother, written at the end of 1923, he delivers a characteristically gentle lecture in the course of defending his vocation as poet and attempting to calm her agitation and confusion:

> One can live happily on very little, I have found, if the mind and spirit have some definite objective in view. . . . If I can't continue to create the sort of poetry that is my intensest and deepest component in life—then it all means very little to me, and then I might as well tie myself up to some smug ambition and "success" (the common idol that every Tom, Dick, and Harry is bowing to everywhere). But so far, as you know, I only grow more and more convinced that what I naturally have to give the world in my own terms—is worth giving, and I'll go through a number of ordeals yet to pursue a natural course. . . . I, too, have had to fight a great deal just to *be myself* and *know myself* at all. . . . Suffering is a real purification, and the worst thing I have always had to say against Christian Science is that it wilfully avoided suffering, without a certain measure of which any true happiness cannot be fully realized.[6]

There is something almost jaunty in Crane's sanguine acceptance of suffering. His remaining years tested his mettle, his staying power, and his willingness to live himself out for his art. Although the burden wore down his faith that "one can live happily on very little," especially when he had to take on hackwork to eke out a living, to a remarkable degree Crane hewed to the independent and courageous task he set of knowing and being himself. "It is to be learned—/This cleaving and this burning,/But only by the one who/Spends out himself again," Crane wrote in "Legend." He learned the cost of "this cleaving and this burning," in his bones, but he never found the artist's role as suffering servant of an unachieved ideal congenial or a badge of spiritual superiority. He never believed in the "holiness of failure" [7] (to use Waldo Frank's phrase). When his resilience finally snapped and he could not make a new beginning, he chose, as we know, to die, but it was neither an inevitable nor a martyr's death. It was the culmination of a peculiarly American life.

The man—dreams, blemishes, misjudgments, abundance, and all—is in the poems. Their appeal lies in the romance of experience they convey, in the glamor and color with which Crane invests his own interior voyages. Crane's consciousness, though compulsive, is open-ended, unfinished, constantly in the process of being remade for the sake of a rich and jubilant state of being he calls Cathay and upon which he confers the attributes of divinity and infinitude. The adventures which find the poet living at his nerve endings and spending himself out again and again generate suspense and drama: will his gamble succeed? and, overcoming the "brutality of circumstance," [8] will he be crowned with the transcendent vision he longs for? or the death he must confront and defy? The poems have the ceremonial grandeur of a Pageant of Being. They speak with a directness and intimacy that are as rare as they are authentic. Their occasional swagger is not that of a poseur but of a Blake who with inspired rage denounces all the false gods and creeds that inhibit joy and the emergence of the whole man. All unpleasant facts that jeopardize his salvation are not willfully excluded but are resolutely incorporated into the poet's experience and the poem itself. Crane's major theme, like Blake's, is how to bring about in every man the "lineaments of satisfied desire."

II

The New Criticism and Verbal Excess

That Crane's rank in twentieth-century American poetry is still unsettled is not surprising, since his poetic achievement, though large, is uneven. Crane's reputation among poets as diverse as Dylan Thomas,[9] Louis Simpson,[10] and Robert Lowell has remained steadily high. Lowell, for example, has admired the "tremendous power" and the "fulness of experience" in Crane's poems.[11] And even Crane's most violent detractors, Yvor Winters foremost among them, concede that Crane possessed a lyrical gift of uncommon magnitude. The case against Crane's verbal excesses has been made by America's leading magistrates of New and Moral Criticism—R. P. Blackmur, Allen Tate, and Yvor Winters—[12] who, while acknowledging Crane's talent and the continual spell his poems cast, have argued that he let words manipulate him, that he put forward incoherent ideas, and that as a result, he was a magnificent failure: a rare exotic bird, nice to have around for his colorful plumage, so long as he kept away from the other birds in the poetic aviary.

It is not easy to write about Crane, for his poetry is so vilified and misconstrued, is so ticketed with ideas and intentions, by partisan and opponent alike, that the feeling or experience in the poem is often lost or overlooked. The poems are seen as coded messages of some vague mysticism or as grandiose metaphysical and mythical pronouncements.[13] He is castigated as an obscurantist, a solipsist, a sentimental idealist, an irrationalist, a pernicious influence on other poets, and a purveyor of hokum. Or he is talked of as an Aesthetic Roaring Boy (his nickname in the twenties) who failed in his bid to become a latter-day Whitman.[14] There is just enough truth in these accusations to make calm critical judgment difficult; and there is also something uncompromising about Crane's poetic style and moral conduct that seems to affront a critic like Winters, who patronizes, hectors, and censures him as if he were a naughty schoolboy.

This discomfort with his work and moral outlook is often a discomfort with Romanticism and idealism, both of which are deemed dangerous and deplorably immature, especially in Crane's version of them. To his critics, Romanticism is a heretical doctrine, "spilt religion," [15] as T. E. Hulme called it, that is responsible for unloosing chaos on the modern world. When the poet no longer anchors himself to a stable community with a fixed body of values, so the argument runs, he ends up recreating the discarded order in his mind and attaching too much importance to personality. This misguided effort to secure personal salvation at any cost results in sloppy feelings and the imprecise language of bad poems. The Romantic indulges in bravado and self-deceit, in what Randall Jarrell once wittily named Crane's "Rube Goldberg rhetoric." [16]

Crane would have agreed with Wallace Stevens' maxim that "A dead romantic is a falsification," [17] and he would also have approved another Stevens adage, "the romantic exists in precision as well as in imprecision." [18] How one stands on this crucial issue affects one's evaluation of Crane. For he is incontrovertibly a Romantic poet. In genre, theme, structure, and language, his art resembles, continues, and modifies that of the great nineteenth-century Romantic poets, from Keats and Shelley to Whitman and Rimbaud. Like them, he chose to ignore some of the middle range of experience in favor of evoking narrower and more intense states of consciousness. That is why his poems seem to have the texture of dreams and reveries—layers of images, associations, displacements, condensations, and symbolic transformations. These properties belong to the Romantic poem, as do Crane's preoccupation with vision and knowledge, and the high place assigned poetry as subject of his struggle for self-definition.

The other specific errors Crane is accused of propounding are laid down most forcibly in Yvor Winters' essay on Crane. First of all, Crane accepted uncritically the ideas of Emerson and Whitman that reason was "the source of all evil" and "the adversary of impulse" and that "the automatic man, the unreflective creature of impulse, is the ideal." [19] Second, he believed that man and indeed all creation are good and infallibly progressing towards future perfection. This "optimistic system," [20] according to Winters, led Crane to "glorify change as change";[21] in pursuit of mystic sensations, he cultivated the ideal of gratifying all impulses. Most dangerously, if one follows Crane's vague theories, he is led to a moral relativism in which all values and subjective guesses are interchangeable: a state of anarchy. Crane was "a saint of the wrong religion." [22]

"The poet," Emerson remarked, "will tell us how it is with him, and all men will be richer in his fortune"—[23] and his misfortune, Crane might have added. For Winters and, to a lesser extent, for Tate, Crane was telling ecstatic lies in his poetry, evading experience by taking refuge in a hermetically sealed verbal world that served to satisfy a profound emotional need: poetry as therapy. In effect, his spiritual and poetic folly comes down to advocating mysticism in an hysterical fashion and to coveting unattainable states of being, which somehow destroy the ordinances of reason. Because it is the product of a histrionic sensibility that avoids method or at least comes perilously close to spurning *necessary* fixed and objective boundaries, his poetry is morally unreliable. Its excitability has a palpable design on the reader: to permit him the luxury of an "anything goes" philosophy. The ideal exists only in the shadowy mind of the poet, not in reality, and to make matters worse, he obstinately refuses to see or admit the existence of immutable laws outside the self.

These are serious objections that need to be met squarely at the outset. They rest, I think, on unacceptable premises. For one, all talk of the higher consciousness cannot be dismissed as mystical nonsense or irresponsible hedonism. If the visionary—and he need not be exclusively a poet; he might be an architect like Louis Sullivan or a dancer like Isadora Duncan—feels an unseen power moving in him and affecting the way he sees the world, he is not simply deserting the visible world for the invisible or substituting foresight for sight. Although for the visionary poet, in Stevens' words, "What we see in the mind is as real to us as what we see by the eye," [24] subjectivity is not licensed to say all or show all. One is conscious that the poet's experiences and even the transcendental flights are rooted in, or referred to, a world of fact, not a world of ghostly words. A hard particularity is present even in Crane's most dithyrambic passages. The "pure possession" takes place in a real Bleecker Street. Many of the poems in Key West—"Royal Palm," "O Carib Isle!" and "The Air Plant," for instance—etch the tropical countryside, its flora and fauna, and its unbearable heat with a stunning sensuous exactness.

"No one," Santayana observes in his essay on Dante, "would deserve this name of [visionary] poet . . . if real sights and sounds never impressed him; and he would hardly deserve it either, if they impressed him only physically, and for what they are in themselves. His sensibility creates his ideal." [25] Santayana then goes on to rebut the charge of moral relativism:

> to have an ideal does not mean so much to have any image in the fancy, but rather to take a consistent moral attitude towards all the things of this world, to judge and coordinate our interests, to establish a hierarchy of good and evils, and to value events and persons, not by a casual personal impression or instinct, but according to their real nature and tendency. So understood, an ultimate ideal is no mere vision of the philosophical dreamer, but a powerful and passionate force in the poet and the orator. It is the voice of his love or hate, of his hope or sorrow, idealizing, challenging, or condemning the world.[26]

A fervent votary of the ideal, a Platonist aspiring to the highest good, Crane did not deny things as they are for the sake of that ideal, even though reality was for him often intolerable. The epigraph to "Quaker Hill," taken from the "sublime" Isadora Duncan's *Autobiography,* strikes the correct rueful note of aware disenchantment: "I see only the ideal. But no ideals have ever been fully successful on this earth."

Most of Crane's poems register this pattern of aspiration and imperfection, of assurance and despair, of tension and stoical resignation.

Crane or the Romantic poet or the idealist, then, does not set up the sovereignty of impulse and waywardness that Winters ridicules. Quite the contrary. "The one true hierarchy of values in the world is the hierarchy of consciousness," [27] Waldo Frank wrote in *Our America,* a book that strongly influenced Crane's thinking; the poet is selective as well as inclusive. Winters has misconstrued Crane's utopian moods by dismissing them as shallow and naïve proclamations of a world Crane does not believe really exists. This willful misunderstanding can perhaps be traced to the hybris of reason in Winters' scheme. In a wonderful letter Crane himself pointed out to Winters that if he were guilty of an "alert blindness," Winters was the victim of a "blind alertness" that masks under the guise of logic an impulse to authoritarian order. Crane adroitly handled Winters' moral bullying, warning him to "Watch out . . . that you don't strangulate yourself with some countermethod of your own!" [28]

The fears of a conservative rationalist like Winters are warranted in only one thing: the visionary does indeed wish to overthrow the authority of rules in order to set in its place some unprecedented (but carefully meditated) edifice, a new form of experience that expresses both the individuality of the artist and the finest instincts of the community. "We must somehow touch the clearest veins of eternity flowing through the crowds around us," Crane wrote to Alfred Stieglitz, "or risk being the kind of glorious cripples that have missed some part of their inheritance." [29] Crane seldom spoke cant about freedom. He was reacting to more than his own emotions. Like Blake he conceived of the poet as a revolutionary whose task was not canonizing the self, but challenging and condemning the faulty values of established society that are frequently rationalized as immutable laws when in fact they are expedient social arrangements. The poet articulated a new social ideal that hopefully might bring into being a humane and reasonable order. This fact must be stressed if we are not to misunderstand Crane's attitude to the machine. Almost alone among the poets of his generation he grasped the need for poetry to venture into the harsh domain of contemporary technology. He was not merely awed by the power of the machine, for by itself that power was amoral, but it was a new spiritual *fact* in human life that could not be disregarded or wished away and that could be a useful educative force. Crane recognized that change is as much a law of life as repetition or habit, but this is not an automatic preference for the new over the old. Crane was not a mindless idolator of change. It was evident to him, as it was to other artists at the time, that in the wake of the First World War the old order was dying. He believed that a "new order of consciousness" could rise phoenix-like from the ashes of the old. "What is now proved was once only imagined," Blake had said. (Blake, it should be remembered, was one of Crane's self-styled heroes.) "The great energies about us cannot be transformed . . . into a higher quality of life," Crane explained to Stieglitz, in a letter of great eloquence and camaraderie, by staying within "predetermined and set boundaries," by walking "ably over an old track bedecked with all kinds of signposts and 'championship records.'" What is needed is the visionary artist, who, possessed by an "intense but always misty realization of what *can* be done if potentialities are fully freed, released," gathers "together those dangerous interests outside of [himself] into that purest projection of [himself]. It is really not a projection in any but a loose sense, for I feel more and more that in the absolute sense the artist *identifies* himself with life."[30] This Stieglitz had done with his camera and Crane wished to do with his poetry.

Thus in contrast to Eliot, Crane tried to come to grips with a new age in a more prophetic way. Long before he announced himself a convert to Classicism, Royalism, and Catholicism, Eliot had written that Blake had been sorely mistaken in overturning orthodox tradition and inventing a new one to replace it replete with its own sacred books.[31] Comparing Crane's position with that of Eliot and Hulme, from the distance of fifty years it is plausible to argue that their conservative reaction, with its literary dogmas and politics of nostalgia, in many ways was a spiritual retreat and as great a denial of reality as anything Crane put forward, and surely fulfilled an emotional need for order above all else. This does not mean, of course, that Crane was Eliot's intellectual peer; rather, that he was a truer spokesman for his age and a harbinger of the future. In his untidy way, Crane measured the crisis of modernism with real distinction, and his search for new syntheses deserves a sympathetic hearing.

Crane's prescience and intelligence in describing the cultural changes around him have not as yet been adequately appreciated. The letters amply document his keen appraisal of the dilemma even though he does not offer a program of social particulars to implement these changes:

> The validity of a work of art is situated in contemporary real-
> ity to the extent that the artist must honestly anticipate the
> realization of his vision in "action" (as an actively operating
> principle of communal works and faith), and I don't mean
> by this that his procedure requires any bona fide evidences
> directly and personally signalled, nor even any physical signs
> or portents. The darkness is part of his business. It has al-
> ways been taken for granted, however, that his intuitions were
> salutary and that his vision either sowed or epitomized "ex-
> perience" (in the Blakeian sense). Even the rapturous and
> explosive destructivism of Rimbaud presupposes this, even his
> lonely hauteur demands it for any estimation or appreciation.
> (The romantic attitude must at least have the background of
> an age of faith, whether approved or disproved no matter).[32]

This extract is a typical statement of Crane's, and reveals a number of essential facts of his position. Crane's own "roman-tic attitude" was situated in a faithless age; the validity of his vision would and did inevitably arouse opposition and misun-derstanding, as he well knew. The poet, in the words of Whit-man's "Passage to India," launches "superior universes" through the imagination's excursive powers. This of course is precisely the Romantic enterprise that Hulme mistrusted and wished to legislate against, but it is not that voyage of the ego soaring giddily through space in its verbal balloon that Hulme derided. It has social and political consequences rooted in the immediate present. From Emerson and Whitman on, the con-ception was popularized that the poet had a valuable social job to perform: to give graceful shape to the inchoate mass, the stunted Genius of the States. The poet stood at the center of his people's life, even if ignored by them, ministering to a felt need: his "primal warblings," [33] in telling of new "auroras," provided an antidote to the sloth and materialism of the masses. He was a spiritual pioneer who redirected and humanized the will. Artistic activity turned forward and back: back to a usable past and forward to a better future; Whitman's "rondure of the world" was America in the present.

For Crane, the visionary and the aesthetic were inextricably tied to social rehabilitation. Like such cultural journalists as Van Wyck Brooks, Paul Rosenfeld, and Waldo Frank, he, too, found the technological civilization America had built up deficient in beauty and vision. The engines of denial set in motion by the Puritan mentality had to be stopped, to be replaced by the nonutilitarian satisfactions of the spirit. For Frank and for Brooks, though not for Rosenfeld, the machine was the villain, the latest and most capital Puritan engine. When Crane first arrived in New York in 1917, the reexaminations of American tradition and the sorting out of which legacies were useful for the new urban communities were in full swing, and he undoubtedly was affected by the debate. If American civilization were truly to come of age, Crane insisted, it had to annex the machine to poetry.

I am not suggesting that Crane held his ideas with a serene confidence in their absolute truth and certain adoption by American society. Certainly his thoughts fluctuated; certainly he had moments of gaudy optimism that the evils of the American present would be soon ameliorated; and certainly the new had a magical allure for him because he lived in an atmosphere of contingency. He was not, however, a moral epicurean or an intellectual hypocrite, and for these reasons his faithfulness to the spirit of modernism is so vital. The erosion of his faith in the futurity of an America he had championed, coarse perhaps in its energies but expanding into a commodious, vital culture, and spiritualizing its material resources, can be traced to his troubles with the composition of *The Bridge.* As usual they were signaled by his temporary attraction to Spengler's ideas, toward which he was generally hostile, about the inevitable spiraling downwards of civilizations. Prompted by his reading of the pessimistic German, Crane reassessed the positive purposes underlying *The Bridge.* In a letter to Waldo Frank from the Isle of Pines, on June 20, 1926, where he had gone to renew his depleted energy, he remarked with incisive coolness that "intellectually judged the whole theme and project seems more and more absurd." [34] He explained to Frank that he had lost faith that the forms and materials he wished to use existed in the world. He was "emptied of vision." *The Bridge* was a patchwork. His dream of being the American Virgil, the poet-colonist who would establish the links between his nation's past, present, and future, who would carry its household gods in his utterance to a new civilization where they would flourish, had to be set aside. It was not repudiated. Crane's way of handling the crisis sheds light on his character. Even amid despair, he never flatters himself or loses an element of detachment and self-irony. He finished *The Bridge* and resumed his guarded faith, much like Whitman's in *Democratic Vistas,* that America would stir from its stupor. Vision, needed more than ever in its collective life, was not another expendable commodity.

III

A Touch of Genius

In modern American poetry the lyric customarily records the confessional impulses of a tormented sensibility, often in an overwrought rhetoric, in a poem of and about self-consciousness. In these journals of pain, the poet's forcing of feeling sometimes induces a forcing of syntax and a taxing of language. Each poem is an unfolding of contraries, a religious-erotic experience. In Crane's poems, the points of pressure are often the sublimated equivalents of the pressure of feeling in his life: the swings from hurt to joy and from exaltation to despair, the air of tense, distraught eagerness to will love into being and to war with death in the self. This drama of both unfulfillment and transfiguration is played out to a dazzling, driven music.[35] The language sweeps along lyrical currents—jammed, excited, buoyant, involuted, majestic.

The immediacy and verve of Crane's poetry or its complicated verbal surface cannot be denied. Many of his readers feel that they are looking through a frosted window and are only dimly if tantalizingly aware of what is behind that window. But, as T. S. Eliot said, it is a test that "genuine poetry can communicate before it is understood." [36] What is not sufficiently accepted is that Crane was a good poetic workman, devoted to his craft and continually refining his tools. He is not an unschooled rhapsode. There are pattern, sense, and method in his poems, and indeed his rapid change from a

jejune poet to a strongly original one is a fascinating chapter
in American literary history. My purpose is to look at particular poems and explain how they are put together.[37] There
has been a dearth of concrete information about Crane's
poetics and style. Crane wished to write a handful of poems
that would survive the vagaries of fashion. In this he succeeded because he mastered the techniques of his craft. "The
value of genius to us," Emerson declared, "is in the veracity
of its report. Talent may frolic and juggle; genius realizes
and adds." [38] Crane's poems have a touch of genius in them,
because they report honestly his strivings after being and add
to our knowledge of all that obstructs us from assuming our
full humanity.

CHAPTER 2

Early Poems

In structure and subject matter Crane's most representative poems closely follow the great Romantic odes; they record, after the fact, an ascent from dejection to a moment of acute vision or pleasure and its aftermath, a descent into the dark sight or shortsightedness of daily life. His poems, like Wordsworth's and Keats', are poems of crisis, in which the poet, assailed by self-doubts, tries to come to terms with the wanings of his emotional and poetic powers by devising complicated strategies to coax the influxes of joy into being. Since Crane experienced these transfiguring moments rarely—they were spaced among long intervals of despondency during which his perceptual powers were inactive or dulled—he valued them the more highly. The experience contains an air of uncertainty. Alternating between waking and dreaming states, Crane, like Keats in "Ode to a Nightingale," has great difficulty holding in memory these fugitive, heightened feelings, and so he turns the poem into a reconstruction of the spiritual voyage, with the inner narrative, as in "The Broken Tower," continually being interrupted by self-interrogations.

For the Romantic consciousness this longing to fix a perishable experience, this solace of self-expression, involves a special struggle with, and special attitude toward, language. The language must range through a succession of moods from high to low; it must be pitched at a level of intensity that will sustain the moments of exaltation, and it must be sparse and simple to fit the fallings off into despair when the loss of the visionary gleam is most keenly felt. It must be graphic and vague. Thus in Crane's poetry, whether the experience described is earthly love, as in *Voyages,* or visionary ecstasy induced by wine, as in "The Wine Menagerie," or Columbus' journey to the New World and his discovery of vast new spiritual possibilities, as in the "Ave Maria" section of *The Bridge,* the poet is in search of the "incognizable Word" that witnesses and survives the devastations of time. But the poet must use words to embody the Word, and they, together with his memory, are unruly and unreliable. Because the experience is real *and* indistinct, the poem's language must be both explicit and full of implications. In order to achieve this amalgam, the poet must free his language of some of its denotative strictness, substituting the more associative processes of the imagination.[1]

The reader of Crane's poetry immediately notices the many oddities of vocabulary—Crane's verbal manners and mannerisms—that are the hallmark of his style. The words, taken by themselves, are not very strange, though their juxtapositions sometimes are. The effect at times of crabbed rhetoric, of knotty language, seems due to this bundling of unexpected elements. Crane learned from Eliot and the French Symbolists the habit of dropping out transitions and logical connectives and choosing words for their sonority or sensuous allure.

This concentration on the emotive reverberations of words, especially in rhapsodic passages, in part to represent sudden shifts and veerings in thought and feeling, occasionally submerges clarity. But as R. P. Blackmur has pointed out, Crane had a "profound feeling for the hearts of words, and how they beat and cohabited." [2]

One is also struck by the sweep of Crane's diction: an elevated rhetoric proper to incantatory and invoking moods, to the litany of rapture and suffering; nervous, playful jazz words; coinages; the language of the street; an abstract, polysyllabic, and technological nomenclature; and at his worst, though he usually avoids them, stilted and embarrassing poeticisms. Crane shares with Wallace Stevens an ear for the precise yet unorthodox opulent word.

Since the radical fact about Crane's poetic career was the abruptness of his maturing, much is to be gained by tracing chronologically the development of his characteristic idiom from its unpromising beginnings through *Voyages* in 1924 (after which there is no major change of manner), examining along the way the decisive poetic influences on his rhetorical style. In Chapter 6, I shall classify the most important and frequently used words in his vocabularly, and explain the reasons for their choice.

II

The Apprentice's Workshop

Although Crane's early poems, written between 1917 and 1920, are not easily distinguishable from the run-of-the-mill verse being produced at the time, and contain few hints of the personal style that would emerge fairly soon, it would be wrong to patronize them. They are, as might be expected from a boy of seventeen, conventional and sentimental, and tinged by an effete melancholy. Their mood is shot through with a languid self-pity charged slightly with self-irony, a vague paganism, and a dandyism that strikes poses of precocious worldliness about the flurries of love and the fickleness of women. Crane pretends to suffer from a "bleeding heart." The poems are heavily descriptive yet almost disembodied: an atmosphere suffused in moonlight is evoked, and then the speaker comments dreamily on his emotions. The vocabulary is relatively free of literary or mythical allusions—except for Venus and Ophelia—although Crane dips frequently into the stock phrases of *fin-de-siècle* Romanticism: "The bleeding heart" that "Humanity pecks, claws, sobs and climbs"; "Mercy, white milk, and honey, gold love—("The Hive"); "the shiver/Of the first moth's descent"; "The moans of travail of one dearest beside me" ("Annunciations"); and "A Dove's wing clung about my heart last night" ("Carrier Letter"). The emotional dynamics are limited.

Prim and decorous and elegant, muted in tone, dreamy and controlled, these early poems bear the faint musty smell of the drawing room. A feminine narcissism hangs in the air, redolent of perfumes and dim lights, tears and inarticulate emotion, and an oversolemn, pallid epicureanism. The diction is picturesque and vague and coolly sensuous, full of "opal pools" ("Echoes"), "long mellowed wines/Of dreaming" ("C 33"), and "grey and gold amenity" ("Interior"). At this period, Crane's chief literary models were the poets of the 1890s, especially Wilde, Dowson, and early Yeats, whose poems abound in pale lilies, sweet, sickly passion, "lost innocence," sighs, and drooping heads. It is a poetry that seldom raises its voice above a whisper. A typical example is Ernest Dowson's "Spleen":

> I was not sorrowful, I could not weep,
> And all my memories were put to sleep.
>
> I watched the river grow more white and strange,
> All day till evening I watched it change.
>
> All day till evening I watched the rain
> Beat wearily upon the window pane.
>
> I was not sorrowful, but only tired
> Of everything that ever I desired.
>
> Her lips, her eyes, all day became to me
> The shadow of a shadow utterly.
>
> All day mine hunger for her heart became
> Oblivion, until the evening came,
>
> And left me sorrowful, inclined to weep,
> With all my memories that could not sleep.

As a young aesthete in New York, affecting a cosmopolitanism and a nonchalance taken in part from the fashionable Yellow-Book style that still had its admirers and imitators in such magazines as *The Pagan* and *Bruno's Bohemia* (in which Crane published his first poems), Crane undoubtedly found such sentiments appealing. They offered to the inexperienced adolescent a style of weary wisdom he had not really earned and a Romantic worship and sorrow (and elsewhere a religiousness) he probably had not felt deeply.

"Legende," a poem that came out in *The Modernist* of November, 1919, is an example of this emotional attenuation, this retreat into memory, where at several removes the poet safely examines the failure of love:

> The tossing loneliness of many nights
> Rounds off my memory of her.
> Like a shell surrendered to evening sands,
> Yet called adrift again at every dawn,
> She has become a pathos,—
> Waif of the tides.
>
> The sands and the sea have had their way,
> And moons of spring and autumn,—
> All, save I.
> And even my vision will be erased
> As a cameo the waves claim again.

As in the Dowson poem, the poet both welcomes and is resigned to oblivion. Crane chooses words like "waif," "adrift," "surrendered," and "erased" that he feels will suggest his helpless passivity and the inevitability of death. The extinction of personality is mirrored in the words, but the "I" has no body, as though drained of blood and emotion, and the waves have no force.

Knowing the vigorous declamatory language of Crane's later periods, one is taken aback by the discretion with which sense experience is presented; even lovers' quarrels are muffled. One looks in vain for signs of Americanness in Crane's language. Apparently he had not yet read Whitman or Emily Dickinson, for he lacks the boisterous oracular energy of the former and the gnomic wit of the latter. Nor is he depicting a particularly American landscape or people, as Frost and

Edwin Arlington Robinson were doing at the time. Never-theless, the liquid handling of words he copied from Dowson and Wilde was valuable to the apprentice poet, since it gave him the confidence and fluency needed to begin subduing a subject to a style. And amid these salon clichés, these en-ervated and posturing lovers, we can discern foreshadowings of brisker phrasing and a fondness for odd couplings:

> The anxious milk-blood in the veins of the earth,
> That strives long and quiet to sever the girth
> Of greenery.

Crane's lifelong personification of the sea as a woman and his obsessive use of the color white first appear in the poem on Cezanne's *The Bathers*:

> Only simple ripples flaunt, and stroke, and float,—
> Flat lily petals to the sea's white throat.

The "sea's white throat" describes the white-capped waves with flowers floating in their midst, an image which antici-pates the "floating flower" of *Voyages II*. "Carrier Letter," a somewhat mawkish poem about lovers' separations and the poet's constancy contains one characteristic phrase:

> And with the day, distance again expands
> Between us, *voiceless as an uncoiled shell.**

Rather somberly, after a tryst that ends in "farewell," the speaker, love's acolyte, observes his estrangement from his lady as being both spatial and "voiceless." They no longer communicate: the gulf between them expands, and he puts the "uncoiled shell" to his ear but hears no sound.

* My italics.

"Modern Craft" describes a woman suffering from a sort of emotional anemia, like the woman in Eliot's *The Waste Land* who, from ennui, engages in perfunctory sexual relations: a case of modern love where feeling is missing, and the woman is consumed by no passion though she can provoke lust in men. Crane displays erotic tenderness for the woman, despite the fact that "Too many palms have grazed her shoulders." The diction of the first stanza, though it combines its disparate elements rather tentatively, is instructive:

> Though I have touched her flesh of moons,
> Still she sits gestureless and mute,
> Drowning cool pearls in alcohol.
> O blameless shyness;—innocence dissolute!

Crane's gallantry is evident in "blameless shyness," and the oxymoron "innocence dissolute," while not violent, sums up his mixed attitude toward the woman. The first two lines play off the poet's Romantic and sexual naïveté against the woman's lack of response or animation. The third line joins words into a mood of voluptuous remoteness.

One poem, "October-November," seems to be working in the sparer style of the Imagists; Crane paints with pastel watercolors the play of Indian summer lights:

> Indian-summer-sun
> With crimson feathers whips away the mists,—
> Dives through the filter of trellises
> And gilds the silver on the blotched arbor-seats.
>
> Now gold and purple scintillate
> On trees that seem dancing
> In delirium;

Then the moon
In a mad orange flare
Floods the grape-hung night.

The poem is like a miniature triptych; it moves in space more
than in time. Three pictures are presented: a sunset so gos-
samer-like yet powerful that its feathers can *whip* away the
mists; a panel of gold and purple lighting the trees in such
movement that they seem "dancing in delirium" (a hackneyed
phrase); and the moon coming out and as it were demonstrat-
ing its superior colorful light by driving out the gold and
spreading its dominion throughout the purplish dusky sky.
The poem is purely an exercise in the palette of words. Crimson, gold, silver, purple, orange, and grape please the senses,
as if to show that the resources and power of art are equal to
those of nature, that the young poet is up to the demands of
painting them.

These Imagist and Impressionist poems are not ordinarily
a vehicle for the expression of complex emotion or thought.
They depend too much for their effects on merely reporting
phenomena, thereby removing the imagination from actively
contributing to the poetic act. Crane rejected most of these
early poems from *White Buildings,* but to the student of his
stylistic development they are invaluable documents, the
workshop of a gifted poet. Two quasi-Imagist poems, however, were admitted into the first volume—"In Shadow" and
"North Labrador." They are predominantly skillful mood
pieces that play with light and dark to different ends. The first
three stanzas of "In Shadow" are like a Monet painting. The
lady is revealed obliquely through the effects of light and
shadow on her parasol, lace dress, and hair. The scene is again

deliquescent; the words catch the stealthy silence, the confused, suspended ominousness of the woman's identity. When she finally speaks in the last stanza, she shatters the mood of perfumed twilight and dress, and the vocabulary shifts from impressionistic colors to cultivated conversation. The "amber afternoon" and "green twilight" and "the parasol pale as a balloon and white as a moon" are verbal devices that create an emotional tonality, in this case, a dying out of feeling; "furtive lace" reflects Crane's practice of choosing oddly attributive adjectives. The rest of the language is rather insipid (the poem is more interesting for its rhythmic effects and its manipulation of syntax).

"North Labrador" is a tight, terse, almost denuded poem, a rendering of visionary terror. The poet first sketches in the image of an ice-blocked land embraced by "plaster-grey arches of sky" moving silently and timelessly and then personifies the northern country as a woman with "glittering breasts" and without memory, unvisited by any suitor. The question he poses her cannot be answered. This eternal movement toward nothing represents the inhuman remorselessness of Nature. The diction, deliberately bleak and neutral, successfully depicts the spiritual horror, the meaningless process, and the eerie light of "Darkly Bright." "North Labrador," unlike "In Shadow," is masculine and grimly ironic in its courtship of abstraction.

In 1920, Crane's experiments with new verbal forms, or more accurately, with the mixing of different kinds of words, led to two curious poems, "Porphyro in Akron" and "The Bridge of Estador." "Porphyro" especially, as the title suggests, is an exercise in ironic reminiscence, a burlesque counterpointing of the spirit of romance and poetry with the wasteland spirit of manufacturing Akron. The machines that so fascinated and repelled Crane are briefly alluded to—the axles and monkey wrench are symbols of the unrewarding, dehumanizing work of the men, mostly immigrants, who trudge daily to the rubber factories, far removed from the previous harmony of their labor with the plough—but it is primarily the cultural aridity that depresses the young Porphyro, Crane's mocking name for himself as the Romantic hero in America. However valorous he may be, he will be balked by the business ethos of a milieu sottishly opposed to poetry—"in this town, poetry's a/Bedroom occupation." The corruption of the American Dream, particularly its baneful effects on foreigners who "will be Americans/Using the latest ice-box and buying Fords," dispirits him: he realizes that, unlike Keats' hero, he is unlikely to steal away any Madelines from Akron. Each of the three sections evokes the noises and drudgery of this "unreal city"; time moves from dawn to noon to wintry night. Though there are echoes of the language of T. S. Eliot's "Preludes" and "Prufrock" in the poem ("I will go and pitch quoits with old men/In the dust of a road."), the language is more abrupt and concrete, more anecdotal, and more colloquially fluent than in any of Crane's other poems to this point.

Section II recounts a pleasurable moment amid the drabness of Akron life. The words are flat, naturalistic:

> I remember one Sunday noon,
> Harry and I, "the gentlemen," seated around
> A table of raisin-jack and wine, our host
> Setting down a glass and saying,—

> "One month,—I go back rich.
> I ride black horse. . . . Have many sheep."
> And his wife, like a mountain, coming in
> With four tiny black-eyed girls around her
> Twinkling like little Christmas trees.
>
> And some Sunday fiddlers,
> Roumanian business men,
> Played ragtime and dances before the door,
> And we overpayed them because we felt like it.

Crane's rhetorical flair often precluded his using this low-keyed conversational style. Unlike Frost, he was not interested in making poetry exclusively out of the speech of daily life, yet he could inflect speech with a musical cadence, as the above passage and, particularly, the good-natured bravado of the last line prove. Such speech is employed sparingly, and usually to lower the pitch from a passage of intense feeling to a passage of calm reflection, as in *Voyages V*. It is also an antidote to sentimentality, as in the idealized yet humorous drawing of the warm family picture. In Part III the memory of his mother's singing recalls his gesture of homage, "To find the only rose on the bush in the front yard," but its maudlin language, after the quotation from Keats' "The Eve of St. Agnes," is rudely scotched by these lines:

> But look up, Porphyro,—your toes
> Are ridiculously tapping
> The spindles at the foot of the bed.

In short, the poem reveals a distinct loosening in Crane's handling of quotidian details, a concern for the human fact and the disclosure of personality through speech and act, and a search for a viable style that would bring sentiment and wit closer together.

"The Bridge of Estador" is subtitled "An Impromptu Aesthetic Tirade," but it seems neither impromptu nor an aesthetic tirade nor a unified expression. Nevertheless, it does provide a clue to the direction Crane's language would take. "How can you tell where beauty's to be found?" he asks. How can the realistic data, the ugly "dun/Bellies and estuaries of warehouses,/Tied bundle-wise with cords of smoke," be transformed by the imagination into something coherent and beautiful? If art can make us see things anew, is it enough to set down the objects that the eye sees:

> I have heard hands praised for what they made;
> I have heard hands praised for line on line;
> Yet a gash with sunlight jerking through
> A mesh of belts down into it, made me think
> I had never seen a hand before.
> And the hand was thick and heavily warted.

This realistic poetry has "a soul, an element in it all," but Crane plumps for the poet who waits high on the bridge, "Where no one has ever been before," for visions that may or may not come, visions of "things irreconcilable" that twist those who, venturing among the stars, dream the impossible synthesis. He argues that "though you have never/Seen them again, [these visions], you won't forget," which I suppose is intended as consolation, but calling himself "Beauty's fool," he seems to cast doubt on the wisdom of the visionary enterprise. In any case, though the issues are not finely drawn, this is a central debate for Crane. The best parts of the poem are the descriptions of objects rather than their visionary application. The poem is a failure, as Crane realized, but he integrated the best fragments into "Praise for an Urn." Crane was now ready to enter the next stage of his poetic development.

III

Laforgue and "Chaplinesque"

These "songs of minor, broken strains" continued to be written while Crane impatiently sought to deepen and complicate his style, and to move away from the somewhat bland, somewhat derivative language of neo-Swinburnians and Romantic manqués. Crane realized that he needed a more rapid and charged diction, one capable of functioning on reciprocal and complementary levels, roughened and ironic, to replace the soporific uniform language of most of the early poems. "North Labrador" had pointed to a sparer density and a more mysterious relation between surface and overtone that might accommodate metaphysical speculation within a realistic frame. At this point Laforgue replaced Oscar Wilde, Dowson, and early Yeats as the model for poetic emulation. While Crane continued to write poems like "Pastorale" and "My Grandmother's Love Letters" with their almost cloying femininity as exercises in the delicate elaboration of sensibility, he was thinking, reading, arguing aesthetics with his friends and excitedly making plans for newer, bolder poems.

Crane's translation of Laforgue's "Locutions des Pierrots" served him well in the forging of his style. There are a crispness and spiritedness to the language, a gaiety and a tenderness that are new. Almost every fresh departure in Crane's development was followed by a swift consolidation of the technical (and hence expressive) problems of his medium. Crane admired Laforgue's Gallic impudence and mischievous wit, and attempted to adapt them, as we shall see later, in "Chaplinesque." Crane's diction captures the chivalric mockery, the elegant quizzicalness of the original, the queer blending of extravagance and aloofness; it postures, it capers, it laughs at its romantic silliness and suffering: passion is deflated, but not entirely. This is a long way from the moping debilities of "Interior" and "Annunciations!" The pale lady swaddled in parasol and shadows, paragon of mystery to the young man, is gone; in her place a woman more mysterious, a *femme fatale*—"Eve, Gioconda, and Dalila"—whose frivolous changeableness and ladylike acting elicit from the speaker-lover light banter and mock-heroic self-perplexity:

> Your eyes, those pools with soft rushes,
> O prodigal and wholly dilatory lady,
> Come now, when will they restore me
> The orient moon of my dapper affections?
>
> For imminent is that moment when,
> Because of your perverse austerities,
> My crisp soul will be flooded by a languor
> Bland as the wide gaze of a Newfoundland.
>
> Ah, madame! truly it's not right
> When one isn't the real Gioconda,
> To adaptate her methods and deportment
> For snaring the poor world in a blue funk.

The diction here is interesting for the way the poet undercuts the clichés of the love situation: the cruel distant Courtly

Lady is scolded in a cajoling voice for her dilatoriness. Crane is able to indulge his penchant for apostrophe ("O prodigal and wholly dilatory lady"), for portentous overstatement ("Ah, madame!" and "For imminent is that moment when, . . ."), and for soft sentiments ("Your eyes, those pools with soft rushes"), only to subvert them by conjoining wryly incongruous words: "The *orient moon* of my *dapper* affections"; the soul "flooded by a languor" like the soulful gaze of a sheep dog; and a word as inappropriate to a love poem, "adaptate," as the woman's "blue funk" is to love. Finally, the placing of abstractions and the tying of them to concrete verbs is well done. Here, in Part I, and in Parts II and III, Crane leavens the poem with sonorous Latinate words: "perverse *austerities*," "To *adaptate* her methods and *deportment*," "True, I nibble at *despondencies*/Among the flowers of her domain/To the sole end of discovering/What is her unique *propensity!*" and "Oh, by the *infinite circumflex*/Of the archbeam of my cross-legged labours,/Come now—appease me just a little/With the why-and-wherefore of Your Sex!" Thus, the importance of these translations was that Crane learned how to contrast the vocabulary of sentimental effusion with the vocabulary of pungent and vivacious wit, or, as R. W. B. Lewis points out, to exploit the comic and pathetic aspects of the Pierrot tradition.[3]

Laforgue had a liberating influence on Crane's verse, injecting a more hale and sardonic strength into the language, but in the long run Crane could not write poems in this manner. For one, Laforguean irony was too suspiciously scornful of impassioned speech, of feeling itself, for a person of Crane's temperament; he probably thought it not the highest flight of which the imagination was capable. For better or for worse, Crane was attracted to metaphysical and spiritual subjects, and to a more celebrational mode of poetry than the gifted cynical Frenchman. Defeat was too painful and omnipresent to be treated with facetious distance; and Crane felt he must convert his feelings of love and despair into poetry that would be a "stay against confusion." The brio never disappears completely, it is sublimated. A racy casualness and a knowledgeable satire, so fresh and given full rein in the letters and in his conversation, only appears in a few places, most notably, "Bacardi Spreads the Eagle's Wings," Part II of "Faustus and Helen," and parts of *The Bridge*.

"Chaplinesque" is Crane's most Laforguean poem, but it is subtly modulated into many other things—a tribute to the balletic slipperiness and the mimetic genius of Chaplin; a comment on the poet's indestructible power of transforming neglect, misunderstanding, poverty, and even the sureness of death into the triumphs of art; the artist's ability to survive "the fury of the street," and American society's crass indifference to and persecution of excellence. Chaplin, Crane felt, had managed to protect his sympathies from brutalization and coarsening, to hug the truths of the heart to his tattered, absurd rags. There is bitter awe at the poet's adaptability, at his unconquerable innocence, and bitter protest at his beleaguerment and isolation:

> The game enforces smirks; but we have seen
> The moon in lonely alleys make
> A grail of laughter of an empty ash can,
> And through all sound of gaiety and quest
> Have heard a kitten in the wilderness.

The artist's "meek adjustments" and "random consolations" take on the character of a holy act, for in the face of huge obstacles, the poet is engaged on a quest for his own and his society's salvation.

Crane's friends found "Chaplinesque" puzzling and obscure, and so, as usual, he explained it to them with defensive patience. It is hard to see why the poem gave so much trouble, provided that the reader was familiar with Chaplin's films. Their appeal for Crane was great. As master of the bittersweet, Chaplin could distill in one gesture the comic-pathetic antics of the tramp, a hero who endures humiliation with dignity and amazing resiliency, an "infinitely gentle, infinitely suffering thing." As Crane remarks, "Poetry, the human feelings, 'the kitten,' is so crowded out of the humdrum, rushing, mechanical scramble of today that the man who would preserve them must duck and camouflage for dear life to keep them or keep himself from annihilation." [4] The "famished kitten" on the step or in the wilderness is not only an apt symbol for the artist's plight, it also illustrates Crane's withholding of allegiance to Laforgue.

The language of the poem's surface gathers together the details of Chaplin's tramp routine, the gestures of the clown, his stage props, his eloquent shabbiness and radiant goodness: the "fine collapses," "The pirouettes of any pliant cane," "warm torn elbow coverts," the "slithered and too ample pockets" of his baggy pants, the "puckered index" and "dull squint" with which authority (the police) greets the vagabond. The words are simple and supple, sometimes concrete as with the cane and sometimes indirect as with "fine collapses." These are combined with the abstractions—"adjust-

ments," "consolations," "obsequies," "enterprise," and words of
a quasi-religious and moral nature—"meek," "doom," "innocence," "grail," and "wilderness"—that are the key signatures
of Crane's poetry.

CHAPTER 3

The Singing Masters

Despite his admiration for Laforgue, Crane found him ultimately of only partial help for another reason: Crane could not adopt the conventions of the dramatic monologue that Laforgue and Browning and Eliot employed to present feeling. There are almost no personae in Crane's poems. Crane's voice is heard in dialogue with himself unmediated by ironic distance. Moreover, while he was an admiring student of the Eliot of "Prufrock" and the "Preludes"—"I must have read 'Prufrock' twenty-five times and things like the 'Preludes' more often," he remarked to Allen Tate[1]—he could not subscribe to Eliot's vision of life or the style that so masterfully embodied it. When *The Waste Land* appeared in 1922, Crane read it at first with subdued enthusiasm and then with critical skepticism and disappointment: "It was good, of course, but so damn dead." [2] Nevertheless, *The Waste Land* was midwife to the birth of "Faustus and Helen"; and if he quarreled so forcefully and even belligerently with Eliot's outlook and practice, it was to avoid being submerged by the older poet's influence, as Allen Tate was. "Having absorbed him enough," Crane writes to Tate:

. . . we can trust ourselves as never before, in the air or on the sea. I, for instance, would like to leave a few of his 'negations' behind me, risk the realm of the obvious more, in quest of new sensations, *humeurs*. These theories and manoeuvres are interesting and consolatory,—but of course, when it comes right down to the act itself,—I have to depend on intuition, 'Inspiration' or what you will to fill the page.[3]

These candid admissions of method and intent have been pounced upon by Crane's critics to prove that he abandoned all control over his material to some dubious fitful inspiration. But Crane meant by the term "intuition" a painfully slow gestation, that patient clarification of his purposes, themes, and perceptions by which any poet, whether Classical or Romantic, labors to give life and form to his verse. The process is not helter-skelter: the poet sometimes stumbles upon the right word, patches, transposes, erases, and adds in revising. Crane took almost two years to complete the three sections of "Faustus and Helen." We must learn to read Crane's exuberant statements of intention cautiously.

"Faustus and Helen" marks a turning point in Crane's career, for in it he establishes the lineaments of his idiom, and in a large sense invents a flexible language to encompass the great themes of poetry—war, love, death, beauty, knowledge—that did indeed, as Crane claimed, introduce "new timbres" that were poignant, gay, and feverish, hymn-like and reflective. Brimming with confidence, he fired off a letter to Tate that helps explain the mood and conception of his first major poem:

The poetry of negation is beautiful—alas, too dangerously so for one of my mind. But I am trying to break away from it. Perhaps this is useless, perhaps it is silly—but one *does* have joys. The vocabulary of damnations and prostrations has been developed at the expense of these other moods, however, so that it is hard to dance in proper measure. Let us invent an idiom for the proper transposition of jazz into words! Something clean, sparkling, elusive! [4]

Since the revolution in poetry in Crane's day of which he approved to a degree was, among other things, a revolution against Romantic diction, his age was likely to be hostile to his proposal to revive the Romantic vision in fresh modern dress. That Crane was willing to undertake this difficult, some might even say impossible, synthesis and risk almost certain unpopularity is proof of his courage and imaginative independence. Whether he succeeded in "Faustus and Helen" is arguable, but to judge it fairly we must acknowledge its ambitions and innovations, its daring fusion of ragtime and metaphysics, of the colloquial and the ornate. It is, as Crane called it, "a work of youth and magic," [5] a poem "Striated with nuances, nervosities"; it is also an erratic poem, with its share of the pretentious diction Crane could never wholly keep out of his verse. But before we examine these vices and lapses and the linguistic charm of "Faustus and Helen," we must backtrack a moment to discuss the way Crane's reading of the Elizabethan and Jacobean poets (prompted by Eliot and Pound) and of Keats prepared for the breakthrough in "Faustus and Helen."

In order to express satisfactorily the multifariousness of a speeded-up world, the modern poet, Crane argued, must ransack the vocabularies of the literatures of the past. "The modern artist needs gigantic assimilative capacities, emotions— and the greatest of *all—vision.*" [6] In keeping with his own assertion, Crane borrowed freely from the Elizabethan and Jacobean playwrights. He found in them a manual of rhetoric and a sensibility close to his own—eclectic, inventive, lyrical, witty, and gorgeous—which encouraged him to go beyond the surface evocativeness, the impressionism, of his early verse. The grandiloquence and flamboyant virtuosity of Marlowe and the quiet concise melancholy of Webster had a bracing influence on Crane, since they checked a tendency in his verse toward softness and blur whenever he expressed emotion or touched on erotic-metaphysical subjects. Writing to Gorham Munson on November 26, 1921, Crane refers to his "Elizabethan fanaticism" and "long-standing friendship" with Marlowe,[7] Webster, and Donne—it is a recurring subject of his letters during the formative period 1920–22—singling out for comment their "verbal richness, irony and emotion." [8] As Emerson puts it in "The Poet," "The young man reveres men of genius, because to speak truly, they are more himself than he is. They receive of the soul as he receives, but they more." [9]

An analysis of the following typical passage from "Tamburlaine the Great, Part II" will show why Marlowe's diction, "Cambyses' ranting vein," impressed Crane deeply:

> Through the streets with troops of conquered kings,
> I'll ride in golden armour like the sun;
> And in my helm a triple plume shall spring,
> Spangled with diamonds, dancing in the air,
> To note me emperor of the threefold world,
> Like to an almond tree y-mounted high
> Upon the lofty and celestial mount
> Of ever-green Selinus quaintly decked
> With blooms more white than Erycina's brows,

Whose tender blossoms tremble every one,
At every little breath through Heaven is blown.
Then in my coach, like Saturn's royal son
Mounted, his shining chariot gilt with fire,
And drawn with princely eagles through the path
Paved with bright crystal and enchased with stars,
When all the gods stand gazing at his pomp,
So will I ride through Samarcanda streets,
Until my soul, dissevered from this flesh,
Shall mount the milk-white way, and meet him there.[10]

What would undoubtedly dazzle and interest the young
poet is Marlowe's sensuous ornamentation, the lyrical excess
with which the Scythian potentate celebrates his victory and
in which the sounds of the words appeal to the ear almost independently of their relation to particular meanings. But only
almost, for there is a pictorial exactness, a tactile and visual
immediacy, and a rhythmic urgency created by the language
that corresponds to the poet's intensity of feeling—and satis-
fies it fully. The poet is a god, a visionary magician who can
conjure up the magnificent spectacle of his own triumph so
complete that even the gods are transfixed by the procession.
The words, like Tamburlaine himself, shimmer with light,
from the spangled diamonds of the plume to the roadway
paved with crystal and embedded with stars. We share Tamburlaine's exultant conviction of his forthcoming apotheosis
because Marlowe has been able to yoke rare words, his
"princely eagles," to draw the chariot of the imagination. The
swagger of the language is redeemed from monotony by its
formal ceremoniousness, as of a cosmic pageant of supremely
varied and extravagant order. The words, assembled, as it
were, for a sumptuous display of verbal royalty, are redundant

but dynamic. Marlowe takes us to the outermost edge of the poetic sublime, and as such his style is peculiarly suited to Crane's temperament, as we shall see in the final section of "Faustus and Helen."

Quite different from the pomp, multitudinousness, and extroverted beauty of Marlowe's verse, but equally admired by Crane is Webster's blend of "irony and emotion," of derisive jest and passionate simplicity. The atmosphere of Webster's plays is one of extremes: darkness relieved only now and again by flashes of light, lurid scheming and vicious evil beleaguering the helpless good. "Webster was much possessed of death/And saw the skull beneath the skin. . . . He knew that thought clings round dead limbs/Tightening its lusts and luxuries," T. S. Eliot wrote in "Whispers of Immortality," in lines that Crane probably knew. Webster, like the other Elizabethans, was very much in the modernist poetic mind, and Crane, whose antennae picked up clearly whatever cultural news was in the air, recognized that Webster's style might help deepen his own. Webster indeed affords an important clue to the workings of Crane's eclectic, "assimilative" mind. At first glance it seems odd that at the very moment Crane was hammering out the first draft of "Faustus and Helen," a poem in which he wished to make a resounding affirmation of life and counter the pessimism of his age, a poem, moreover, that would involve a sequence of styles, all permeated by a language of "Dionysian splendor," he should be writing to Allen Tate in this vein about Webster:

So you are in love with the dear Duchess of Malfi also! How lovely she speaks in that one matchless passage [III, ii, 66–70]:

> "Doth not the colour of my haire 'gin to change?
> When I waxe gray, I shall have all the Court
> Powder their haire with Arras, to be like me;
> You have cause to love, I entred you into my heart
> Before you would vouchsafe to call for the keyes."

Exquisite pride surrendering to love! And it was this that faced all the brutality of circumstance in those hideous and gorgeous final scenes of the play. The old betrayals of life, and yet they are worth something—from a distance afterward.[11]

One solution to the paradox of Crane's enchantment with Webster's charnel world may be found in F. L. Lucas' observation that the characters in Webster's plays are the sort "for whom life is a fever tormented with hopeless dreams of happiness, whose lucid moments are both haunted and fascinated and repelled by the thought of the quiet and final rest of death. . . ."[12] This is a remarkably apt description of Crane's own character, and only the hostility of some critics has perpetuated the notion that he denied the "brutality of circumstance." Thus just as Marlowe expressed Crane's aspiration for a colorful and plentiful style of poetry and being, so Webster expressed his sense of the ordeals of idealism and the limits of our "conscript dust," the "nameless gulfs" that separate us from our better selves. When Crane says in "The Wine Menagerie" "Between black tusks the roses shine!" it is a sentiment or belief Websterean in mood he has learned on his pulses.

The qualities of Webster's diction to which Crane responded in the Duchess of Malfi's speech above or in Ferdinand's line "Cover her face: Mine eyes dazzle: she di'd yong" are the understated wit, the concentrated gravity, and the unexpected flaring of "that terrible intensity with which his utterance trembles." [13] Those cruel, despairing diatribes that Webster's villains repeat like a catechism of treachery in swift, virile phrases are tempered and modulated, and this is the lesson Webster taught Crane, by quiet, plain-spoken, inward-turning words. Crane's wit, generally taken for uninhibited verbal ingenuity, has been underestimated. Crane realized from his reading of Webster that, in Lucas' words, "the implied strikes always so much deeper than the said." [14]

The third of Crane's Elizabethan-Jacobean "singing masters" was John Donne. That Donne was a favorite of Crane's, even an obsession, his letters bear witness to: Crane always used his correspondence to set down his immediate reactions to and judgments of his current reading. Two letters quite specifically explain why Donne's poetic style attracted him as a model. To William Wright, he confesses:

> I admit to a slight leaning toward the esoteric, and am perhaps not to be taken seriously. I am fond of things of great fragility, and also and especially of the kind of poetry John Donne represents, a dark, musky, brooding, speculative vintage, at once sensual and spiritual, and singing rather the beauty of experience than innocence.[15]

And to Sherwood Anderson, almost three months later:

> What I want to get is just what is so beautifully done in this poem, ["The Expiration"]—an "interior" form, a form that is so thorough and intense as to dye the words themselves with a peculiarity of meaning, slightly different maybe from the ordinary definition of them separate from the poem.[16]

Now Crane's preoccupation with style, as these letters indicate, extends beyond such crucial matters as what words to use to questions of subject matter, emotion, and verse form. What this informal manifesto announces is that he wishes to hazard a kind of poetry that combines heterogeneity, sharpness, and daring. The lyric fragility of early poems like "In Shadow," "Pastorale," and "My Grandmother's Love Letters," he felt, was too soft, too innocent, too restrictive; it could not convey simultaneously the range and depth of his experiences, the exhilarating conflict of the sensual and the spiritual. What his verse needed was a masculine roughness, so that with an instinct for the aesthetic preference and balance that would aid him in strengthening his poems, he turned to Donne. In an article on Donne in 1923, T. S. Eliot formulates the reasons for the influence of Donne in the modern age, and what must have been Crane's view:

> One of the characteristics of Donne which wins him, I fancy, his interest for the present age, is his fidelity to emotion as he finds it; his recognition of the complexity of feeling and its rapid alterations and antitheses. A change of feeling, with Donne, is rather the regrouping of the same elements under a mood which was previously subordinate: it is not the substitution of one mood for a wholly different one. . . . The range of his feelings was great, but no more remarkable than its unity. He was altogether present in every thought and every feeling.[17]

The trappings of Romantic diction are, of course, to be found everywhere, in Crane's early and late poetry, since he is by nature a Romantic, but the poems are saved from nebulousness, from floating in "the circumambient gas," [18] by a stylistic knack, reflected in the diction, of stiffening the idealism, panegyrics, and visionary transport with fact and com-

mon sense. Readers often overlook this nervous particularity
in Crane's verse. Donne's poetic speech (and vocabulary)
blended the language of concept with the language of passion; it taught Crane how to vocalize internal debate and
avoid sheer vagueness, how to line the vatic coat with the
fibres of realism. If the verbal texture in Crane's poems is not
as wiry or intellectual as Donne's, that is owing to the lack of
the brusque discursive logic that stitches Donne's love poems
together.

If we set side by side the passages from Donne's poems that
Crane quotes approvingly in his letter to Sherwood Anderson
with "Black Tambourine," the one early poem that Crane
felt adequately approximated Donne's experiments with connotations and "interior" form, we can discover how Crane's
hospitality to a wide range of words enriched his verse and
incidentally increased the possibilities of metaphor in "Faustus
and Helen." The Donne texts are "The Expiration" and three
lines from the "Second Anniversary":

THE EXPIRATION

So, so, breake off this last lamenting kisse,
    Which sucks two soules, and vapors Both away,
Turne thou ghost that way, and let mee turne this,
    And let our selves benight our happiest day,
We ask'd none leave to love; nor will we owe
    Any, so cheape a death, as saying, Goe;
Goe; and if that word have not quite kil'd thee,
    Ease mee with death, by bidding mee goe too.
Or if it have, let my word worke on mee,
    And a just office on a murderer doe.
Except it be too late, to kill me so,
    Being double dead, going, and bidding, goe.

SECOND ANNIVERSARY

Thou shalt not peepe through lattices of eyes,
Nor heare through Labyrinths of eares, nor learne
By circuit, or collections to discerne.

Crane's poem "Black Tambourine" follows:

The interests of a black man in a cellar
Mark tardy judgment on the world's closed door.
Gnats toss in the shadow of a bottle,
And a roach spans a crevice in the floor.

Aesop, driven to pondering, found
Heaven with the tortoise and the hare;
Fox brush and sow ear top his grave
And mingling incantations on the air.

The black man, forlorn in the cellar,
Wanders in some mid-kingdom, dark, that lies,
Between his tambourine, stuck on the wall,
And, in Africa, a carcass quick with flies.

What Crane recognized in Donne's poetry[19] was a method of exploiting the overtones of words. Since words, in Emerson's phrase, are "the archives of history," and derive their meanings from their context, the poet, by putting them in a *new* setting, ends up arranging new configurations of meaning. Thus in "The Expiration" Donne plays on the double meanings of kill and death, equating the sex act with death, and even recharges the simple words "goe" and "bid" by introducing them as Romantic executioners of dark commands. The excerpt from the "Second Anniversary" employs a reversal of associations. The surrounding context establishes the illusion of sense experience, the imperfect knowledge it gives; the "lattices of eyes" are associated with lovers gazing raptly at each other as in sexual intimacy, but true celestial vision is not confined like this squinting of earthly lovers (the lattices being eyelashes), nor is the pure spirit lost in labyrinthine sounds that deter perfect hearing and understanding.

Crane's originality lies in his ability to induce words to create a network of meanings, something akin to a chromatic scale of moods. These depend, first, on the selection of words, and, second, on their groupings in the poem. In "Black Tambourine" the predicament of the black man is dramatized by juxtaposing words that connote geographical and historical space with words that signify his claustrophobic world, his being immured in the slum cellar: the imagination roves from Africa to the closed mid-kingdom of his mind; from Aesop's discovery in Ancient Greece of heaven to the grave; when the "roach spans a crevice in the floor," the words ironically suggest a bridging of large space in the dank narrow cellar room; cellar implies cell. Similarly, in the phrase "carcass quick with flies" Crane puns on the word "quick," counterpointing the life-in-death with the black man's death-in-life and with the tardiness of tortoise and judgment. Crane's skill in devising these intricate verbal collages and endowing them with meaning grew with extraordinary celerity.

Keats' influence on Crane's poetry is on the surface less visible than, and not as easily verifiable as, that of the Elizabethans, yet it is crucial. Crane does not talk much about Keats in his letters; there are indeed only two references to him, one in 1921 at the beginning of the transitional period when Crane was reading voraciously and absorbing a host of poets of diverse styles, and the second in 1930 when the critical attacks on *The Bridge* and its brand of Romanticism aroused in Crane not only a measure of gloom and a prickly sensitivity but also a sturdy defense of the principles of American Romanticism. But, as always, Crane's comments contain a wealth of suggestive ideas that enable us to read his mind and to understand his "poetic creeds."

On October 17, 1921, at a time when his own style was unformed or incompletely formed, Crane wrote an ebullient letter to his friend William Wright, scolding him for liking such weepy women poets as Sarah Teasdale and Edna Millay, and listing his own poetic preferences. To a New Critic, Crane's "catholic admirations" would constitute a bewildering and perhaps amusing confraternity: "Messrs. Poe, Whitman, Shakespeare, Keats, Shelley, Coleridge, John Donne!!!, John Webster!!!, Marlowe, Baudelaire, Laforgue, Dante, Cavalcanti, Li Po." [20] This is an unexceptionable gallery of poets, most of whom had received the imprimatur of Pound and Eliot, the chief arbiters of modernist taste. What matters is Crane's inclusion on this list of Shelley and Whitman, Keats and Coleridge, whose poetry was generally excluded from the canons of acceptable taste because of ostensible failings: Romantic interior decorating, imprecision, transcendentalism, lack of irony and paradox. Crane, however, was no simple-minded literary idolator. He knew that his own sensibility leaned toward just this serious Romanticism of intensely personal expression upon which his contemporaries frowned.

It was Allen Tate's conviction, and Yvor Winters', that the Romantic tradition was a dead end. In 1930, with excusable bitterness and his customary fair-mindedness, Crane took issue with them for advocating the idea that poetry was a moral cure-all and for contracting its expressive scope. "Poetry as poetry," he remarks,

> (and I don't mean merely decorative verse) isn't worth a second reading any more. Therefore—away with Kubla Khan, out with Marlowe, and to hell with Keats! It's a pity, I think. So many true things have a way of coming out all the better without the strain to sum up the universe in one impressive pellet. I admit that I don't answer the requirements. My vision of poetry *is* too personal to 'answer the call.' And if I ever write any more verse it will probably be at least as personal as the idiom of *White Buildings* whether anyone cares to look at it or not.[21]

Crane's allegiance to "the positive and universal tendencies,"[22] remains undiminished. This is more than a quarrel about the proper morality of aesthetics. Crane is defending the poet's privilege to pursue his vision without tying it to doctrines, to explore the extinction of the self, in the manner of the sublime, if he pleases. It is no exaggeration to call Crane's position heroic, for unlike Keats, his poetic peers disapproved of his focusing on emotion as self-indulgence and bathos, as if *emotion* mattered that much.

Keats' use of synaesthetic imagery and his contrivance of an odal stanza that permitted a pleasurable counterpointing of irregularity and order were lessons not lost on Crane. But it is in the area of diction that Keats exerted a pull on Crane's verse. Keats had criticized Shelley for his dispersed diction, telling him to "load every rift with ore," and this dispersed vagueness was the chief fault of Crane's early poems. Keats' own diction, marked by sensuousness and intensity, lushness and concentration, was the vehicle of a complete and sympathetic rendering of the things of the world, without effacing his own identity. Indeed the poet's emotions, his jubilations and sorrows, interest him so much that he constructs out of them a lyrical drama whose language is ceremonial and apostrophizing (not Wordsworth's language of common men). These are the natural artifices of self-conscious poetry, of waking dreams, and when the modernist school reacted against it, querying the authenticity of the overstatement and the concern for self, it was truncating not only the sublime mode of poetry but often feeling itself.

Take the familiar middle stanzas from Keats' "Ode to a Nightingale":

> I cannot see what flowers are at my feet,
>   Nor what soft incense hangs upon the boughs,
> But, in embalmed darkness, guess each sweet
>   Wherewith the seasonable month endows
> The grass, the thicket, and the fruit-tree wild;
>   White hawthorn, and the pastoral eglantine;
>   Fast fading violets cover'd up in leaves;
>   And mid-May's eldest child,
>   The coming musk-rose, full of dewy wine,
>   The murmurous haunt of flies on summer eves.
>
> Darkling I listen; and, for many a time
>   I have been half in love with easeful Death,
> Call'd him soft names in many a mused rhyme,
>   To take into the air my quiet breath;
> Now more than ever seems it rich to die,

To cease upon the midnight with no pain,
While thou art pouring forth thy soul abroad
In such an ecstasy!

Still wouldst thou sing, and I have ears in vain—
To thy high requiem become a sod.
Thou wast not born for death, immortal Bird!
No hungry generations tread thee down;

Despite Keats' melancholy assertion that he cannot see or hear well, that his response is inert, the words contradict him; especially in stanza five, he luxuriates in the rich abundance of nature, describing it with the accuracy and joy of a botanist savoring favorite specimens. There is a feeling of surfeit in the soft and perfumed air; the surrender to the spell of nature is a surrender to the spell of death: the poet is embalmed by the dark potency of life, the fading violets are covered by new leaves. The very pleasures of life contain the seeds of their dissolution; the poet's ecstasy cannot last. Death, rich, painless, and easeful, is directly confronted in the next stanza. Where before Keats' desire to die was concealed even from himself, now he muses over its timeliness, as though an idea that had been stored in memory, even caressed, now emerges, and he courts death as a half-eager lover. In stanza five, he names the creations of nature that die; in the next stanza, he calls death itself "soft names." But even though the I-eye in the fifth stanza plays over concrete objects and in the sixth gazes inward, in both stanzas the poet, like the nightingale, is "pouring forth [his] soul abroad/In such an ecstasy." Because the poet's attention is divided and distracted, as he moves leisurely from a mood of ripeness to despair to anger, the diction moves from a high, almost Marlovian externality to taut generalizations, from declaration to exclamation to direct address. Crane incorporated into his own poems this circuit of alternating verbal tension and relaxation through which his emotions could pass.

Crane, like Keats, comes to emphasize not so much his reaction to external reality, as his inspection of inner reality. The poem is a lyrical report on what happens inside the person—his enthusiasms (his intensity), his unique perceptions of beauty and truth that leave a permanent impression on him.

CHAPTER 4

"Faustus and Helen"

"Faustus and Helen" is Crane's "Ode to Psyche." In it he boldly announces that he will dedicate his imagination to the service and homage of the muse, and like Keats "build a fane/ In some untrodden region of [his] mind." The poem is therefore a festive solemnizing of his vocation as a visionary poet; a meditation on abstract beauty and the poet's aspiration to create a fully imagined world that will compensate for and overcome the experience of defeat. Critics of the poem, uncomfortable with its tacit Platonic orientation, its historical and symbolic analogues, and its variegated language, have argued that Crane's scheme is untrustworthy because it posits a faith that denies the actual. Vincent Quinn, for example, remarks that "the experience offered in the poem is generally weaker than the assertion made about it." [1] But this is to misunderstand the Romantic design of "Faustus and Helen." The poem is not so much an epithalamion as it is a disciplined, fervent preparation for the fulfillment of the ideal. The perplexed faith, the exhortation, the promise of commitment— these are typical of the Romantic poem, as is the belief that the requital of desire is always problematic. The poem stands

on its own without the symbolic parallels to the Trojan War
that Crane draws in his letters. The only alchemy in the
poem is, in Henry James' phrase, the alchemy of art, in which
the Faustian poet transmutes the material into forms of spiritual perfection and absolute beauty.

The poem's organization, Crane wrote, was symphonic, and
he supplied what amounts to a Romantic program in the manner of Bruckner or Mahler:

Part I
Meditation, Evocation, Love, Beauty

Part II
Dance, Humor, Satisfaction

Part III
Tragedy, War (the eternal soldier), Resume,
Ecstasy, Final Declaration[2]

This slightly grandiose sketch hints at the complexity and
range Crane was aiming at and the variety of moods for
which he needed to find proper language; his solution was to
pack the poem with "tangential slants, interwoven symbolisms." [3]

The epigraph from Ben Jonson's "The Alchemist" hints at
the stylistic medley Crane will try in the poem: a superior
bombast alternating with an expressive simplicity. Against the
barbarian hordes, with their materialistic forces and babel of
voices, the Faustian poet will "raise the building up/Of
Helen's house," that is, rescue poetic beauty from the confusions of modernity. He commits himself to a quest for a
language that will resourcefully combine the naked force and
vividness of "profane Greek" with the more special involutions

and archaisms of "Talmud skill." Brom Weber is right in seeing an ironic purpose in this spoof of the "poet—misunderstood, ridiculed, sensuous, anxious for beauty and wealth—who persists in his role despite the abuse and contempt which are heaped upon him." [4] The irony cuts even deeper, for Crane, exercising his ingenuity ("Talmud skill"), sometimes uses a large number of bizarre and unfamiliar words that seem to trip off the bawdy tongue of Doll Common herself: "bluet," "graduate opacities," "hiatus," "nervosities," "incunabula," "hypogeum," and others.

The poem begins forthrightly criticizing the dull democratic average which afflicts the modern mind, for to Faustus the food that the masses take as the communion of their lives— the "baked and labeled dough"—is dreary and quantified and formulaized: stock quotations, baseball scores, memoranda. A cheap bread indeed! (Faustus' is the "white wafer cheek of love.") To represent what is inimical to visionary activity, the diction is dryly abstract and deliberately ponderous:

> The mind has shown itself at times
> Too much the baked and labeled dough
> Divided by accepted multitudes.
> Across the stacked partitions of the day—
> Across the memoranda, baseball scores,
> The stenographic smiles and stock quotations
> Smutty wings flash out equivocations.
>
> The mind is brushed by sparrow wings;
> Numbers, rebuffed by asphalt, crowd
> The margins of the day, accent the curbs,
> Convoying divers dawns on every corner
> To druggist, barber and tobacconist,
> Until the graduate opacities of evening

> Take them away as suddenly to somewhere
> Virginal perhaps, less fragmentary, cool.

Slanting across these apathetic certainties, "Smutty wings flash out equivocations." Though the birds' wings are covered with the soot of the city, the dirt is able to shine and flash out a message, unlike the daily messages from Wall Street and the ball park, of possible illuminations available to the unfettered human consciousness, of the "Imagination eluding its daily nets, self-consciousness." [5] Like the birds in Stevens' "Sunday Morning" they signify freedom and emotional tranquility. Crane's way with words is evident here not only in the juxtaposing of the concrete and abstract ("wings" and "equivocations") but in the clever exploiting of the adjective "smutty." "Smutty" suggests the grime of the city, the color of the birds' wings, and also the fact that the mind capable of new insights is unconventional, though deemed obscene by the earthbound multitudes. It is this cumulative effect, this refining of meaning by redundancy, that Crane frequently strives after in his poetry.

The pattern of equivocations is worked out in stanza two. "Numbers" may refer to the flocks of birds crowding the city streets during the long commonplace day and suddenly disappearing, as evening approaches, to their nesting places in the eaves of skyscrapers. But the "numbers" are primarily the undifferentiated mass of men who, rebuffed by the hard asphalt, the unpleasant environment of the city, lead lives of busy desperation, marginal in the sense of being superficial and concerned with spiritual bookkeeping and "stenographic smiles," all of which accent the "curbs" or limits of their lives. Without vision, their minds are dismembered, their senses atrophied: they suffer a "disintegration of experience." Yet, some hope remains, for if "the mind is brushed by sparrow wings," as the hot glare of the day dissolves gradually into the "opacities of evening," the mind can escape into a realm "Virginal perhaps, less fragmentary, cool"—in short, into the visionary world in which Faustus meets and courts Helen.

The next two stanzas rise in crescendo and sureness, like a chant, to the climactic affirmation of creative solitude, and Faustus' entry into "That world which comes to each of us alone," the world of higher consciousness and transcendental beauty that is untouched by violence, war, or finitude. The poet-Faustus crosses over the inevitable abysses of the "world dimensional"—his limited knowledge, death—into a state of being of supernal beauty:

> Reflective conversion of all things
> At your deep blush, when ecstasies thread
> The limbs and belly, when rainbows spread
> Impinging on the throat and sides . . .
> Inevitable, the body of the world
> Weeps in inventive dust for the hiatus
> That winks above it, bluet in your breasts.

If we restrict ourselves to the denotations of the words, we find it hard to picture them singly or in sequence and make any sense of the passage; individual words and connections (in part as the result of the dislocated syntax) elude the reader. Like Faustus, we must liberate our imaginations to convert the images of the actual, which are reflections of a Platonic world of pure ideas, into meaningful relation. The stanza combines the compression of Donne's metaphysical conceits with Keatsean hyperbole.

Crane is describing the stages of ascent from physical to abstract beauty, "the passage of the soul into higher forms"—[6] his version of the Platonic ladder of vision in *The Symposium.* The world of phenomenal objects is seen as an emanation from the radiant center of Helen's "deep blush." The poet's love for Helen releases in his imagination a flood of new images and perceptions of exceptional beauty. This ecstasy of vision is at first a kind of sexual rapture, but it soon spreads outward to include nature and the cosmos itself ("ecstasies thread/The limbs and belly" . . . "rainbows" impinge). The body of the world, the earth, is contrasted with the hiatus, the space of the heavens which Faustus must pass through to merge in the "eventual flame," the one weeping, the other winking, which suggests that the irreconcilability between man's earthly self and the universe he inhabits is still somehow "inventive," that is, available to the imagination.

"Bluet in your breasts" is ambiguous. "Bluet" is a bluish cloth or a blue flower (Crane does not mean blues, he was upset when the line was misprinted that way), variously called "forget-me-not," "innocence," and "quaker-ladies"! The blue probably refers to the blue sky (the "hiatus") like Mallarmé's *azure,* infinitude, and, audaciously, to the nipple of Helen's breast from which the poet draws sustenance. The innocence and forget-me-not are germane because the poet-Faustus has pledged himself the eternal votary of Helen. Nevertheless, a certain amount of indeterminacy remains. Is the body of the world the outer circumference of the ideal as the soul was the outer circumference of the body for Blake, or is it a covering of that ideal world which man cannot lift, a reading that seems confirmed by the tears of man.

Perhaps the last three lines are a more skeptical view of the
enthusiasm of the first four. In any case, in the rich obscurity
of the passage the balance between denotation and connotation is too sharply broken:

> The earth may glide diaphanous to death;
> But if I lift my arms it is to bend
> To you who turned away once, Helen, knowing
> The press of troubled hands, too alternate
> With steel and soil to hold you endlessly.
> I meet you, therefore, in that eventual flame
> You found in final chains, no captive then—
> Beyond their million brittle, bloodshot eyes;
> White, through white cities passed on to assume
> That world which comes to each of us alone.

In this stanza the poet's enthusiasm for a perfect ideal has
not waned, but he realizes that he cannot hold his vision
"endlessly." The earth possesses a transparency through which
visions pierce, but it glides to death, and so Crane, turning
to Helen, in a tender erotic benediction, vows that he will
share that moment of pure vision—the "white cities" unpolluted by the smutty equivocations of the modern city and
unseen by the "bloodshot eyes" of its citizens—that is the
fiery consummation of death. He contemplates aesthetically
"the secret of the world, there where Being passes into Appearance and Unity into Variety." [7]

Part I ends with a courtly beseeching dedication to ideal
beauty:

> Accept a lone eye riveted to your plane,
> Bent axle of devotion along companion ways
> That beat, continuous, to hourless days—
> One inconspicuous, glowing orb of praise.

The diction mingles in a curious way mechanical and (Platonic) geometrical terms—"bent axle," "riveted," and "plane" —with old-fashioned Romantic epithets—"glowing orb," "hourless days." Sight joins with sound, the silent eye with the harmonious beating of a universal time, in a cosmic praise unlike the "deft catastrophes of drums" the poet will hear in Part II.

II

"New soothings, new amazements"

The second section exploits words for special effects of motion and noise. Written in a deliberately raucous style, quite different from the effusions of the first section, it has what T. E. Hulme called "dry hardness," [8] yet preserves a large measure of sensual implication. Some critics have found the diction contrived, but beneath its Byzantine surface is a dextrous precision and a piquant wit.

The poem is set in a rooftop speakeasy. Dancers skate the floor in self-abandonment while a band plays the latest jazz tunes in frenetic tempos; it is a scene of kaleidoscopic lights and burlesque hilarities. Music pierces everything, introducing "New soothings, new amazements"; hence the "cornets," "drums," "snarling hails of melody," [9] "crashing opera bouffe," "tremolos," and "strange harmonic laws." The language imitates this joyous hullabaloo.

Crane scrupulously catalogues the varieties of intriguing movement. "Glee shifts from foot to foot"; dancers "ricochet from roof to roof." Everything jumps and steps—"White shadows slip across the floor/Splayed like cards from a loose hand"; there are "Rhythmic ellipses," curved and elongated shapes that the body takes, "canters," graceful "falls downstairs" (recalling "poised yet lost in traffic"), "scuddings," "dippings"; relatives "rocked in patent armchairs"; even "the awnings gyrate." The verbs, too, energetically characterize the dance: "shifts," "balance," "lead," and those quoted above.

Crane was fond of witty puns. While describing the frenzied dance, he says:

> Rhythmic ellipses lead into canters
> Until somewhere a rooster banters.

The pattern of the dance leads to unexpected changes, from ellipse to a loping, bouncing gait, and so does the language. "A rooster banters" alludes playfully to the chaffing conversation, the good-humored raillery, that dance partners frequently make, the man preening a bit like the cock of the walk; the phrase also suggests the coming of dawn, and strikes a slightly discordant note, like the horn in "Peter Quince at the Clavier." The atmosphere of the "gardened skies" is done in a style of verbal art nouveau, peculiarly metallic and artificial. Crane liked such poetically outlandish words as "incunabula," "splayed," "striated," and "nervosities" —he often coined them himself—and such unusual ones as "incandescent" and "ricochet"; they are suited to this poem, since the scene stresses the artifices that the poet is heir to, and which he liked to turn into poetry. Crane often, for example, mixed abstract adjectives and adverbs into concrete nouns, as in the "deft catastrophe of drums." The catastrophes are not deft; the drums are deftly played and insinuate some

calamity, as though the drum roll itself were a warning of
the wars and apocalyptic upheavals of section III.

Crane's avowed intention of presenting "Dionysian revels"
and a contemporary version of Helen's seduction is fulfilled
by staging a parodic tour de force, a condensed Fitzgerald-
like scene out of *The Great Gatsby*. Helen has been transformed into a flapper, with a beauty that lacks full consciousness yet imparts a tense promise of paradise. Faustus' eye is
riveted on the "plane" of the "quotidian" world, a fallen world
of physical beauty that merely simulates the beauties of the
ideal, but I do not agree with Brom Weber that the poet
reacts with "lust, the antithesis of the devotion expressed in
Part I." "As poet," Weber goes on, "he observes the desecra-
tion of beauty by modern man. As modern man he is the
ravisher and defamer of beauty." [10] But although this young
Helen is the "siren of the springs of guilty song," and the
poet, gazing at her with affectionate irony, cannot decide
whether she is worth pursuing—had Paris seen Helen dancing
to those jaunty jazz rhythms, he would have abducted her—
the "fall downstairs" is done with "perfect grace and equanimity" and discloses "strange harmonic laws." Indeed, the poet
is both cool spectator and participant in the dance, and the
language follows the mobility of his commitment. The music
is not merely distracting; it is reassuring because it reveals
"New soothings, new amazements." If Faustus is the apostate
of beauty, he is not deaf to the titters hailing the groans of
death; if the "gardened skies" are not as distant or desirable as
the "hiatus" of section I, he cannot frown upon his sexual
revelry. When Crane somewhat pompously, or self-mockingly,
remarks, "I have seen/The incunabula of the divine gro-

tesque," he is showing us the early stages of beauty, the experiences which the imagination will work over, the unformed and potential rather than the already perfected. (Its maturity is presumably described in the communings of parts one and three.) This is in part a "blest excursion," not, as Vincent Quinn suggests, merely "an hysterical escape from frightening realities." [11] The resolution of the "conflict between desire and understanding" [12] is not dodged, it is just postponed. We should remember that Crane projected this section as an interlude of "Dance, Humor, Satisfaction." And this he has done. By widening its range, lightening its texture, and quickening its pace, Crane has created a sardonic, pleasing diction, which he could counterpoint against his solemn and lofty diction.

III

The Lavish Heart

Section III returns intentionally to the more sublime and formal mode of the first part. It is a direct confrontation with death, and in true Romantic fashion, a way of going beyond the tragic to the consolations of the imagination. In a large sense, Crane seeks to redeem mankind from the violent experience of war and free the imagination of his generation from self-pity and a licking of their wounds, so that they can sing again: "We did not ask for that, but have survived,/And will persist to speak again. . . ." The spectacle of war, the terrible wrenching actions of the pilot as he bombs towns and views the sufferings of victims and destroyers, unfolds with a curiously ritualistic detachment, an almost religious melancholy and mute anguish. There is no glossing over of the havoc of war; the planes, like a camera, zoom in on the "rifts of torn and empty houses/Like old women with teeth unjubilant," but by experiencing these horrors and accepting them, the poet achieves a precarious victory and catharsis: "Let us unbind our throats of fear and pity." Section III, he explains to Waldo Frank, is "Dionysian in its attitude, the creator and the eternal destroyer dance arm in arm . . .";[13] and as he writes in his notebook, "the agency of death is exercised in obscure ways as the agency of life."[14] The reference to Dionysus suggests an important motif that recurs in the last lines of "Lachrymae Christi," where the conflated figure of Christ-Dionysus undergoes a violent death that promises the renewal of life, and in the final lines of "Faustus and Helen," where the poet transforms the crucifixion of time, the "volatile/Blamed bleeding hands" that "extend and thresh the height/The imagination spans beyond despair,/Outpacing bargain, vocable and prayer" into a triumph. Like the Bridge, the imagination soars upward into space and, overcoming the shoddy commercialism, the poetic gabble, and the religious reaction of modernity, reaches the center of a new unifying consciousness.

The language of section III presents special difficulties. In the letter to Frank, Crane remarks that "the entire poem is so packed with cross currents and multiple suggestions that I am anxious that you should see the thing as I do. . . ."[15] "Crosscurrents and multiple suggestions" correctly depicts his symbolist technique, as we shall see, but he arrived at this amplitude of inferences by weeding-out obvious phrases, and transposing, highlighting, and condensing others. If we examine an early draft of this part, we can trace not only the evolution of Crane's conception but also the dramatic improvement in diction:

Religious gunman! that died too soon
and in other way that[n] as the wind settles
on the sixteen thrifty bru[i]dges of the city—
your capped and hidden eye succeeds the faun's
as arbiter of bea[u]ty in these streets,
darkly spread out before the motor dawn.
¶What did you ask for; what were you refused?
The privilege of a gift (a goose, tobacco
and cologne; or belles and voices? *that you sought in vain?**

O thief of time! sing *"out"* in the new year;
laugh out the meager penance of their days
who dare not touch the cup that sings!
Clink in with me the praise of all
assembaled near the gasp of desperation
that floods the mind with lovliness released.

Impossible if I deny—yet *"ever" "always"* know
it so that love gives you† more than them *"they"*. . . .
The quenched breath, the substance [*that is*] drilled
shall prophesy your soul in heaven
by the sigh Astarte† [*Astarte's sigh*]—of Astarte, mother of
    beauty—
mother of Saints! *this is your dry crust's lament!*

The lavish heart shall win the rape, in sight,
of ever-virgin Beauty, untouched, unatouchable.

* The italicized words in this draft were handwritten by Crane; the other words were typewritten.
† Crane apparently rejected this word, for the manuscript shows a horizontal line through it.

It shall see, beyond the cautious scan
of mortal wisdom, navel and womb. [*(The) arid relinquish!*]

The aged fire leaps up again, as always,
clearing away the mists of measured hours.
Forgoteen measures are retraced in the grass,
and ancient feasts beabd down the boards.
Primeval presences lick the dews:
inviolable, the soul has twanged its bow!

.   .   .   .‡

There is no light on all the street
to echo now the shimmer of my lamp
against the blackened window [*winter*] pane. . . .
Tower against tower, to build, [*return*] the skies,
glooms out before me in my dreams.
Accuse the wind that sails [*out*] the sun
into your sight, and dawn . . . It is the same.
I do not accuse. Fools come in the dark
to pipe complaints against this (*the*) (*everpresent*) dawn
That brings dismay and beauty to the world

Crane retains very little of this material in the final published version. The episode of the airplanes, for example, the experience of destruction, which is so necessary for clarifying the redemptive role of the "religious gunman," is missing. The very fact that Crane speaks of him in the past tense and asks rhetorically why men spurned his gifts casts doubt on his symbolic effectiveness as "arbiter of beauty." Lines four to six fail of descriptive power because they are too diffuse, but by discarding the faun and the verb "spread out," summoning the "gunman" as a presence in the street, and rearranging the first three lines, Crane gives the first stanza a feeling of mystery in the final version:

‡ These four dots are Crane's.

> Capped arbiter of beauty in this street
> That narrows darkly into motor dawn,—
> You, here beside me, delicate ambassador
> Of intricate slain numbers that arise
> In whispers, naked of steel;
> religious gunman!
> Who faithfully, yourself, will fall too soon,
> And in other ways than as the wind settles
> On the sixteen thrifty bridges of the city:
> Let us unbind our throats of fear and pity.

For the sake of logic and economy, "capped" is transferred to a position modifying "arbiter" rather than "eye." "Capped" eye suggests a closed lid; "capped arbiter" the airman's cap, the *crowned* judge of beauty (Paris) and the savior of the resurrected dead. "Narrows" more exactly than "spread out" represents the slowly encroaching dawn and the deserted street in which Crane strolls with the "delicate ambassador," his doppelgänger. "Numbers" recalls the "numbers" of the first section that "crowd the margins of the day," the legions of the dead the religious gunman will revive, and the Platonic algebra of multiples moving towards eternal unchanging oneness. Even a phrase like "naked of steel" resonates with "multiple suggestions": it looks back to the lines in Part I that explain the elusiveness of Helen's beauty to the questing poet, whose "press of troubled hands" is "too alternate of steel and soil to hold you [her] endlessly." The last three lines of the first draft are reserved for a later passage, and altered in tone and meaning: the goose, tobacco, cologne, bells, and voices become prophecies of heaven, not examples of defeat.

The other changes Crane wrought on his original text are also interesting. First, such banal phrases as "Clink in with me the praise," "dry crust's lament," "the soul has twanged its bow," and "Fools come in the dark/to pipe complaints against this dawn" are eliminated. Second, the cowardice of those meager people who cannot get beyond the "cautious scan" of the "world dimensional" is more sharply demarcated from the bravery of those with a "lavish heart" whose visionary reach and acuteness clears away "the mists of measured hours." The first draft makes clear the contiguity of beauty and dismay, "the gasp of desperation/that floods the mind with lovliness [sic] released," but in revising the poem, Crane assigns the blessing and dismay to Helen: "the ominous lifted arm/That lowers down the arc of Helen's brow/To saturate with blessing and dismay." This consecrating gesture recalls Faustus' previous gesture of homage in Part I: "But if I lift my arms it is to bend/To you who turned away once, Helen. . . ." Moreover, the verb "saturates" is stronger than the earlier "bring," as though man were thoroughly permeated by these antithetical states of being.

"Astarte's sigh" drops out probably because Crane did not wish to introduce into the poem a new mythic reference. The "cup that sings" becomes the "new and scattered wine" and the general categories of "mortal wisdom, navel and womb" are particularized in "Anchises' navel" and "Erasmus' hands." The explicitness of the "rape" of "ever-virgin Beauty" and the "primeval presences" disappear; in fact, Crane excises all specific mention of beauty, instead concretizing it in such images as "gold hair." The one weak passage that Crane retains is "goose, tobacco and cologne—/"Three-winged and gold-shod prophecies of heaven." These terms are too private and limited to serve as substitute emblems for the Christian trinity as auguries of an inviolable spirituality. Finally, Crane replaces the tower that "builds the skies," the projective power of the imagination, with the "volatile/Blamed bleeding hands" that "extend and thresh the height." In all instances, Crane's revisions aim at condensing and coalescing dispersed sensations or ideas.

The diction in the passage describing the planes flying in formation and bombing the town became a matter of contention between Crane and his critics:

> We even,
> Who drove speediest destruction
> In corymbulous formations of mechanics,—
> Who hurried the hill breezes, spouting malice
> Plangent over meadows, and looked down
> On rifts of torn and empty houses
> Like old women with teeth unjubilant
> That waited faintly, briefly and in vain:
>
> We know, eternal gunman, our flesh remembers
> The tensible boughs, the nimble blue plateaus,
> The mounted, yielding cities of the air!
>
> That saddled sky that shook down vertical
> Repeated play of fire—no hypogeum
> Of wave or rock was good against one hour.

Were Crane's intention merely to render an airplane attack in the naturalistic manner, say, of Wilfred Owen, the passage here could surely be ridiculed for its overblown, fancy diction. But Crane was creating a poetry of cosmic space, much like Milton in *Paradise Lost,* and he was right in defending his constructions "corymbulous formations of mechanics" and "nimble blue plateaus" as being exact. "Corymbulous" means cluster, a flat or slightly convex head of a flower, so that the word conveys a picture of the planes flying in geometric pattern and in addition an ironic inversion of organic, beneficent flowering. The planes invading the "hiatus" of section I travesty the proper ascent of this boundless sky; the unity is mechanical, not spiritual. "Corymbulous" is grimly related to "bluet." We are actually given a sharp sense of being in the plane and contemplating the wreckage and feeling the speed. That is why, as Crane noted, the blue plateau is nimble; from the vantage point of the moving plane the plateau is not stationary—and the planes hurry the hill breezes.[17]

"Spouting malice plangent" is a typical Cranesque verbal construction (a curiously Miltonic inversion)[18] that juxtaposes words to force maximum meaning out of a phrase. "Spouting" and "malice" are visually self-explanatory, while "plangent" suggests the deep or loud reverberation of the bombs exploding like tolling bells and the plaintive sound of the airman's regret, both of which contrast with the "bells and voices" that "leaven" the "lavish heart," that is, promise atonement for these destructive acts. "Saddled sky" refers to the slope of the plane as it rains deadly fire upon the meadows, and is related to the "mounted cities of the air" (so unlike the "white cities" Helen passes through in Part I). The "eternal gunman" is here a sort of aerial cowboy.

What prevents such linguistic flights from breaking down or appearing ludicrous and frigid, and it is well to insist again on the decorum of Crane's rhetoric, is their accuracy and placement among simple, homely words which chasten their turgidity. Crane's compulsive apostrophizing, his habit of using the imperative and interrogative modes, traditional conventions in Romantic verse, leads at times to indefensible lapses in taste such as the word "hypogeum" for catacomb. The rationalist critic like Yvor Winters, with his rigid canons of poetic propriety, would rule out this rhetorical diction altogether, which would be a mistake, since Crane's canny ability to reconstruct words from their inside out[19] more than compensates for the occasional inflation or strained wit. The lyric impulse gives direction to the poet's feeling and choice of language.

The eclecticism of Crane's language, with its fondness, in Josephine Miles' phrase, for the poetry of praise, is characteristic of American poets who in seeking an original style feel free to appropriate any tradition. This practice is evident in the passage that ends "Faustus and Helen" on a feverish note of emphasis:

> Anchises' navel, dripping of the sea,—
> The hands Erasmus dipped in gleaming tides,
> Gathered the voltage of blown blood and vine;
> Delve upward for the new and scattered wine,
> O brother-thief of time, that we recall.
> Laugh out the meager penance of their days
> Who dare not share with us the breath released,
> The substance drilled and spent beyond repair
> For golden, or the shadow of gold hair.
>
> Distinctly praise the years, whose volatile
> Blamed bleeding hands extend and thresh the height
> The imagination spans beyond despair,
> Outpacing bargain, vocable and prayer.

The language here is peremptory and incantatory, the poet speaking as the ventriloquist of some spiritual revelation. His sensibility is galvanized, he talks in a voice of command, gathering, as it were, "the voltage of his own blood and wine" to officiate as high priest of the imagination at the sacrament of a new communion. Thus we are not surprised by the scattering of vaguely religious words in the stanza, for some electric current seems passing between the poet and his communicants that will convert grief into joy. This salvation is not possible for everybody, just for those who have dared to share "the breath released,/The substance drilled and spent beyond repair/For golden, or the shadow of gold hair." To achieve this ecstasy requires much effort—a delving upward. And a qualifying note enters this transcendence: Crane is not sure whether spending beyond repair the substance drilled in fact is for the ideal beauty (the golden hair) or merely the shadow of that ideal, though either would apparently suffice.

"Faustus and Helen" marks the place where Crane found his style, and developed a language that had considerable charm, range, wit, and intensity, that could accommodate large themes, rapture, distress, and philosophical speculation. Crane improved and refined his verbal manner in later poems, most notably in *Voyages* and "The Broken Tower," but its characteristic gusto and careful imprecision were laid down in this young man's virtuoso poem.

This "careful imprecision" is widespread in Romantic poetry, and in Crane's. The virtue of cultivating indeterminacy is that it provokes in the reader the considerable aesthetic pleasure of recognizing the significance and immediacy of the experience presented in the poem (the paradisal vision of "Faustus and Helen III," for example). Because the experience is visionary, it cannot always be communicated in exact words. The calculated effect of this indeterminacy is a tantalizing mystery, which can, of course, conceal incompetence or the lack of something worthwhile to tell, just as it can so pull away from concrete realities as to confuse, irritate, and alienate the reader. Crane was willing to risk this last danger. He was unwilling to sacrifice the multitudinousness of his kind of poetic statement. Beginning in "the realm of the obvious," "Faustus and Helen" wins for his poetry, as he had planned, "new sensations, *humeurs*," a "natural idiom" that he "unavoidably stuck to in spite of nearly everybody's nodding, querulous head." [20]

CHAPTER 5

"Voyages"

Crane's lyrical gift expressed itself best in subjects whose feelings he could not feign. His great poems are about himself. Divided and bruised as he was spiritually, it is logical that his poems should plumb and relate his spiritual history and, even more, converge on those moments of relief from pain when that sense of unity which his anguished life missed flooded him with joy. This very vulnerability makes Crane a powerful love poet. There is little humor or relaxed play in his love poems: everything is intense because menaced by time, loss, and fear or knowledge of betrayal. The poems are sensual without being physical; sex is usually spiritualized, though Crane does not omit bodily or erotic descriptions. His gallantry in love is as great as Cummings', but he lacks Cummings' childlike celebration of sex; nor does he see love as an absurd cartoon, as Cummings sometimes did. His consciousness is almost always embattled; the stress is on the psychology of love, on the lovers' mixture of volition and coercion. He is ever warding off defeat even in the midst of pleasure, suspicious that the moments of voluptuous ease will soon end. The demand for some kind of absolute fulfillment is movingly presented, and when the anguished joy ebbs, he seeks comfort and permanence in the poem which is created along with the love and survives it.

The sequence of six love poems, written over a span of three years and collected as one long poem, *Voyages,* is Crane's highest achievement and fascinating to read for its verbal experiments and effects: delicacy, somberness, awe, despair, and a gay wit transfiguring all the dread. What makes *Voyages* so momentous is the new note Crane strikes, or the old note he recovers and makes his own. Cummings' love poetry has a quaint comfortable Romanticism. There are intrusions and adversaries to his enjoyment of love—growing old, inconstancy, and prigs, to name a few—but one does not feel, or feels seldom, in Cummings' love poetry, an intensity springing from making love an absolute. His poems do not report the emotional crises with the personal urgency that Crane's do. The sentiment affirming freedom to love is set in a texture of tender whimsy or light fantasy, but the language, in spite of the typographical novelty, is generally traditional and balladlike. Pound's love poetry, especially his early poems, is marked by an ironic detachment and emotional reticence that effectively steers away from the fatigue, preciosity, morbid romance, and purple passages of the nineties poets—but his language, too, is conventional. In Crane's love poems there is some veiling of the object of his desire, and a curious combination of reserve and confession or importunity. *Voyages* achieves the fusion of masculine and feminine elements in his sensibility that often eluded him. Its astounding vocabulary of love sets him apart from his contemporaries, making available to the praise and endless self-analysis of the love lyric a language that is supple, virile, and encyclopedic. Although Crane lacks Donne's satiric edge and mock-serious courtesies, he shares a similar psychological incisiveness, and has a finer idealism. In addition, the love poetry has an urbanity and rhapsodical calm that are Shelleyan. It is as though Crane took these different kinds of lyrical speech and crossed them to create a third: the love poetry of joinings and sunderings.

The language of *Voyages* is multi-layered, full of unexpected turns and inventions, alternately assertive and diffident. *Voyages I*, written earliest and originally called "Poster," was curtly dismissed by Crane as little more than the "Skull and bones insignia";[1] it is a prelude to the orchestrated themes and feelings that follow, the voyage outward to love and death. It is also one of Crane's most objective renderings of his childhood experience—spare and plain in diction, but beginning those verbal crisscrossings and extraordinary plays with connotations and sounds that make the texture of the poem so rich and clotted. Words echo within a section and forward and backward. And words convey simultaneously tactile, visual, and auditory experiences.

Voyages I starts simply with an image of children swimming in the sea, blithely absorbed in their joyous movements, indifferent to the warning of sea and wave that there are delimiting boundaries to the exploration of self and experience, that death cruelly comes, and that trust in a benign nature is dangerous. The poem is divided into two parts. The first half describes the activity of the children and of the forces of nature; the second half is the poet's direct, affectionate address to the children, in which he admonishes them gently to beware of the sea's treachery: "The bottom of the sea is cruel." The poet's apostrophe is as much to himself as to the "brilliant kids," and it goes unheeded, for in *Voyages III* he plunges into the maelstrom of sea and love and confidently finds in the "steep floor," not death, not carnage, but "the silken skilled transmemberment of song," which assures that the betrayals of lovers can be forgotten and the testament of beauty written in the covenant of "Creation's blithe and petalled Word." In other words, *Voyages I* is a miniature of the remaining poems, introducing the central theme and the central technique: metamorphosis.[2] The children "have contrived a conquest for shell shucks," the husks and unpromising objects that yield up, in the words of "At Melville's Tomb," "The portent wound in corridors of shells." The materials of art, as well as love and happiness, are perishable, subject to the bleachings of time, but the poet's ingenuity, like the children's, circumvents this falling away through the aesthetic ordering of the imagination. It is no wonder that Crane ignored his own advice, for the free, merry, and spontaneous play of the children needs to be complemented by immersion in the depths of the actual, "Must first be lost in fatal tides to tell," even if the tides are perilous, as, indeed, they are for the swimmers of *Voyages VI* who are immersed in their "icy and bright dungeons."

The latitudinarian tendencies of Crane's diction permeate the poem. He loves to exploit different denotations of words in order to establish a series of interlocking connotations. If we consider the following lines:

> Above the fresh ruffles of the surf
> Bright striped urchins flay each other with sand,

we notice the carefulness of Crane's method. "Ruffles" means folds and therefore presents rather exactly the configuration of the sea (a visual image); ruffles also means flourishes of the drum, an auditory image of the pounding surf, so that he is coalescing two sense impressions of the sea. Both meanings are picked up later in this poem and reappear in like or transmuted forms in subsequent *Voyages*. Thus "In answer to the children's *treble* interjections," "The sun *beats* lightning on the waves,/The waves *fold* thunder on the sand." The children do not hear the ominous music of reality, but it accompanies the poet on all his voyages, whether in the seductive "bells off San Salvador" or in the funereal "knells" and "Adagios of islands" he passes.

The "Bright striped urchins" refer to the children but also to the sea urchins tossed up by the sea, and additionally implies either their striped bathing suits or their bodies striped by the sun. The latter meaning is taken up again in "cordage," perhaps the most unusual word in this poem. In the six poems, Crane assimilates numerous terms from the language of sailors and sailing into the fabric of love speech. Crane probably picked them up from various sailors in Brooklyn waterfront dives, and, as we shall see, from Melville. "Spry cordage," the ropes in the rigging of a ship, is likened to the rib cage of the children, and also suggests the images of winding and wreathing that run through all the poems. "The line you must not cross" combines the meanings of cords, equator, and a line of music to be written on by the poet's hand and the sea's and lover's caresses: the "Bright staves of flowers and quills" of *Voyages IV*. And, finally, "lichen-faithful" puns on the words lichen and like to warn of an affection that clings and kills like a fungus.

Voyages II is quintessential Cranesque rhetoric. In its language it encompasses a lyrical discourse, an emotional depth, a density of sensuous detail, an impulsiveness, and a sureness of composition, that is remarkably complete. As always, the language moves centripetally, gathering along the way a host of active and discrete words that join in precarious harmony. Unfolding in hieratic slowness, and evocative of contending moods and ultimate repose, the language is painstakingly precise. The poem is, first of all, a marvelous seascape, seen with pitiless clarity, and second, a spiritual voyage. Although the lovers are adrift on the sea, enclosed by bountiful yet death-dealing elements, they can still snatch a brief concord: beatitude comes out of the recognition of death and transience. The language hangs midway between chant and dream, between passivity and an urgent invoking of the spirit of love to hold out against death; its mood, in spite of excited defiance of an inevitable dissolution, is one of calm, bold rapture. The transitions are accomplished by careful fidelity to the demands of the situation, that is, to coalescing the motions of the sea and the words and images it summons in the poet's consciousness. Each phrase describing the sea is murmured in a thoughtful matter-of-factness which switches abruptly to declamations commanding submission because that is the only means of triumphing over chaos and separation: Take, Mark, Hasten, Bind, Bequeath. This is the process of metamorphosis essential to love and to the creative ordering of the poem itself. It is as though Crane were asserting the power of personality and the poetic will to reach the mastery of craft through struggle and surrender.

The longer one studies the worksheets to *Voyages II*, the more astonishing are the metamorphoses Crane wrought on his original conception, which often verged on Romantic chaos. It is not only a matter of preserving some words from draft to draft while transposing and excising others, since most poets in some measure labor over troublesome words and lines in search of greater clarity or sound effects. Rather, it is Crane's imaginative and careful weeding out of words and phrases that either too quickly give away his meaning or screen the reader from the drama of contending emotions. Because in early drafts both emotion and erotic description are very explicit, as in the doggerel of "In braziered closures strip to dive,/ for it is so, we leap to know," Crane's revisions aim at an impersonality that will make his love experience unique yet universally applicable:

> The emulating tides that stroke
> Our sides and clothe by pawing coves
> the swarty superscriptions of a perfect lust,
> Timeless as your leading towering, falling hair—
> Processioned of continuous me in the gamut, deep
> And sleepless, teeming orbit in their lair—[3]

In this stanza, unlike the last draft, the sea is relegated to a secondary role; its motions emulate the lovers' embraces, putting the seal, as it were, on their "perfect lust." In candidly using the word lust instead of love and praising it as timeless, Crane creates a problem of belief: the reader is likely to hold back assent to this extravagant substitution of terms, lust being a lesser thing than love and unworthy of the title timeless.

Given Crane's idealistic predilections, it is inevitable that he should have shifted the emphasis in the final version. Both the poet and his lover gain a prominence here that is dropped from *Voyages II*. The locution "Processioned of continuous me in the gamut" awkwardly attempts to compress the themes of immersion and the sea as a harmonious musical scale (Crane subsequently changed "gamut" to the less hackneyed "diapason") analogous to the emotional range of the love. The towering, falling hair, likened to the rise and fall of the waves, is clearly a sexual epithet, out of place here but transmuted into the beautiful conceit of *Voyages V*: "In all the argosy of your bright hair I dreamed/Nothing so flagless as this piracy." Besides such banal phrases as "pawing coves" and "teeming orbit in their lair," and the grammatical confusion of modifiers, the passage is pictorially murky. Crane seems to have realized all these faults, and discarded everything except the words "superscription" and "processioned," both assigned, in the final version, to the sea—"samite sheeted and processioned" and "superscription of bent foam and wave."

The examination of another passage may shed light on the methods and purposes of Crane's revisions:

> Take this sea, then. Entangled to learn
> frondages of *dark* islands breathing now
> the crocus lustres of the stars. And though
> in terror of her sessions she enlist us
> to her body endlessly, subscribe. She
> is our bed. Her* Shadowed sceptres roving
> mark gliding shoulders sadly memorized
> as vanished lily groves; and you whose arms

* Crane apparently rejected "Her," for the manuscript shows a horizontal line through it.

> dip now in mine,—anon, you too, in turn,
> to see you dive immeasureably with phantom ease!
>
> Bells ringing off San Salvador *in scrolls*
> *of silver, ivory sentences sustain*
> *Confessions, brimming, O prodigal,*
> *Of which your tongue slips mine,*
> *Poincetta meadows of the tides*
> *Efulgent joy*† [?], *repeated awe*
> *While they are one, sleep, death, desire*
> *Close round one instant in one flower.*[4]

The chief defect of these stanzas is that they are talky and disjointed. Despite the commands and assertions such as "Take this sea, then" and "She is our bed" there is no continuity and little breathing space between words. The language only sporadically communicates the fatal entanglement of terror and love. The lovers are joined intimately in experience of darkly sensuous and cosmic beauty: the tropical palms are imagined exhaling the perfume and light of the stars. This lush synaesthetic phrase disappears in later drafts, possibly because Crane thought it more logical that the "bells off San Salvador salute/ The crocus lustres of the stars," "salute" connoting a mood of good will, established by the "wink of eternity," a gesture duplicating the sea bending toward the moon in ceremonial harmony. Moreover, "Entangled to learn" again says too much, points a moral, and was wisely eliminated.

In the third sentence, the sea is explicitly a siren luring the lovers to a fatal embrace, and though aware that the sea's magistral severity induces fear, the poet can only counsel submission to the doom: the sea's bed is deadly. The words "ses-

† There is an illegible word, handwritten, after "joy".

sions," "enlist," and "subscribe," however, do not fall together in semantic logic or achieve the verbal nuances Crane was seeking.

The fifth sentence is disfigured by the trite phrase "vanished lily groves," which Crane surprisingly retained through most of the drafts. The poet strains to provoke the reader into feeling the sadness of his memory of time's swiftness. "Shadowed sceptres roving/mark gliding shoulders" is a too busy sentence that blocks up the verbal music. Crane therefore breaks up clusters of words for the sake of rhythmic vitality and freedom. As a beginning, he transposes "sceptred" to a position modifying "terror": "the sceptred terror of whose sessions rend," like a king's or judge's power to execute a subject. Since in several other drafts he had the phrase "silhouettes of sceptres roving," he apparently wished to picture the dance of light and shadow on the waves, but finally rejected both "shadows" and "silhouettes." In "Mark how her turning shoulders wind the hours," Crane salvages the personification of the sea as a woman, sharpens the picture of the waves unfurling, and conveys a sense of the lovers hemmed in by time.

Crane suppresses altogether the last three lines of the first stanza and the fourth line of the next stanza, "Of which your tongue slips mine," mainly because they are embarrassingly specific in physical description, and platitudes at that. Of the rest of the second stanza, Crane eliminated "effulgent joy," "brimming," and "repeated," and for reasons of euphony replaced "ivory" with the alliterative "snowy": "On scrolls of silver snowy sentences." "Sustain" becomes "complete" and the reference to "prodigal" kept. "Poincetta meadows of the tides" undergoes slight changes in spelling and pronoun, but with "crocus lustres of the stars" possesses the opulence Crane loved in his words. His verbal style being essentially periphrastic, he needed to control this impulse toward excess.

Crane's handling of theme and his choice of words produce a kind of stylized tension between argument and the bardic, between plainness and the bizarre. Crane wishes to create a spell, a mood, and to locate the juncture of the private self and the external or cosmic, and still avoid preciosity and Romantic chic. There is, for example, the conscious effort to revive or renew archaic poeticisms, such as "spindrift," "minstrel galleons," "undinal,"[5] as if he were calling forth from the past some splendor nearly disappeared, which, decked out in a modern sensibility, has yet some beauty to give. (Some of these words, thrown up from the unconscious, are borrowings from Melville and Rimbaud.) They are lyrical emblems of his special exaltation, and in context extend the emotionally rich states of being in which menace and faith survive together: "sleep, death, desire,/Close round one instant in one floating flower." Consider the "minstrel galleons."

Galleons were stately sailing vessels, often men-of-war or trading ships; their capture was a great prize for the pirates. The poet is cast upon the sea of chaos and wanders drunkenly in his enchanted boat through the lovely meadows and islands of the Caribbean. This ship, this state of being, is obviously a rich one; love is imagined as booty, and the enemy is both time (the sea) and the lover's unfaithfulness. This links to the piracy of *Voyages V*: "In all the argosy of your bright hair I dreamed/Nothing so flagless as this piracy." And "minstrel" is apt because it refers to Crane's musical and poetic roles. All of these meanings are relevant to the poem.

By using these words Crane is not trying to destroy the logic of fact or to swaddle his feelings in the language of riddle. The poem is not, after all, constructed according to a recondite blue-print, nor is it a glorifying of psychological irrationalism. Rather, it is an attempt to face the truth of flux and to open up multiple perspectives. The Romantic poets do not like to prescribe boundaries or rules to their experience, but this does not mean that they give themselves up to amorphousness and indefinition. For them as for Crane, words have a symbolic power; the search for self is equally a search for the order and essence of language, the comprehension of an unspoken idea, "the incognizable Word." The language moves waywardly in keeping with the poet's wayward moods and perceptions. This may be an ambitious and unattainable ideal—it does at times lead to obscurity—but it is not a stupid one, for it corresponds with some deep human need to express a sense of wonder before the twin mysteries of selfhood and world and unify them. Thus Crane is obsessed with naming (it is perhaps the major theme of the *Key West* poems), with isolating the object or feeling and identifying with it in order to master it. It is like wrestling with the angel of incomprehension and forcing him to yield his blessing: a coherent, durable poem, which is a naming of sorts.

It is necessary, however, to stress that Crane did not drive logical clarity out of his poetic utterance. His casual associations of the connotations of words contain a structural pattern. In apprehending and arranging sensuous or mental experience, he recognizes that the discursive function of language *may* interfere with the non-discursive. One part of a metaphor may be submerged, but we can divine it in the words scattered in the poem. This does not mean allowing autocratic liberty to the reader's intuition or inviting promiscuous interpretation; it does mean a more patient ferreting out of meanings concealed in unexpected words or sequences of words, of noticing, that is, the peculiar displacements poetic language is prone to.

Voyages II is a case in point. Its language is molded to fit those moments of visionary intensity, danger, and quietude that are mirrored everywhere in the poem: in the sea, in "The seal's wide spindrift gaze toward paradise," in the "lovers' hands," and most poignantly in the poet's own mind. The language, in fact, is almost liturgical, for passages of praise expressing stately joy and repose alternate with passages of stern otherworldliness expressing a sense of inescapable doom. Although there is no concept of God, there is a succession of cosmic referents, something like the Psalmist's sense of the regality of nature, of the world made in love and terror. Time and eternity, the grave and paradise, are the nodes at which the poem intersects. The slowness of the poem is due to Crane's metrical markings and syntax—the movement is clearly an Adagio—and the procession is almost funereal in its musical language, as if some great public figure were being mourned with much pomp. The procession is, of course, lyrical and inward and meditative; the urgency the poet feels is dissipated in the hush of "bent foam and wave" and the approach to consummation.

Unusual words are most frequently employed to render the seductive touch and appeal of the sea. The sea is personified as a woman—her body, as it were, is sculpted by the poet, limb by limb, belly, eyes, breasts, shoulders, and hands—who is infinite, shimmering with beauty, erotically ebbing and flowing, fathomless, enfolding, and impenetrable. (She emerges from the bottom of the sea, transmembered, as Venus, in *Voyages VI.*) She is "Samite-sheeted," a silky shroud, an undine, a coquette who laughs at the "wrapt inflections" of human love. "The poinsettia meadows of her tides" are alluring tropical archipelagos for the peripatetic lovers, yet they merely delay the coming of apocalyptic violence when the throes of love, the universe-casting gaze for paradise, will receive its answer, its knowledge, its fulfillment and release: death. Few American poets have so desperately realized this entwining of love and death. One thinks of Whitman's "Out of the Cradle Endlessly Rocking" and its elegiac consolations. For Crane, desire is sacred, but it springs simultaneously with death. In *Voyages II*, he is momentarily sustained by his piety, his heart is filled with reverence, and his ears are filled with the echoing bells that salute the stars like a music of the spheres; his prayer is directed to a creator who is either absent or only fitfully guarantees human wholeness. Eyes glancing at the sea's infinite space, Crane courageously admits the "dark confessions her veins spell." The pathos of the finite is that completion means death, completeness the poem.

The language of *Voyages II* is saturated with the language of *Moby Dick,* just as the theme of the poem explores favorite Melvillean themes. At the time he began writing *Voyages* Crane had just finished reading *Moby Dick,*[6] so that it is no surprise that his mind should be brimming with its Shakespearean richness, miscellany, and energy. There are specific borrowings, a kind of unconscious quotation which proves that Melville cut deep into Crane's imagination, and there are similar verbal processes, particularly Melville's practice of beating abstract words into a concrete sentence. Melville's metaphysical conceits may serve as glosses on difficult textual fragments in *Voyages*.

First of all, some of the marine vocabulary bears the imprint of *Moby Dick*. The poinsettia meadows are like the fields of brit through which the *Pequod* cruises, and the mildness and fecundity of the sea the voyagers coast along resemble the sea-gardens in which the whales spawn. In fact Crane's evocation of the infinite sea room, and the soft and dirge-like main, as well as his sense of the sea's magnanimity and treachery correspond with Melville's, as in the following passage: "These are the times of dreamy quietude, when beholding the tranquil beauty and brilliancy of the ocean's skin [as though it were "samite sheeted"], one forgets the tiger heart that pants beneath it; and would not willingly remember that the velvet paw but conceals a remorseless fang." [7] The word "leewardings" and possibly the "penniless rich palms" derive from this description of Moby Dick: "such lovely leewardings! They must lead somewhere—to something else than common land, more palmy than the palms." [8] The exquisite line "On scrolls of silver snowy sentences" seems close to the following extract from the chapter on "The Spirit-Spout":

It was while gliding through these latter waters that one serene and moonlight night, when all the waves rolled by like scrolls of silver; and by their soft suffusing see-things made what seemed a silvery silence, not a solitude.[9]

And the two lines from the last stanza "Bequeath us to no earthly shore until/Is answered in the vortex of the grave" [10] recall "the lashed sea's landlessness," [11] two of the troubled seekers of *Moby Dick,* and the catastrophic ending of the voyage. Ahab's boat spins in the vortex of his grave (via the agency of the white whale) and then sinks, Ishmael alone riding out the whirlpool on the periphery. Crane's fate is something like Ahab's. And Crane, like Bulkington, is an outcast from the safety of the shore compelled to explore, in the very jaws of death, the possibilities of the wild, unknown regions of the self, fleeting transcendental ideals, and untrammeled visionary experience and knowledge.

If the feminine face of the sea is described in a vocabulary of romantic wonder and smoothness, its darker masculine face is expressed in a vocabulary of austere nobility and graphic wit. Legal and royal terms abound. The sea is personified as a magistrate presiding sternly over a courtroom in which the lovers are on trial for their lives.[12] The emblems of authority are on display, formal and chastising, as are the paraphernalia of an indictment: "processioned," "knells," "sceptred terror," "sessions," "demeanors" (implying misdemeanors), "dark confessions," "superscription," "sentence," and finally the "grave." What is startling about these subtly accumulating legal words is that they apply equally to a description of the motions of the sea. This plasticity of reference and inserting of solemn Latinate words into a lyrical context is a leading characteristic of Crane's diction.[13]

This technique depends for its success on the spacing of connotations in irregular patterns throughout the poem; the words themselves are not split into emotive and mental units, but the reader picks them up as they impinge on his consciousness and lets them reverberate against each other. Sometimes it is the eye that joins the parts, sometimes the ear. Thus in stanza one the sea bends to the moon in the tide's movement, and in stanza three the underwater bells in the Caribbean salute or echo to the north (the crocus grows in cold climates); this motif is picked up, in slightly modified form, in the first stanza of *Voyages III* in the image of light retrieved "from sea plains where the sky/Resigns a breast that every wave enthrones." And *Voyages IV* brings back the images of distance joined and cold-warmth from *Voyages II* (San Salvador—crocus) in "wings/Whose circles bridge . . . (from palms to the severe/Chilled albatross's white immutability)."

The linguistic principle at work is one of weaving, of following a word or image through its successive protean changes: the "wink of eternity" suggests an eye, which is taken up in "rimless floods" and then dropped until the last line when it reappears as "The seal's wide spindrift gaze toward paradise," the spindrift (continuous driving of spray) insuring that the gaze be not entirely clear. The "rimless floods" and "*unfettered* leewardings" of the sea are contrasted with the "*wrapt* inflections" of the lovers. Similarly with the legal terms, as we saw, and with the musical words. The "diapason" of the sea, that is, its concord or entire compass, knells, tolls, summons by bells the lovers to their trial and death; these bells anticipate and differ from the enticing bells off San Salvador with their promise of a durable love. Finally, as Crane notes,[14] "Adagios of islands" refers to the rhythm of their intoxicated boat as it rocks gently through the sea, the lovers an island surrounded by the destructive element.

Crane also exploits the potential for puns and complementary meanings; the multiple characteristics of the sea are injected into the nature of language, rime becoming rhyme. When the sea mockingly laughs at the "wrapt inflections of our love," it is laughing at the self-enclosed isolation of the lovers, but also at the lovers so rapt by their emotions that they do not see its impending dissolution or the sea's exemption from such restraints. Crane is obviously punning on the words, he is not merely being an amusingly bad speller as Philip Horton has said.[15] "O my Prodigal" again offers this doubling of meaning: the lover is like the prodigal son who leaves his home, and the love itself is prodigal. Lastly, in "her penniless rich palms," a brilliant oxymoron, "Palms" functions as the tropical tree, as a symbol of victory (this is both straightforward and ironic), as a reminder of "the pieties of lovers' hands," and as the blade of an oar (*Voyages III*).

Voyages is inexhaustibly rewarding to the student of Crane's diction. So many diverse terms are brought together in the poems: sailing terms, some familiar, some not, kelsons, tides, bays, harbors, estuaries, navigation, and the like; the flowers of the tropics; and the impressions that sky, sun, and wind give at sea. They ballast the poem much as the factual chapters in *Moby Dick* anchor Melville's allegory. Crane's idiom is strengthened further by transposing nouns into verbs and verbs into nouns (a trick he may have picked up from Melville): "In this expectant still *exclaim*," and "Or as many waters *trough* the sun's/Red kelson. . . ." His verbs and verbals are strongly transitive, thereby imparting thrust to the sentences—"vastly now *parting* gulf on gulf of wings"; "No stream of greater love *advancing* now/Than, *singing*, this mortality alone/Through clay aflow immortally to you." This energy probably arises from the dramatic action of the mind, the inner restlessness which is the impetus of his psychological lyrics.

The abstractions add an element of distance, an intellectual edge, and an eloquence to the poems; they also add an element of surprise by virtue of their conjunctions with concrete words. In *Voyages* words like "immutability," "irrefragably," "logically," "insinuations," "infrangible," and "inviolably" chime with a tragic presentiment or resigned sadness.[16] They have special metrical value, of course, but they are not line fillers, nor are they flattened out and denotatively inexact. "Immutable," "infrangible," "inviolable," and "irrefragable" all mean indestructible, unchangeable, inseparable, which is in keeping with the poet's fierce assertion that love will endure, though it is immortal only in the poem itself:

> The imaged Word, it is, that holds
> Hushed willows anchored in its glow.
> It is the unbetrayable reply
> Whose accent no farewell can know.

The quasi-religious overtones of Crane's vocabulary, the spiritualizing of the secular that typifies the Romantic poem, and which he used as early as "Chaplinesque," is illustrated by *Voyages III*. This, the most richly ceremonial poem of the sequence, is a hymn; in it the poet dons priestly robes, enters the sanctuary, and performs the ritual act that binds him to his lover. He has a vision of supernal grace in which death is transcended by a series of sea changes. In his guise of chaste petitioner, he attains the sacramental perfection of "infinite consanguinity" with the sea, his lover, death, and poetry; it is a state of being that is like Keats' "happy pain." "Consanguinity," "laved," "reliquary," and "transmemberment" are the religious terms used.

These words provide an exact picture of the interplay of light and dark on the surface of the waves, of the swellings and recedings of the waves; and they build to a vivid yet reticent description of the erotic experience. The line "admitted through black swollen gates" refers both to the ship passing into the trough of the sea and Crane into his lover. "Ribboned water lanes" recalls "samite-sheeted" (also "silken skilled transmemberment") "cordage," and the many words of winding and wreathing. The vortex is brought back in the phrase "whirling pillars." Finally, Joycean traits appear.

Crane was an early and ardent reader of James Joyce's *Ulysses*. When it appeared in installments in *The Little Review* and later in book form, he seized upon the novel as a breakthrough of consciousness and as an emblem of the modern artist's power to create, in magnitude and abundant detail, "the epic of the age." [17] Crane begged Gorham Munson to smuggle in a copy of the book from France so that he could read it in its entirety. A subsequent reading confirmed his sense of the novel's genius. He found it an ingratiating if bitter book with "a strong ethical Nietzschean basis." [18] The *Letters* record a rancorous and complicated experience which upset Crane considerably: his mother told him that a friend had borrowed the book and never returned it; Crane was convinced the book either was sold or confiscated. This loss is unfortunate, since we cannot examine Crane's annotations;

nevertheless, the influence of *Ulysses* is evident explicitly in the poetry, especially in *Voyages*. More indirectly but pervasively, it captivated Crane's imagination and influenced his language.

The external evidence is interesting but inconclusive, since many of the following words and images might have reached Crane independently or through other reading. The "two little curlyheaded boys, dresed in sailor suits with caps to match and the name H. M. S. Belleisle printed on both," whom Bloom sees "dabbling in the sand with their spades and buckets, building castles as children do . . . happy as the day was long" [19] remind us of the "Bright striped urchins" of *Voyages I*. Belle Isle, which appears in *Voyages II* and *VI*, may derive from Whitman's *Specimen Days* (it is a Southern prison hospital) or from a place in Newfoundland. The "one floating flower" of *Voyages II* is reminiscent of the passages in *Ulysses* that describe Bloom's pubic hair in the bath as "dark, tangled curls of his bush, a languid floating flower." [20] Bloom's vision of a lazy, hot, flowery Far East, with its lethargy and sleeping sickness in the air[21] is like Crane's tropics. And the fusion of sea, word, and harpstring in the following passage is similar to the "Proem" and "Atlantis" sections of *The Bridge*: "Whitebreast of the dim sea. The twining stresses, two by two. A hand plucking the harpstrings merging their twining chords. Wavewhite wedded words shimmering on the dim tide." [22]

But clearly what Crane responded to most was the novel's technical experimentation and linguistic élan. There was, first of all, the astonishing diversity and flow of verbal materials: words seem able to sing and dance, add and subtract, think and feel, to have life of their own. Second, Joyce was as syncretic a writer as Crane, roaming through the verbal universe and mingling slang and the scientific, the lyrical and the didactic, the journalistic and the language of dreams. This must have bolstered Crane's already strong faith that language might perform any feat. Perhaps most instructively, Joyce was an inventor and magical manipulator of words— puns, palindromes, anagrams, and portmanteau words testified to Joyce's bravura gifts. That Crane learned from these devices and assimilated them into his poetry is hard to doubt.

When Crane writes, in *Voyages III,* of "the silken skilled *transmemberment* of song," he creates a brilliant new word that expresses the tension in the poem between creative and destructive process, between love and death. The word, like the love, is made up of transubstantiation and dismemberment, the one impossible without the other. The poem requires a similar reconciliation of opposites: the "imaged Word" fulfills a memorial function by preserving the love even after it has ended. In the same poem the phrase "This *tendered* theme" suggests both the act of giving and the tenderness with which the love is offered. *Ulysses* is filled with such coinages: "blandiloquent," for instance.

In the "Proem" to *The Bridge,* Crane, addressing the bridge and invoking its powers, says, with a Joycean pun, "And of the *curveship* lend a myth to God." "Curveship" refers to the cluster of circle images in the poem that stand for unity and the harmonizing of fact and value, self and world; and it also looks ahead in its pictorial aspect to the curved ship that Columbus sails in the next section, "Ave Maria," and, by extension, Crane's belief that he can sail metaphysical seas.

Another such pun occurs in "Lachrymae Christi": "Thy Nazarene and *tinder* eyes." Crane here fuses the meanings of tender and tinder to suggest the sacrificial joy and tenderness of Christ that leads to the fiery renewal of man (Christ is associated with Dionysus). Last, the cultural montages in *The River* stem from Joyce's diverting coinages: Uwantit, dubiosity.

CHAPTER 6

Diction

What I have been describing as Crane's habitual verbal method is close to that of the Symbolist poets, and his language, like theirs, relies for its organization primarily on musical and associational modulations. Its antecedents go back even further: to the language and structure of the great Romantic odes. Under the pressures of emotion, whether great pleasure or dejection or states in between, the language of the Romantics at times precludes moderation. The proximity of these states of exaltation and despondency to dream and nightmare, which was an important discovery of the Romantic poets, meant that if the poet were to be true to the experience he was describing, he had to give up some of the rational explicitness of the waking mind. His language would not be that of everyday talk. This is not to defend obscurantism or emotional incoherence, but to suggest that the linguistic propriety of such poems will not be the same as that of, say, Dryden's poems. C. S. Lewis is right, I think, when he remarks that "poetry most often communicates emotions, not directly, but by creating imaginatively the grounds for those emotions. It therefore communicates something more than emotion; only by means of that something more does it communicate that emotion at all." [1] The Romantic expression of emotion may be disliked, but the fact that its dominant verbal moods—declamation, invocation, and apostrophe—and its agitated utterance proceed from definite laws of form should be recognized.

Poets before the Romantics wrote psychological lyric poetry, most notably John Donne, but the fundamental difference between Metaphysicals and Romantics lies in the greater self-consciousness and endeavor of the Romantics to chart an exit from that self-consciousness: one feels a more provisional self in a Romantic poem than in a Donne poem. Because they were aware of their fluctuations of feeling, because they believed (and this belief verged on doctrine) that, as Paul Valéry remarks: fragments lead to a whole, the disorder of consciousness gives birth to the beginnings of order, and *accidents provoke essences,* their vocabulary and mode of combining words were influenced by these notions. Valéry further describes this process:

> . . . deep states of disturbance or emotion give rise to inexplicable bursts of expressive activity whose immediate effects are forms produced in the mind, rhythms, unexpected relations between hidden points in the soul which, although remote from each other until that moment and, as it were, unconscious of each other at ordinary times, suddenly seem made to correspond as though they were parts of an agreement or of a pre-established event.[2]

Those who are uncomfortable with the excitations of feeling that preoccupied the Romantic poets have scornfully dismissed their poems as "rhetorical," [3] meaning that the Romantics depart from the limits imposed by reality to pursue the thrills of autointoxication and destroy in the process both the mind's equilibrium and its grounding in the ordinary: they abolish the social functions of language. From this viewpoint, the poet's language must submit to the test of its closeness to everyday speech, a speech that is paraphrasable. What is preferred is a poetry of deflation and wry irony, like Frost's, that stresses the limits of knowledge and, thereby, what can be put into a poem. This leaves little outlet for visionary poetry or a poetry of overstatement which springs from a desire to venture beyond the limits of what is already known. In this kind of poetry, the poet turns his thoughts and feelings inside out in order to discover truth. As Wallace Stevens says, "The poet is the priest of the invisible." [4] He does not pump up his heart with empty feelings; rather, he gropes for the meaning of his erratic insights. That is why he is willing to risk inflation and banality, to essay the sublime.

What, then, is the relation between speech and music? Are formal and colloquial discourses irreconcilable? What is lost by turning away, even in part, from the speech of one's contemporaries? What is gained? In short, how free is the poet to screen out vulgar speech and to set in its place a more artificial language? The answers are problematical. It is not easy to find a viable compromise between talk and gorgeous rhetoric. The Symbolist poets, seeking to create a pure poetry, that is, a poetry isolated from utilitarian meanings which would assimilate poetry to music, pushed Romantic self-consciousness to a dangerous extreme. For them, the poem was an artifact and its language could be crammed with curiosities drawn from anywhere that the poet's mind cast its net. The danger in "pure" poetry is that it becomes a hot-house flower, its language stilted and aging rapidly, or else remains a private utterance (though indirectly this involves profound criticism of and withdrawal from society). The weakness of poetry that returns to the axis of common speech is that it rests snugly in the commonplace; it too much narrows the boundaries of inquiry into the nature of reality. For all Frost's greatness as a poet, one feels that in refusing to push into "metaphysical" areas he shackles his poetry; something is missing, some chancing of impossibilities, some resonance. He is too self-approving. Yeats is the one modern poet who manages to wed these two languages.

For the most part, then, Crane belongs to the Romantic-Symbolist tradition. It sanctioned his lyrical explorings of his tortured sensibility, and gave him a way of making poetry out of his emotional impasses and of attaining, if only occasionally, that oneness with the world that he ever chased and that eluded him. This fact is important because it explains the timbre of Crane's poetic voice and the main subject matter of his verse—the intense, almost Brahmsian emotionalism and shy boldness with which he expresses the battering against frustration and temporal defeat, and those rare moments of extraordinary fluency and calm when he was released, by music, love, alcohol, or poetry, from the tormented round of self-destructive acts. At its best, as in *Voyages*, Crane's rhetoric is dazzling and full of ramifications; at its worst, as in "Indiana," it is bewildering, willful, and mawkish.

There is a tradition in American rhetoric which, while never deserting common speech, countenances plucking words from every linguistic tree: Whitman's poems sprinkle, with outlandish rather than elegant effect, French words into the American idiom, or introduce scientific terms, with complacent humor, that convey the power and the pulse of the contemporary industrializing spirit. In the democratic future which Whitman envisioned for the United States, confidently at first and doubtfully afterwards, the poet would weave together the multicolored strands of the American people.

This inclusiveness reflects not only a basic attitude toward life, but a conception of what it is to be an American, American identity being conceived as an aggregate of several identities. Crane shared these views and practices. He, too, wished to write a "Song of Myself," but unlike Whitman, he was generally unable to incorporate the external world so heartily into himself or to project imaginatively more than one or two selves. In his poetry he could not move easily from self to world, and while he shared Whitman's gregarious conviction that the poet was representative man gathering up the divergent and contradictory claims of America and stamping some life-enhancing unity on them, Crane was too honest to deceive himself that twentieth-century America would listen to such a visionary poet. His age in its aimless activities had become too enamored of its pursuit of material rewards to heed a plea for spiritual wholeness, especially when couched in a difficult rhetoric. It was out of harmony with "the absolute direction I always seek, often miss, but sometimes gain." In this hostile atmosphere, he had to satisfy himself that his poetry gave a "true record of such moments of 'illumination' as are occasionally possible. A sharpening of reality accessible to the poet. . . ." [5]

II

The "imaged Word"

A study of Crane's key words reveals a striking bias toward a Romantic diction and, not surprisingly, a diction that expressed his personal dilemma: how to break out of an unhappy life and its corollary of how to find a stable and reassuring faith. The linguistic features of Crane's poems are formed by the pressures of this quest. If the statistics and charts of the principal nouns, verbs, and adjectives English and American poets have used, which are in the appendices to Josephine Miles' book, *Eras and Modes in English Poetry*, are compared with the words Crane used twenty or more times, some interesting facts and conclusions are revealed. The chief fact is that Crane stands apart from almost all modern poets in his choice of diction.

The following is a list of the forty most frequent words in Crane's poetry:

1.	eye-eyes	74	9.	wind	43
2.	time	55	10.	still	39
3.	know	52	11.	hear	33
4.	see	48	12.	light	33
5.	death-dead-die	47	13.	sky	32
6.	white	45	14.	sun	32
7.	day-days	44	15.	take	31
8.	one	43	16.	lift	31

17. love	30	29. shadow	24
18. night	30	30. bright	23
19. dream	29	31. heart	23
20. back	28	32. stone	23
21. sea	28	33. dawn	22
22. moon	27	34. green	22
23. all	25	35. smile	22
24. beyond	25	36. bleed-blood	21
25. hand-hands	25	37. black	20
26. hold	25	38. slow	20
27. star-stars	25	39. water	20
28. wing	25	40. world	20

Of the major words on the list, seven are particularly concerned with seeing or with the conditions in which the poet can see best: eyes, see, white, light, sun, bright, and dawn. They are almost always associated with a birth of hope, a beneficent life force, and a fullness of being. Their negative counterparts include death, night, shadow, and black. Crane sometimes reverses the values attached to these words. Sun, for example, in many of the *Key West* poems is a harsh force that beats down the will and coerces Crane into seeing the stark cruelty of nature. In these poems, the visible object world, though rendered sharply, seems untransmutable by the imagination. Similarly, shadow or night may be neutral states in which dim apprehensions, intimations of the eternal, take place; they do not always threaten annihilation.

This obsession with seeing has two dimensions. In the first the poet is Seer, the prophetic spokesman for the community of the unseeing and the partially seeing, who exhorts, chastises, and makes the past fully conscious by outlining its continuity with the present. A reader of auguries, Whitman's heir, who spiritualizes American values and imbues the drama of American experience with an ethical and aesthetic meaning —this is an enticing role to Crane, and the goal he set himself in *The Bridge*. But he only intermittently succeeds in finding a language that could report his vision and support the massive theme of the poem. Imaginatively, he can see beyond the conflicts and mean expediencies of his age (and the American past) to an Atlantis where deformations and venality are replaced by purity and love. Yet when he tries to delineate this paradisal vision clearly, his view is constantly being blurred by the inhumanity around him and by his own unhappiness. He cannot achieve the impersonality needed for the narration of these public events; his private world intrudes too often. The unity he longs for is absent, or is just wish fulfillment.

In a more modest way, in the shorter lyrics, Crane finds the manner of the "egotistical sublime" a suitable style. Aspiring to see better, and searching for the grace and clarity that will pierce the unknown with illumination he is a poignant figure. Crane was fond of quoting Blake's aphorism that one should see *through* the eye, not *with* it, and for Crane, as for Blake, the perceiving mind is more significant than the objects it perceives.

The boundaries of Crane's quest for insight were marked by two perils, time and death, both of which haunted him during his mature years. These are, to be sure, hoary topics. What poet has not written about the transitoriness of time or meditated on the death of a friend or his own death? But Crane felt them with special intensity, since he was haunted by the feeling that he had wasted or misused his poetic gifts.

In bondage to time, which meant mostly entrapment in bitter humiliation and disquiet, he seemed to welcome death as consolation and the one moral certainty, and more importantly, as a precondition to the transfigurations for which he so ardently yearned.

"White" figures centrally in Crane's vocabulary for two reasons. First, it is pictorial, as in such phrases as "the meteorite's white arch" and the "white sand" of Carib Isle. Second, it mirrors his search for a state of purity and unity (the bridge is called "whitest Flower"); it is often opposed to lust, as in this passage from "Recitative":

> Look steadily—how the wind feasts and spins
> The brain's disk shivered against lust. Then watch
> While darkness, like an ape's face, falls away,
> And gradually white buildings answer day.

Literally these lines picture dawn breaking over New York skyscrapers—Crane is a superb evoker of New York's clangorous spirit—but figuratively they present the emergence of the poet's mind from the hallucinatory fog of debauchery into the clear morning of intact selfhood, which permits him at the poem's end to "walk through time with equal pride." In a peculiar way Crane was an idealist of the senses, and the fact of his homosexuality may have caused him to return so often to the word "white," since it probably connoted a holy desire unvitiated by guilt or mortification.

Therefore, "white," with its corollaries "bright" and "dawn," and the word "smile" are used honorifically in Crane's diction. They are often heralds of salvation bringing the gift of momentary wholeness or fixing the permanence of the poem, like Venus' eyes "That smile unsearchable repose"; or they are gestures and tokens of love, such as the lover's "bright hair," or affectionate innocence, such as the "bright striped urchins." Only rarely does the word carry the ambiguity Melville, Poe, and Emily Dickinson give it. In *Voyages V* where "Together in one merciless white blade—/The bay estuaries fleck the hard sky limits," estrangement is signaled by this reversal of connotations. Nonetheless these changes do not cancel out the essential moral radiance these words have for Crane.

The paradox of the one and the all lies at the heart of Crane's poetry, just as it lies, unresolved, at the heart of his life. Seldom feeling this oneness with all things, always striving to get in touch with the generative forces in himself and in nature, he eagerly prays for that awakening in which "What I hold healed, original now, and pure. . . ." that is, the reconciling, of one and all, will last. This yearning, with its hint of a dying into life, is offered in its most distilled form in "A Name For All." Wrestling with slippery words, which seems a maiming of creation by the names "we have, even to clap on the wind," Crane has a vision of individuality merged into a harmonious world order: all in one and one in all:

> I dreamed that all men dropped their names, and sang
> As only they can praise, who build their days
> With fin and hoof, with wing and sweetened fang
> Struck free and holy in one Name always.

This may be interpreted as an urge to escape the discipline of craft and his own imperfections as poet and man by melting into a kind of Pantheistic universe, but it is typical of Crane to want to build a higher synthesis that, under the shelter of a divine power, includes good and evil. Crane's deepest instinct was to sing these songs of praise; his tragedy, as man and poet, was to feel his self splintered and adrift in the vortex of disunity. He could not hold together for long. The songs he sang were of praise forced out of pain.

"Sky," "sea," "moon," "sun," and "stars" are the stock words of the Romantic poets, who rove the world of nature looking out for analogies and equivalents of their inner moods: the world of outer space is an extension of the self's inner space. This handy, overused shorthand is liable to become a preposterous solipsism, but Crane intends it, daringly, as a literal claim for the existence of unsystematic shifting links between man and the world. In *Voyages II* Crane's vision of the sea in its dual role as creator and destroyer corresponded with the lovers' own feelings. Similarly, the moon that in *Voyages II* shines benevolently on, and moves in tune with, the tides changes in *Voyages V* to "deaf moonlight," to a tyranny, a tidal wedge that separates the lovers. Stars and sky often intimate an unbridgeable cosmic distance. Crane's skill is in revitalizing these overworked words.

"Wind" is like the "correspondent breeze" of Wordsworth's *Prelude*: the creative spirit that visits and leaves the poet, that blows and lists, as his moods vary. In "Recitative," for instance, it is a symbol of the fugitive potent force that can waken the listless poet to creative endeavor and love. In the *Key West* poems, the wind is mostly becalmed, "little," or "knots itself in one great death—/Coils and withdraws," until it rides in the hurricane as a chisel that batters at creation in a frenzy of liberating destruction.

Of the remaining words on the list, only "hands," "wing,"

and "stone" need be mentioned.* Hands are usually symbolic of intimacy ("the pieties of lovers' hands") or purification ("The hands Anchises dipped in gleaming tides"); "wing" is symbolic of Crane's many efforts to soar, like a bird, into the highest reaches of consciousness; and "stone" is symbolic of the intractable despair and resistant will that blocked him from writing or loving; in "Possessions," the "fixed stone" of lust is contrasted with the "bright stones wherein our smiling plays." It also refers to the inhumanity of modern technological civilizations:

> Because these millions reap a dead conclusion
> May I presume the same fruit of my bone
> As draws them towards a doubly mocked confusion
> Of apish nightmares into steel-strung stone?

If we consult Miss Miles' chart of major adjectives for the modern period, we find that Crane employs only two of the five main adjectives with any degree of frequency: great, little, old, *green*, and *white*. His five favorites are white, green, bright, new, and black. I have already discussed "white." It is understandable that Crane avoids antithetical measuring words like "great" or "little"; they seem irrelevant to the types of experience he is rendering. He also turns his back on "old," which confirms his many announcements that he wishes to affirm life and to seek a substitute for the pessimism of T. S. Eliot, for whom "old" is a major adjective. "Green" is a surprising inclusion because it is the least resonant of Crane's words. In fact Crane's group tends to concentrate on colors, and,

---

* Nine of the nouns most often found in Crane's poems do not appear in Miss Miles' list of twenty-one principal nouns—wind, sky, sea, star, dream, stone, wing, shadow, and dawn.

except for "black," which he associates, traditionally, with evil or melancholy, they speak to states of being that are unpolluted, fresh, undimmed, with a potential for, or flourishing with, life.

"New," however, has an incantatory charm for Crane; it peals out whenever he has had a sudden seizure of insight or joy, whenever an exceptional feeling has passed into him and he wildly acclaims its presence: "new soothings, new amazements." "The pure possession, the inclusive cloud/Whose heart is fire shall come." The Biblical imagery indicates that some divine revelation is near. Perhaps the most joyous outburst occurs in "The Wine Menagerie": "New thresholds, new anatomies . . . new purities snared." Crane's fervor for the new is associated with those moments when the "scattered chapter" of his wasteful acts and the "livid hieroglyph" of his self can be bound up and read—when, in short, he can escape the beckonings of the past and make a new beginning toward wholeness.

III

The "multitudinous Verb"

Crane's verbs are even more interesting. Seven of the fourteen most common verbs do not appear on Miss Miles' list: lift, hold, leave, remember, die, turn, and sing. The reasons are not hard to find. These words have a special meaning to Crane; they are inextricably tied to the quandaries of his richly contradictory moral experience. Like the air plant, Crane "Is pulmonary to the wind that jars/[His] tentacles, hor-

rific in their lurch." And like the royal palm, he "Climbs up as
by communings, year on year/Uneaten of the earth or aught
earth holds." This blend of wildness and patience, of aspiration and inertia, is characteristic of American poetry—of
Whitman, Melville, and Poe, for example—but Crane carries
it to an extreme, yet he possesses enough inner strength and
integrity to somehow keep himself from suffocating in his
private world: he can make poetry out of his problem. As
Robert Lowell sympathetically remarks:

> . . . he was at the center of things in the way that no other
> poet was. All the chaos of his life missed getting sidetracked
> the way other poets' did, and he was less limited than any
> other poet of his generation. There was a fulness of experi-
> ence; and without that, if you just had his mannerisms, and
> not his rather simple writing—which if done badly would be
> sentimental merely or just his obscure writing, the whole thing
> would be merely verbal. It isn't with Crane. The push of the
> whole man is there.[6]

With his habitual tact and good sense, Lowell looks at the
poems as human documents. Those critics who have taken
Crane to be a metaphysician or a mystic manqué have sophisticated or falsified him, and made the poems inaccessible to
the reader. Crane is a Romantic visionary, but this means
that his visionary terror is real terror, just as his visionary
ecstasy is real ecstasy. Like the Romantics, he sought to embody the vagaries of his emotional and perceptual life in an
idiom of self-communing.

The verbs tell the story of Crane's struggles. "Lift," for
example, appears in one form or another thirty-one times, almost always in a context emphasizing a straining for tran-

scendence, a desire to be lifted, by a kind of spiritual levitation, above the clogs of his earthly state. That is, to reach a
sublime knowledge through intercourse with the divine. This
is not fanciful, since "lift" connotes erotic movement, as well
as the burden of the will as it tries to raise itself. Last, it connotes a beseeching, prayerful gesture, the search for deity, as
Crane explained the line in "At Melville's Tomb": "Frosted
eyes there were that lifted altars." [7]

This upward movement is repeated in *Voyages VI*, "Where
icy and bright dungeons lift/Of swimmers their lost morning eyes"; the lover, fulfilling the prophecy of *Voyages IV*, is
"now lost in fatal tides," waiting until he can see "Creation's
blithe and petalled word . . . Conceding dialogue" and Belle
Isle. Here the poet emphasizes the impediments to lifting. In
"O Carib Isle" Crane feels only the feeblest sexual or emotional potency: "No, nothing here/Below the palsy that one
eucalyptus lifts/In wrinkled shadows—mourns." The most
striking use of "lifts" occurs in "The Broken Tower," and it
draws on the first two meanings. After the poet has "dropped
down the knell/Of a spent day" in the first stanza, he gradually pulls his powers together, and by entering "the visionary
company of love," in spite of self-doubts, joins his divided
self by an act that involves both a lifting downward and a
lifting upward:

> visible wings of silence sown
> In azure circles, widening as they dip
>
> The matrix of the heart, lift down the eye
> That shrines the quiet lake and swells a tower . . .
> The commodious, tall decorum of that sky
> Unseals her earth, and lifts love in its shower.

The last line recalls the myth of Zeus and Danae.[8] And here, at least for the moment, the marriage of heaven and earth is consummated, and the imagination triumphs. However, the love that sows the poet's imagination and unseals the earth cannot last, for it is silence rather than words that unlocks the self.

The question of how to hold his glimmering perceptions and how to make the promise of beatitude permanent racked Crane his entire life. It is not accidental that Crane affixed these lines from Blake's *Introduction* to *Songs of Experience* as the epigraph to his *Key West* sequence:

> The starry floor
> The wat'ry shore,
> Is given thee 'til the break of day.

During the period of "Faustus and Helen" he could believe that like Anchises he would turn his forced (internal) migration to good end and found a city on the ruins of his hope that would answer all conundrums, and reconcile time and eternity, silence and words, serpent and eagle. (At this time he was also writing the Atlantis section of *The Bridge*, that fantastic Orphic hymn with its lavish music of praise.) Although this euphoria soon disappeared and Crane was left, with the bitter taste of exile, to face his own disintegration, he never lost faith that poetry could root him to life: "The imaged Word, it is, that holds/Hushed willows anchored in its glow." Of course, just as he might be held in joy, so he might be held in pain (but never in hate; even at the nadir of despair, Crane does not hate, or swerve from his conviction that for the imagination to live and grow it must root itself in love). Crane's poems are permeated by a lovely urgency; their rhetorical passion often shields the fragility of his victories and the pathos of his defeats.

"Die" and "sing" should be discussed together because they form a rhythmic motif in Crane's work. While exploring the countries of his mind, Crane experienced countless little deaths, losses of identity, poetic failures—as we have seen, he even came close to believing that death was a necessary condition for insight—but these were followed by resurrections, the recuperation of spent powers, and the return of poetic inspiration. The act of singing was a defiance of death, the song an emblem of his simple human faith in the power of love and art to "gainsay death's brittle crypt."

"Remember," "turn," and "leave," the last three of Crane's chief verbs, recount the entanglements and disentanglements of memory. The past is volatile for Crane, since much of his childhood experience was disturbing, and he understood that his destructive behavior derived from those early days. This accounts for the infrequent bitterness ("I was promised an improved infancy") and the wish to regress back to infantile securities, but mostly he remembers in order to exorcise the wound. However, memory can be estranging or become a paradigm of death, as at the end of "Stark Major":

> Walk now, and note the lover's death.
> Henceforth her memory is more
> Than yours, in cries, in ecstasies
> You cannot ever reach to share.

His restless memory continually brings forth questions he cannot answer. Memory recalls his "long-scattered score/Of broken intervals," his betrayals of himself and his muse, his seasons in hell; but it also brings back, and adds, "The angelus of wars my chest evokes," those elating times he "entered the broken world/To trace the visionary company of love," and found that the word he poured *was* cognate with his finest imaginings. It is therefore clear why "turn" should loom so large to him: he was so often passing between violently anti-thetical emotions, turning away from unbearable agony and turning toward love, beauty, and wonder.

Seeing is not Crane's only way of sensuous perception; his revelations come equally through hearing. There are few poets so alive to sounds and voices, whether from within or from without, whether they are siren calls, delusions, or faulty poems ("banked voices slain") or the message of hope heard on his pulses. They represent part of his mantic and confessional impulses; he hears and tells his visitations and failures to himself and to others.

This survey of Crane's language should demonstrate that contrary to the established judgment of most of his critics, Crane's poetry is not semantically muddled or the work of a gifted but lawless enthusiast. Rather, Crane's diction is pluralistic, colorful, energetic, and sensuous. It ranges from paeans of "cosmic passion" [9] to lyric meditations on the self's difficult pilgrimage to knowledge. One thinks of Wallace Stevens' couplet in "Esthétique du Mal": "Natives of poverty, children of malheur/The gaiety of language is our seigneur." The emotional resonance of Crane's vocabulary is unusual in American poetry, and if his diction deteriorated at times into fustian and the parody of emotion, that fact does not diminish its overall achievement. For there is an amplitude and pathos in Crane's words, a grandeur and eloquence, that rise out of an intricate humanity. The verbal redundancies come from an emotional abundance itself springing from deprivation. Crane's poetry of praise, with its vocabulary of physical presence, ceremony, and pleasure,[10] embraces Romantic and American modes, especially the "egotistical sublime," in order to dramatize episodes in the poet's spiritual biography. The language, even when pictorial, is actively shaped by the poet's struggles and confrontations with chaos. It does no disservice to Crane to say that the verbal fabric is at times forced and arbitrary, and strays from a normative prose-like rigor. In most cases, there is a reason for the deviation. The method of a Crane poem is progression by accumulative associations: its flexible and musical language binds the lyric of dream to the rich circumstantiality of this world.

CHAPTER 7

Imagery

The reader of Crane's poetry is often made uneasy by a seemingly unsolvable quandary. Acknowledging the beauty, power, and even coherence of particular images, he cannot be certain that his analysis has in fact uncovered the sense of the whole. He feels lost in a maze, baffled, and irritated. He has perhaps read Crane's poems as the Rabbis read scripture: convinced that the word was a hidden allegory whose meanings could be ferreted out by inspired and dogged exegesis, that every word, every jot and tittle, had a reason for being and would yield up its secret if only the intellect were exercised long enough and hard enough over chapter and verse. The reader, however, soon discovers that intellectual discipline and the aid of a good dictionary, necessary though they are, take him only halfway toward understanding an image or a complex of imagery. He needs also intuitive skill and lucky guesswork. He must get the feel of Crane's imagistic world, linguistic habits, and sleights-of-hand, and, finally, he must rely on a knowledge of Crane's entire output.

The common reader's complaint that poetry is not a cryptogram or a secular bible, that obscurity is an inexcusable vice, has of course been raised against most modern poets, but most vehemently against Crane. Critics like David Clark, for example, have claimed that Crane's images are willfully recondite, logically confusing, arbitrary, and irrational:

> Term and referent become indistinguishable. One cannot tell the central point from the circumference to which imagery has expanded it. One is afraid that there are many centers and many circumferences, areas whose circles are not completed within the poem's subject or whose center-points lie outside that subject, thus disintegrating the poem's total effect.[1]

Such criticisms were commonplace when Crane was alive, so that he had not only to defend his practice in particular poems but to develop a theory of metaphor that would account for the three chief features of his imagery: the extreme condensing of images, the use of synaesthesia, and the organization of images in mosaical form (the three are sometimes found together and sometimes alone). The three basic texts are the essay "General Aims and Theories," (1925) a kind of retrospective summing up of his purposes in *White Buildings* in which he defines the "logic of metaphor" and the liberties the poet can take with figurative language; his cordial exchange with Harriet Monroe, who hesitated printing "At Melville's Tomb" in *Poetry* magazine until Crane cleared up the poem's obscurities (October, 1926); and the letter of March 17, 1926 to Gorham Munson.[2]

The letters of 1920–22 are filled with allusions to a decisive crisis in Crane's poetic development.[3] Dissatisfied with his early Impressionist poems, and groping for a more complex and arresting style, he had already begun moving in the direction of the Symbolist fused metaphor. Poems such as "Pastorale," "My Grandmother's Love Letters," and "In Shadow" seemed slight and pallid. Characteristically, Crane poses the issues, his "new verities, new inklings," as part of a quarrel with T. S. Eliot. Although not alone in being haunted by Eliot's formidable presence—William Carlos Williams truculently deplored Eliot's verse, especially *The Waste Land,* as "the greatest catastrophe to our letters" because it gave "the poem back to the academics" [4]—he felt that he had to exorcise that presence if he were to establish his own style and subject matter. Yet, paradoxically, it was Eliot's verse that served as the model for the fused metaphor Crane was to bring to refined art. On January 5, 1923, Crane frankly confessed to Gorham Munson:

> You already know, I think, that my work for the past two years (those meagre drops!) has been more influenced by Eliot than any other modern. . . .
>
> There is no one writing in English who can command so much respect, to my mind, as Eliot. However, I take Eliot as a point of departure toward an almost complete reverse of direction. His pessimism is amply justified in his own case. But I would apply as much of his erudition and technique as I can absorb and assemble toward a more positive, or (if [I] must put it so in a skeptical age) ecstatic goal. I should not think of this if a kind of rhythm and ecstasy were not (at odd moments and rare!) a very real thing to me. I feel that Eliot ignores certain spiritual events and possibilities as real and powerful now as, say, in the time of Blake. Certainly the man has dug the ground and buried hope as deep and direfully as it can ever be done. He has outclassed Baudelaire with a devastating humor the earlier poet lacked.[5]

In "Faustus and Helen" Crane succeeded in applying Eliot's "erudition and technique" toward a more "positive and ecstatic goal"; yet while breaking away from Eliot's "poetry of negation" and inventing "something clean, sparkling, elusive!" his poetic mode still employed Eliot's "tangential slants and interwoven symbolisms." After "Faustus and Helen," there is little alteration of the Symbolist trope.

Crane's images are difficult, but they are not unprecedentedly so—in his correspondence with Harriet Monroe he dryly points to difficult images by Blake and Eliot that escape the censure of obliquity.[6] I sympathize with Crane's exasperation. He was, after all, writing in the mainstream of contemporary poetry, and while he was perhaps a more erratic if more striking inventor of images than Pound or Eliot, he did not jettison method or logic from his poems. Metaphor is the discovery of likeness in unlikeness, of the relation between two or more seemingly unconnected objects, and thus by its very nature taxes the reader to follow its direction. A Symbolist metaphor tends further to submerge term or referent, as Clark says, and its principle of organization is sometimes elusive, but a principle exists *within* the structure of the poem, not outside it. For the Symbolist poet, the gain in vividness and connotative richness, in elasticity of meanings, is worth the loss in strict prose denotation.

The limitation of the Impressionist method, Crane argues, lies in its lack of formal and spiritual ambition. The Impressionist is content to record the events of the moment—he is a sort of unofficial journalist of fashion—to project:

> . . . certain selected details into his reader's consciousness. He is really not interested in the causes (metaphysical) of his materials, their emotional derivations or their utmost spiritual consequences. A kind of retinal registration is enough,

> along with a certain psychological stimulation. . . . The
> impressionist creates only for the eye and for the readiest
> surface of consciousness.[7]

Impressionist poetry is to be shunned because it aims at
"decoration or amusement," at rearranging the already known;
it is an inferior mode of vision that does not much alter the
reader's consciousness. Its images are too explicit and un-
resonant, too complacent a jotting down of externals, too easy
to decipher.

"Absolutist" poetry, on the other hand, aims at incarnating
the previously unknown and effecting a permanent change in
the reader. It begins with the raw data of our "real" world
and then proceeds to make:

> . . . at least a stab at a truth, and to such an extent may be
> differentiated from other kinds of poetry. . . . Its evocation
> will not be toward decoration or amusement, but rather
> toward a state of consciousness, an "innocence" (Blake) or
> absolute beauty. In this condition there may be discoverable
> under new forms certain spiritual illuminations, shining with
> a morality essentialized from experience directly, and not from
> previous precepts or preconceptions. It is as though a poem
> gave the reader as he left it a single, new word, never before
> spoken and impossible to actually enunciate, but self-evident
> as an active principle in the reader's consciousness hence-
> forward.[8]

This visionary program aligns Crane with the Romantic poets.
The mind's eye is directed inward to the shifting life of the
emotions; in the course of these "psychic explorations"[9] the
poet has sudden unmediated glimpses of an underived or

unique truth about reality. What are these precious "spots of time" (to use Wordsworth's phrase), these "absolutes" Crane wishes to set down in the poem? He indignantly denied Munson's charge that they were a kind of "psychological gaming," a predictable alternation between "gutter sniping" and "angel kissing." [10] Crane himself calls that absolute which "approximates a formally convincing statement of a conception or apprehension of life that gains our unquestioning assent, and under the conditions of which our imagination is unable to suggest a further detail consistent with the design of the aesthetic whole." [11] In recording the vicissitudes of a man's struggle for self-knowledge and for visible signs of the grace and beauty of a rich consciousness, his best poems offer much evidence of the emotion he attached to the attainment of that knowledge. To present this complex and changeable "apprehension" an "absolutist" poetry requires a luminous imagery that flashes multiple meanings through its linked associations.

This aesthetic debate about Impressionist and "Absolutist" poetry bears directly on the nature and function of Crane's imagery. In seeking a new kind of metaphoric relationship that might capture "the more imponderable phenomena of psychic motives, pure emotional crystallizations," Crane had to "rely even more on these dynamics of inferential mention":[12] that is, on the Symbolist technique of indirection. This technique comparatively neglects the "logically rigid significations" [13] of words and invites ambiguity, ellipsis, the "bundle of insinuations" [14] he cited as his goal in "Black Tambourine." While admitting that "much fine poetry may be completely rationalistic in its use of symbols," [15] Crane opts

for the Symbolist and Romantic poem because, by bypassing
literalism, it achieves the utmost ramification at a minimum
sacrifice of clarity.

Crane went to great lengths to stress that his condensed
metaphor was not a private juggling of associations and did
not annul logic. Although words and images in a poem do
not adhere to the strict rules of discursive language, they
possess a logic of their own that gives the impression of
necessity. The poet's intention is manifest; the reader intuits
the sense and finds the semantic connections, partly by con-
sulting his own experience and partly by noting the context
of images. This is not special pleading or an attempt to trans-
fer the responsibility for coherence to the reader. When Crane
submitted "At Melville's Tomb" to *Poetry* magazine, he received a letter from Harriet Monroe asking him to justify
certain "illogical" and "obscure" images. He eagerly seized
the opportunity to expound his theory of poetic language
and dispel the conclusion that because he is interested in "the
so-called logical impingements of the connotations of words
on the consciousness (and their combinations and interplay
in metaphor on this basis)" [16] that he merely shuffled images
together until he found something "novel or esoteric." [17]
"The process," he goes on to say, "is much more predetermined and objectified than that": [18]

> Its paradox, of course, is that its apparent illogic operates so
> logically in conjunction with its context in the poem as to
> establish its claim to another logic, quite independent of the
> original definition of the word or phrase or image thus em-
> ployed. It implies (this inflection of language) a previous or
> prepared receptivity to its stimulus on the part of the reader.

The reader's sensibility simply responds by identifying this inflection of experience with some event in his own history or perceptions—or rejects it altogether.[19]

This, perhaps Crane's most reiterated (and sophisticated) aesthetic point, is a defense of an image that is indefinite for the sake of its suggestibility and yet is intellectually as well as sensuously precise. His favorite motto, taken from Donne, was "Make my dark poem light, and light." Writing to Allen Tate, Crane remarks, "I have always been working hard for a more perfect lucidity and it never pleases me to be taken as wilfully obscure or esoteric." [20] At this point let us examine Crane's practice of the imagistic strategy of condensation in "At Melville's Tomb."

Crane's profound affinity with Melville, commented on in the discussion of *Voyages*,[21] is nowhere more evident than in the dirge "At Melville's Tomb," his poetic tribute to his visionary predecessor. Like Crane, Melville is a watergazer for whom, in Ishmael's words in *Moby Dick,* "meditation and water are wedded forever." [22] The tomb of the title is the sea, later to become Crane's own grave, to which Crane comes as elegist and weaver of philosophical reveries:

> Often beneath the wave, wide from this ledge
> The dice of drowned men's bones he saw bequeath
> An embassy. Their numbers as he watched,
> Beat on the dusty shore and were obscured.

Melville is imagined standing on some solid projection, perhaps the bridge of a ship or a promontory. From his vantage point, like Ishmael in the masthead or Columbus in his "loft of vision," he is able to see deep beneath the waves where the sea keeps its cruelest secrets, and "wide," comprehensively, as it were beyond the horizon. His long view enables him to watch the bones of the shipwrecked sailors ground up like dice and flung by the ocean currents far from the scene of the original calamity. Their numbers, meaning both the multitudes who underwent a watery death and the numbers on the dice, reach shore and are blotted out: their identity is forgotten. In *Voyages II*, Crane had requested:

> Bequeath us to no earthly shore until
> Is answered in the vortex of our grave
> The seal's wide spindrift gaze toward paradise

hoping for a postponement of death until his visionary testament had been inscribed, but the sailors in "At Melville's Tomb" have their testament obscured on the "dusty shore."

How "The dice of drowned men's bones" could bequeath anything, let alone an embassy, troubled Harriet Monroe. As Crane explains it:

> These being the bones of dead men who never completed their voyage, it seems legitimate to refer to them as the only surviving evidence of certain messages undelivered, mute evidence of certain things, experiences that the dead mariners might have had to deliver. Dice as a symbol of chance and circumstance is also implied.[23]

Voyage being Crane's central image for the heroic and restless reconnoitering for knowledge and revelation, the fact that the voyage is unfinished and the content of the sailors' messages undelivered is a tragic event. Very likely Crane is referring also to the undelivered message in the Town-Ho episode when Radney, killed by Moby Dick, does not receive the letter from his wife. The grim embassy, then, is the communication of the ubiquitous death that catches men unawares and buries their thoughts in the sea. Only Melville or the visionary poet can piece these lost fragments together and give them meaning, a theme taken up in the next stanza:

> And wrecks passed without sound of bells,
> The calyx of death's bounty giving back
> A scattered chapter, livid hieroglyph,
> The portent wound in corridors of shells.

The wrecks of assorted voyages, like those of the *Pequod*, pass by Melville's perch, but instead of the bells off San Salvador that seemed to cheer the lovers forward in *Voyages II*, only a solemn silence greets the procession of the dead, thereby emphasizing the bitter anonymity of their life and death. Yet, as so often with Crane, death is not terminal but initiates a process of renewal. The calyx, whorls of leaves, is explained by Crane as an ironic reference both to a "cornucopeia and the vortex made by a sinking vessel." [24] Death is bountiful, a horn of plenty, made out of a swirling, agitated sea, that spills out its "livid hieroglyphs" (blue icons), hidden symbols that form a "scattered chapter," as if Melville's imagination can put the numbers, like pages in a book, into a semblance of consecutive order, and thus supply the only "complete record of the recent ship and her crew" [25] that survives. The poet acts as surrogate for the dead men; he delivers their embassy, probates their will. The "portent," the mysterious and marvelous sign that the poet alone is qualified to decode, is wound in labyrinthine "corridors of shells," to be heard by putting the shell to one's ears, though since Crane remarks that "about as much definite knowledge might come from all this as anyone might gain from the roar of his own veins," [26] he may be momentarily pessimistic about interpreting the hieroglyph. The "calyx" is imagistically related to the "corridors of shells" in shape and circular tracery on a surface, and as the outercovering of some substantive truth (in the sea's roar and the shell's):

> Then in the circuit calm of one vast coil,
> Its lashings charmed and malice reconciled,
> Frosted eyes there were that lifted altars;
> And silent answers crept across the stars.

R. W. B. Lewis has justly remarked that this stanza is "one of the great religious statements of modern poetry." [27] In place of the dead faiths, scattered like the bones of the dead sailors, Crane offers his vision of a beatitude and sacramental repose in which the old livid order is healed and the hieroglyphs of the natural and supernatural worlds yield up their meaning. "The circuit calm of one vast coil" is rich in condensed but concatenated meanings. The whirlpool has quieted, and its destructive circles have become a circuit with all the sense of unity that word conveys for Crane. The questing voyage outward is successfully completed. The sea stretches round the vast space of the globe as if in a series of continuous concentric rings (a Platonic image of wholeness). The lashings of the sea and of Melville's mind have been miraculously calmed; for Melville is able to accept the malice of the sea and, by analogy, his own awareness of the proximity of chaos, manifest in the "dice of the drowned men's bones." A new, peaceful dispensation is thus ushered in.

"Religious and visionary thought is thought about perfection and the way to perfection; and symbols are the only things free enough from all bonds to speak of perfection." [28] Yeats' comment aptly describes Crane's visionary act in this stanza and especially in the line, "Frosted eyes there were that lifted altars." Harriet Monroe was rather literal-minded in complaining that she could not visualize this act. Crane said that it "refers simply to a conviction that a man, not knowing perhaps a definite god yet being endowed with a reverence for deity—such a man naturally postulates a deity somehow, and the altar of that deity by the very *action* of the eyes *lifted* in searching." [29] Crane's definition fits his own philosophical temper as well as Melville's: the "ungodly, godlike man" seeking a faith that could thaw the cold of his metaphysical isolation. The eyes are frosted from the long sojourn in the sea, covered by white spray like "The seal's wide spindrift gaze toward paradise" in *Voyages II.* "Lift" connotes the motion of the religious impulse upward. "Altars" is appropriate because it suggests that the sacrifice of the dead mariners is not in vain, that loss is another "sea-change" turned to gain, and that the spirit needs sacred objects with which to worship the deity: the dispersed numbers form a community presided over by the poet. As if in response to the beseeching, "lifted" eyes, "silent answers crept across the stars." To the visionary scanning the skies, to the navigator charting strange seas of thought, answers, though silent, are given. The poetic imagination is the visionary instrument, the "compass, quadrant and sextant" of the last stanza, that measures in the circuit of the stars a cosmic harmony:

> Compass, quadrant and sextant contrive
> No farther tides . . . High in the azure steeps

> Monody shall not wake the mariner.
> This fabulous shadow only the sea keeps.

The compass, quadrant, and sextant are nautical instruments used, respectively, for measuring distance, altitude, and latitude, whose basic unit is some part of the circle, of the "one vast coil." Crane explained this difficult image to Harriet Monroe in the following way:

> Hasn't it often occurred that instruments originally invented for record and computation have inadvertently so extended the concepts of the entity they were invented to measure (concepts of space, etc.) in the mind and imagination that employed them, that they may metaphorically be said to have extended the original boundaries of the entity measured? [30]

Like Ahab's, Melville's intellect is so keen and innovating that it can contrive or repair a shattered compass or set its course without a quadrant and still guage the farthest movements of the sea; unshackled by convention, it extends our knowledge of the godhead postulated in stanza three. The "azure steeps" refer to the blue troughs of the waves. No funeral song intrudes upon the sleeping mariner; the mood of silence and order sustains itself. The last line ends the poem on a note of serene mystery: the sea alone is the worthy keeper of the visionary records and the transcendental intimations that are Melville's great achievement. Melville is the fabulous spirit (shade) casting the long shadow.

The sublimity of "At Melville's Tomb" derives from the moving "inflections" of the condensed imagery (and the formal perfection of the quatrains). There are no cerebral tricks, just unforced religious emotion and lyric revery.

II

"the orphic strings"

Most poets have used synaethesia at some place in their verse, but it is the peculiar habit of the Romantic poets to rely heavily upon it for communicating feelings that are intense and indefinable. Most Romantic poets begin with the concrete data of sense experience and then proceed to a conceptual conclusion. Neo-classic poets begin with a concept and then proceed to embody it sensuously. Since Romantic poetry aims at condensing sensory impressions for emotional intensity, it does not intend the image to be an exact objective equivalent of a feeling; it even courts a certain degree of blurring for the sake of projecting internal voices. For a poet like Crane, synaesthesia is a means of escaping what he takes to be a falsifying literalism. Its concentration can arouse the reader to an awareness of the interplay of impulse and sensation—it can shock him into looking at himself and the world in a new way. Reason is not abrogated, but it is subordinated to the effort to render the living "inscape" of consciousness or of words themselves. "What we see in the mind," Wallace Stevens remarks, "is as real to us as what we see by the eye." [31] Synaesthesia helps make real that insight:

> The equation for successful synaesthesia takes this general form: a stimulus, perceived by one sense, is metaphorically apprehended by another. The method of synaesthesia holds considerable potential for emotional violence; the sigh that

runs in blood and the fragrances soft as oboes affect us with
great and peculiar power—peculiar, because the sensuous
derangement of a Blake or a Baudelaire conducts a shock of
sudden insight.[32]

Synaesthesia involves the interchanging of one sense for
another; describing sounds in terms of sight, sights in terms
of smells, smells in terms of sounds, and so on. This mode
accorded well with Crane's highly pictorial and auditory
imagination. Crane's colorful imagery is a kaleidoscopic presentation of his teeming mind. It is inclusive and nimble, its
synaesthetic qualities emerging in rhapsodic and exultant
passages when Crane feels secure of an integrated consciousness.[33] Consider the following passages:

> Take this Sea, whose diapason knells
> On scrolls of silver snowy sentences,

The sound of the waves is imagined here as writing sentences on "scrolls of silver," the frothy white-caps, and the
sea, in its guise as magistrate, passes severe judgment on the
lovers, which is recorded on scrolls. This beautiful coalescing
of visual and auditory images calls to mind a host of images:
the pelting of the waves, the tolling of a funeral bell, and the
poet's writing a harmonious poem as a stay against time and
as a means of immortalizing his love.

Another such interchange, this time of sight, sound, and
taste, occurs in "The Broken Tower":

> Have you not heard, have you not seen that corps
> Of shadows in the tower, whose shoulders sway
> Antiphonal carillons launched before
> The stars are caught and hived in the sun's ray?

The poet in addressing himself recalls his uncreative labors, his writing of poems that were only shadows of his imaginative conception—the imagery of shadows and light is a central one in Crane's poetry, deriving from his interest in Plato—not worthy of Apollo's craft.[34] The intricate image in the quatrain describes, first of all, the sunrise, the moment when the last stars of night mingle with the first rays of dawn. The stars "caught and hived" are gathered into a place of dazzling light, which is an omen of a new beginning towards fulfilling his talent, and contrast with the shadows imprisoned in the tower, visions inadequately embodied in poems. The hive also suggests honey and sweetness, the pleasureable product of imaginative activity, the proper utilizing of his prodigal imagination (Crane's mind secretes images as the bee secretes honey). The "corps of shadows" [35] is personified as shoulders which move and produce the alternating music of the bells and then merge back into the light and taste images. The image is like the "swift peal of secular light" that the bridge echoes.

The decorum and compactness of Crane's synaesthetic images, the easy passing from one sensuous perception to another, is best illustrated by the "Atlantis" section of *The Bridge*. The aim of this section is to recapitulate themes, motifs, images, and submerged notes while adding new material, and to weave them into a new and comprehensive unity (the image of the shuttling loom is a dominant one in the poem).[36] Thematically, "Atlantis" seeks to reconcile history and myth, time and space, time and eternity; like "Faustus and Helen," it is an epithalamion for the marriage of earth and heaven. Since the poem lacks a running prose

commentary or some other purely logical continuity to link
the various parts together, it depends on the imagery to connect the loose ends. It should be noted that *The Bridge* is a
rhapsodical epic, like Shelley's "Prometheus Unbound," which
deliberately ignores any strict narrative chronology, so that
the reader himself traces out the correspondences between
clusters of images. The texture is rich, complicated, mysterious. In the first three stanzas of "Atlantis," the synaesthetic
image is most concentrated:

> Through the bound cable strands, the arching path
> Upward, veering with light, the flight of strings,—
> Taut miles of shuttling moonlight syncopate
> The whispered rush, telepathy of wires.
> Up the index of night, granite and steel—
> Transparent meshes—fleckless the gleaming staves—
> Sybilline voices flicker, waveringly stream
> As though a god were issue of the strings. . . .
>
> And through that cordage, threading with its call
> One arc synoptic of all tides below—
> Their labyrinthine mouths of history
> Pouring reply as though all ships at sea
> Complighted in one vibrant breath made cry,—
> "Make thy love sure—to weave whose song we ply!"
> —From black embankments, moveless soundings
>   hailed,
> So seven oceans answer from their dream.
>
> And on, obliquely up bright carrier bars
> New octaves trestle the twin monoliths
> Beyond whose frosted capes the moon bequeaths
> Two worlds of sleep (O arching strands of sound!)—
> Onward and up the crystal-flooded aisle
> White tempest nets file upward, upward ring

With silver terraces the humming spars,
The loft of vision, palladium helm of stars.

On first reading, this passage seems a chaos of beautiful sounds. There is a feeling of uncontrolled, self-delighting exuberance, a cascading of images. Nevertheless, after careful examination the images become coherent. A choral paean, "Atlantis" aims after an inclusive amalgamation of several unfolding images. Missing one link in the chain of associations is not fatal, since the principal method of Crane's imagery, like that of such books of the Bible as *Psalms, Song of Songs,* and the Prophets, is periphrasis and parallelism. The epigraph to "Atlantis," taken from Plato, prepares the reader for the poem's transcendentalism and its stress on music: "Music is then the knowledge of that which relates to love in harmony."

The first thing that the poet sees when he emerges from the gloom of the "subway scuttle" and the dark night of his soul is the arching curve of the bridge. The eerie blackness of the tunnel turns to light, and the babbling grating voices of the weary subway riders change to a harmonious choir of "orphic strings"; as if in thanksgiving, Crane releases a flood of song as he contemplates the bridge, and like Apollo's priest interprets its emblematic architecture as an augury of beatitude and oneness. The bridge is both presence and concrete edifice, and, possessed by its beauty, Crane tirelessly draws it again and again. As in John Marin's drawings, the bridge is seen from a slightly odd angle, blurred and outlined, curving sensuously and nervously upward to the twin towers dominating the bay. With a reckless yet intuitive sureness, the cables are imaged in several ways: as the strings of a harp, as a shuttling loom, as cordage, as staves, and as wires.

The scene is pierced with light, as the moon presides benevolently over this vesper hymn; the dawn of the "Proem" has faded into the incandescence of night. This exact picturing of the sweep of the bridge is reinforced by the irresistible momentum of the syntax and by the frequent reiteration, like "antiphonal whispers," of the words "up" or "upward." This ascent is Crane reaching for transcendental unity; for a few moments, something like the music of the spheres fills the cosmos,[37] and he is in touch with the indwelling spirit of the universe.

The bridge is alive with motion. The very cables are animated by the breath of the poet's faith and love into the "Psalm of Cathay." The bridge speaks excitedly and convincingly of the grand synthesis, "the circular, indubitable frieze/Of heaven's meditation" achieved in one song; the voyage is consummated and strife and death ("sweet torment") overcome, the guerdon won. In this revelatory experience, light is transposed into sound, and sound into light. The synaesthetic transferences are carefully handled. In stanza one, for example, the cables which are like the strings of a harp and the shuttling moonlight "syncopate/The whispered rush." This recalls the apostrophe in the "Proem": "O harp and altar, of the fury fused," and the alignment of the "choiring strings." His *éclaircissement* is then transmitted in "telepathy of wires," which is in contrast to the "telegraphic night coming on Thomas/a Ediford" and the wires "that span the mountain stream" in the Dakotas, in *The River*; the image marks Crane's spiritual conquest of the mechanical transmissions, the ugly negations of the industrialization that destroyed the wilderness and substituted "a world of whistles, wires and steam." The poet and his country have suffered through a scarring division, but clairvoyantly the poet reads and hears a message of hope in the bridge, "As though a god were issue of the strings." The next epithet, "gleaming staves," has two meanings: the cables are likened to rungs of a ladder and to a musical staff, while still retaining their radiance which is conferred on his own stanzas (staves). Their visual and tensile perfection—it is the "index of night, granite and steel" —produce a special kind of music: "Sybilline voices," which express Crane's confidence in his apostolic mission to reveal, in his poetry, "Deity's glittering pledge" and "Deity's young name." These "gleaming staves," which both talk and flash out, then modulate to their visual function alone—the *flicker* of "Sybilline voices."

In his protean imagination the cables next take on the shape of "cordage," the ropes or riggings of a ship. The image, which is pictorially exact, is a reminiscence of the "Ave Maria" section, and Columbus' voyage of discovery. Through the cordage is heard the call of "One arc synoptic of all tides below." This is again a complex synaesthetic image. The arc, a symbol of unity, of the artistic ordering of time's flux and history's confusions, calls and threads, thus combining the circle, music-speech, loom, and sea imagery. The labyrinthine ways of history are not meaningless. The "seven oceans" (nature) and "all ships at sea" (exploring man) plight their troth and join in a joyous credo that there is a universal moral design. This is the answer to the poet's vision of chaos in "The Tunnel"; he is no longer "Tossed from the coil of ticking towers." ("Atlantis" reverberates with answers.)

The third stanza continues the meshing of visual and

auditory images. "New octaves trestle the twin monoliths" —literally, this refers to the beams that support the twin towers, the distinctive feature of the suspension bridge and Roebling's great innovation, but figuratively, the image refers to the music and poetry that brace his vision of a divine concord that is, mysteriously, both immanent and transcendental. The movement radiates outward, beyond the bridge to "frosted capes" and the end of history, and to a new beginning.

The upward spiraling does not stop. In each stanza and sometimes twice within a stanza the eye gazes at the curve of the roadway and the cables. Thus "White tempest nets," yet another visualization of the cables, like an Aeolian harp give off sounds of storm and music, and march upward in martial order. This complicated synaesthetic image has two meanings: the nets "ring," or encircle, the tiered bars, at the top of the bridge and ring, or make music, on the humming spars. The "loft of vision," Columbus' perch as he scans the horizons for signs of land, is the attainment of his visionary goal. Similarly, "the palladium helm of stars" evokes Athena safeguarding Odysseus and steering with perfect control his voyage home: the completion of his quest. It is also a crown of stars, a protective orderly universe.

The cross-checking of images within a stanza and the pointing out of their antecedents in other parts of the poem could be continued, for these interchanges of sensuous referents are a conspicuous part of Crane's style.[38] "Atlantis" is an extremely difficult poem, but even though individual conceits seem to resist analysis, the interplay of correspondences is not anarchic, not a matter of surmise alone. Hints are strewn throughout the poem, and even if a local image is obscure, either the context illuminates it or the reader grasps the gist of the passage and its dominant feeling.

III

"the circular, indubitable frieze"

I have suggested that the proliferation of images is not so bewildering as a first reading might discourage one to believe. The succession of images is woven into a network of meditated meanings. The development is not left to chance. Occasionally, an image will be introduced and then dropped, while the poet goes on to elaborate another strand of imagery, but he will nearly always return to his earlier image and interlock it with the others. The structure is that of a mosaic: the gem-like fragments are attractive by themselves, but it is only when all the pieces are put together that the pattern and the whole may be seen. This mosaic structure of Crane's imagery, so essential to his style and his music, is tested in the "Proem" to *The Bridge.*

The "Proem" is not only an apostrophe to Brooklyn Bridge, it is a prelude to the rest of the poem. It functions like an overture to an opera, distilling the major themes, melodies, and rhythms; incarnating the drama in brief, fleeting phrases. This material is developed fully later on. The poem has an air of mystery, beginning at dawn and in a particular place but *in medias res:*

> How many dawns, chill from his rippling rest
> The seagull's wings shall dip and pivot him,

> Shedding white rings of tumult, building high
> Over the chained bay waters Liberty—
>
> Then, with inviolate curve, forsake our eyes
> As apparitional as sails that cross
> Some page of figures to be filed away;
> —Till elevators drop us from our day . . .

Syntactically, this sentence resembles a coil, with no proper completion. We are given a set of contrasting images and asked to piece out their order. On a cold winter dawn from the water, the seagull soars upward, an emblem of freedom and unhampered motion. Like the bridge, the bird builds high, but unlike the bay waters below, it is not shackled. The seagull's wings shed "white rings of tumult," that is, first, the excited cries of the gull wheeling, and second, a Platonic circle of perfection, which anticipates the "inviolate curve" of stanza two. "White" is found everywhere—in the gull, the sail, the "page of figures," the silvery paint of the bridge—suggesting the purity of his vision. But the vision is tentative, and elusive, as though we were vouchsafed only a brief glimpse of a permanent liberty. The seagull flies out of sight, and to our vision, perhaps blurred by the fog that hangs over the harbor dawn, the gull seems like an apparition. The image then splices into another, but manufactured, apparition, a cinematic montage. This kaleidoscopic technique, "panoramic sleights," the rapid appearance and disappearance of images, describes fairly accurately Crane's formal imagistic procedure. The "Sails that cross/Some page of figures to be filed away" are hallucinatory, a dream of escape from the world of mundane fact and dull business routine to which the masses of men are enslaved. The sail of Columbus will heave into view in the very next poem, "Ave Maria," and of course the sails of the clipper ships which have been filed away in the surreal memory of the drunken sailor in "Cutty Sark" pass again before his eyes.

Then follows an abrupt transition, a frightening disjunction. "Elevators drop us from our day,[39]—although this image indicates a momentary release from the drudgery of daily work —recalling the opening of "Faustus and Helen"—the drop is sinister, because it collects a group of nightmarish associations: the plunge of the suicide into the bay, the careening of the subway down into the tunnel under the river, which is really the poet's descent into a mad phantasmagoric world, into the hell of his own mind. The people hurry to seek refuge in the fantastic fictions of the cinema, seeking some epiphany, some revelation that will invest their life with meaning, but the motion is too quick: the magic is unreal and transitory. Man is irresistibly drawn to appealing stopgaps that recur again and again, but nothing of value is disclosed to him.

The bridge is then directly addressed:

> And Thee, across the harbor, silver-paced
> As though the sun took step of thee, yet left
> Some motion ever unspent in thy stride,—
> Implicitly thy freedom staying thee!

The bridge stretches across the harbor, paradoxically both freely moving and unmoving. The sun's motion seems to be measured by that of the bridge. The vaulting stride of the bridge, from Brooklyn's shore to Manhattan's, is linked to some stasis, yet some great unused power is latent in it:

This paradox of the still form compounded from motion produces the bridge, held in place by the active conflict between its lifting cables and its dragging span, "stayed" by its freedom, and imitated by the seagull above it which moves in an "inviolate curve" and which builds above the bridge, "over the chained bay waters," "Liberty." [40]

But if the bridge stands for unity and liberty, it is also the stage on which death is enacted, a death it is impotent to prevent.[41] The "subway scuttle," a coal bin, vomits up a "bedlamite," one of the rejects of a mechanical civilization, who speeds to the edge, teeters momentarily, and then jumps into the "chained bay waters." "A jest falls from the speechless caravan" is a brutally ironic image, which may refer either to the people on the bridge at the time who laugh at the suicide or to the suicide himself, reduced to a jest, the bridge being the "speechless caravan."

In stanza six, time has moved from dawn to the slow leakage of noon, and the scene has shifted to the city that shelters underneath the bridge. "A rip-tooth of the sky's acetylene," in its juxtaposition of nature and machine images, vividly pictures the jagged bolt of light that harshly cuts and sears the New York skyline. "All afternoon the cloud-flown derricks turn. . . ."—the derricks, like the bridge, hum with activity and penetrate space, reaching toward the realm of the spirit, though the derricks may be a parody of the bridge and the gull (which dips and pivots). "Thy cables breathe the North Atlantic still" means some timeless quiet ("still" also means yet):

> And obscure as that heaven of the Jews,
> Thy guerdon . . . Accolade thou dost bestow
> Of anonymity time cannot raise:
> Vibrant reprieve and pardon thou dost show.

The quasi-divine nature of the bridge is exemplified in this stanza. Although the bridge is man-made, it has become something more than man; it is not exactly otherworldly, but it is not temporal either. It represents an indefinite eternal principle which is without the metaphysical furniture of traditional religions, which indefiniteness is its strength. It is both more and less of a concrete conception; more, because it is a substantial structure, less, because it is anonymous." It possesses the power to bestow peace, honor, pardon, and, ambiguously, the reward of anonymity that is not subject to the erosions of time. (The diction is chivalric and archaic, the praise reminiscent of the Psalms, though the bridge is the "Psalm of Cathay," not of David):[42]

> O harp and altar, of the fury fused,
> (How could mere toil align thy choiring strings!)
> Terrific threshold of the prophet's pledge,
> Prayer of pariah, and the lover's cry,—

The Bridge is filled with apostrophes such as this. The bridge has been built out of prophecy, pioneering engineering, and an exceptional poetic frenzy, involving praise and sacrifice (the harp and altar), and Crane is awed at its terrifying creation and the mind that gave it birth, just as Blake admired and wondered at the force that made the tiger. The bridge is "terrific threshold of the prophet's pledge," an epithet which characterizes the bridge's potent religious status, the entrance to a marvelous temple of the spirit which will fulfill at the end of days, and in the poem at the end of "Atlantis," the pledge of an integrated consciousness and a new dispensation: Jerusalem built on New York's shores. The "prayer of pariah" is ambiguous. It prefigures the beleaguered Columbus' prayer at the beginning of "Ave Maria," but how much the bridge is able actively to shield the pariah is unclear, since the "bed-lamite" who rushes to the parapet is an outcast whose voyage ends in death.

The lights and voices of the bridge are seldom separable, and they appear together in the next stanza:

> Again the traffic lights that skim thy swift
> Unfractioned idiom, immaculate sigh of stars,
> Beading thy path—condense eternity:
> And we have seen night lifted in thine arms.

The lights of the bridge are like strings of pearls, pearls that might "whisper through the Doge's hands." Brooklyn Bridge is a superbly articulated structure, an "Unfractioned idiom," which by transference of epithets means both spiritual whole-ness and the poet's poem which mediates that wholeness to man. The time scheme has shifted to evening, and the lights are compared to an "immaculate sigh of stars," an inviolate exhalation of some divine reality—note once again the syn-aesthetic images—which literally and figuratively "condense eternity." "Eternity is in love with the works of time," Blake said in *The Marriage of Heaven and Hell,* and Brooklyn Bridge, that graceful feat of Roebling's technological skill and unswerving vision, is proof of the truth of Blake's proverb. The last line presents a fine visualization of night coming to the city. Crane personifies the bridge as a parent who lifts and hugs night in its arms, a gesture of love that drives away despair. Lift almost always connotes some kind of aspiration, but here it also suggests that the revelation waited for in vain

by the multitudes in stanza three is given to Crane. This point
is confirmed by the next stanza:

> Under thy shadow by the piers I waited;
> Only in darkness is thy shadow clear.
> The City's fiery parcels all undone,
> Already snow submerges an iron year . . .

If the bridge "condenses eternity," it also attests to the unyielding grip in which time holds man; and if the bridge
is a shimmering light of salvation, it paradoxically can be
glimpsed only in darkness, and then only its shadow. Standing
on shore near the docks of "Harbor Dawn," the poet gazes up
at the bridge, but it imparts to him a note of dark uncertainty.
"The City's fiery parcels all undone" suggests the extinguishing
of the buildings' light, or fragmented urban lives[48] (undone
being a permanent ruin), while "Already snow submerges an
iron year" recalls the heavy load of custom that weighs down
the spirit, as in Wordsworth's "Immortality Ode," though it
is possible that the snow merely conceals the horror of the
city.

The pessimistic interpretation seems correct, however, because it would logically account for the invocation to the
bridge which ends the "Proem":

> O Sleepless as the river under thee,
> Vaulting the sea, the prairies' deaming sod,
> Unto us lowliest sometime sweep, descend
> And of the curveship lend a myth to God.

The bridge, like the Mississippi River which sings hosannas
below (in "The River"), is sleepless; it vaults not only above
the sea, but also extends to the prairie, the earth which waits

its blooming (a foreshadowing of "The River," "The Dance," and "Indiana"). Although the bridge is the eternal incarnate in steel and granite, Crane remains outside its redemptive circle and therefore beseeches the bridge to descend—he has already portrayed its ascent—and lend a myth to God, that is, serve as a provisional organizing principle, or, in John Unterecker's words, "give God a shape contemporary humans can deal with —for God is also ideally both bridge and perfect curve, the chastiser and protector who once had made a covenant with man in the shape of a rainbow." [44] The curveship immediately materializes in "Ave Maria" as Columbus' prowed ship.

The criticism we can bring against Crane is that the bridge is both intercessor for man, like Christ in Christian myth, an instrument of man's transcendence of time, and a concretization of that transcendental principle, yet Crane seems to doubt whether it is either durable or available to man. Like the Romantic poets who were searching for a naturalistic yet transcendent substitute for Christian symbols and modes of salvation, Crane has chosen a symbol that is both bodiless idea and mechanical invention, both in and outside of time. This dilemma is what the rest of the poem seeks to work out. The imagery is intelligible once the reader accustoms himself to its mosaic structure and its extreme condensation.

IV

"Performances, assortments, résumés"

Because Crane's imagery has a nervous, almost obsessive quality to it, it is possible and useful to compile a list of his most frequent images. Familiarity with the classes of imagery is an aid to interpreting the poems and to defining the imaginative world Crane created.

1. THE SEA. The sea is probably Crane's most multitudinous symbol. Treacherous and seductive, the giver of life and the bringer of death, it is the perfect emblem for Crane's polarized self. The sea is somber and cruel, the occasion for tragedy, since its "fatal tides," the inexorable flux of time, splinter man or drive a wedge between lovers, but it is also majestic and iridescent, the occasion for idyll, as in *Huckleberry Finn*, an escape from social pressures and a crabbed, cramped civilization. It is, as Edward Dahlberg notes, an oracle whose riddles Crane spent his lifetime trying to understand and obey.[45] In "Passage," for instance, the sea murmurs its revelations to him and carries him back to childhood memories, a process which is repeated in "Repose of Rivers." Crane early perceived the sea's dualistic nature: destroyer and preserver. As in *Moby Dick,* the sea is the habitat of dolphins and sharks, a marine garden of Eden and a cataclysmic flood. Ablutionary rites which absolve the poet of sin and atone for his falterings are performed in the sea: "The sea lifts, also, reliquary hands," Anchises drips of the sea, and Erasmus dips his hands in the "gleaming tides." The presence of water assures him that his spirit has not dried up. Thus, in "Recitative," the steel buildings "grant/The plummet heart, like Absalom, no stream," whereas in *Voyages IV,* he boldly acclaims the transfiguring surge of erotic passion: "No stream of greater love advancing now/Than, singing, this mortality alone/Through clay aflow immortally to you."

This complex sea-imagery passes through several permutations. The sea is painted, worshiped as a god, despaired of, and of course preferred to land. Voyage is a central image to Crane, of such personal force we cannot measure it. Though a wanderer on the sea's wide expanse,[46] the poet can breathe more freely there, he feels less human shrinking, feels a tranquil acceptance of, and relief from, his distress, even if only for a moment. His mood on the sea, and this most notably in *Voyages*, is buoyed by wonder and prayer, and by a sense of liberty and benevolent, usable space; in spite of his recognition of the sea's terrors, hope quickens.

2. EARTH OR LAND. The sea, though, suggests its opposite: the enclosing shore. And this antinomy has both biographical and literary relevance. Crane sometimes seeks to transcend man's earthly nature and sometimes to celebrate it. His own bodily desires tormented him, clogged his spiritual being, turned him against himself—he calls them "this fixed stone of lust." He was a hungry animal prowling for sensual gratification, and usually thwarted or beaten. Yet he was one of the most extraordinary love poets America has produced. Just as for several heroes of American fiction, the land represented an adversary, a confining, mendacious spirit, and a reminder of man's mortality, so for Crane "The earth glides diaphanous to death" and "weeps inventive dust for the hiatus/That winks above it." "Bequeath us to no earthly shore," Crane asks in *Voyages II*, and identifies himself with the great transcendentalist heroes who flee the known world and the safety of shore in quest of some indefinite knowledge. Was not Crane a composite of Ahab, Bulkington, and Ishmael, and like Ahab shat-

tered by a bolt of lightning, yet appearing whole? America spawns queer kinds of visionaries.

But like his nineteenth-century artistic predecessors, Thoreau, Whitman, Twain, and Melville, Crane had a profound attachment to the American land, seeing it as a grand indubitable emblem of America's (potential) greatness. He delighted in evoking the "continental folded aeons," the geological oddities and natural resources, the huge wealth in minerals and precious stones,[47] the "seething pendant wheat," the abundance of Eden. The body of America, our inheritance from the Indian, is the subject of "The Dance," and Crane had an instinctive feeling for the proper moral ecology. But Crane could not help noticing that the self-seeking, ruthless American soul had pillaged the fruits of a fertile soil, had betrayed their trust, had encroached upon, exploited, and ruined that land (the body). "Quaker Hill" is the threnody for that destruction, whereas "The River," as in the following two stanzas, is the hymn to its might:[48]

> Damp tonnage and alluvial march of days—
> Nights turbid, vascular with silted shale
> And roots surrendered down of moraine clays:
> The Mississippi drinks the farthest dale.
>
> O quarrying passion, undertowed sunlight!
> The basalt surface drags a jungle grace
> Ochreous and lynx-barred in lengthening might;
> Patience! and you shall reach the biding place!

3. FIRE AND AIR. Of the other natural elements employed by Crane in his imagery, fire and air occupy a lesser place. Most images have their parodic opposite, as we have seen. Crane's

apocalyptic vision of the bridge consumed in fire is the consummation of *The Bridge,* but it comes after passing through
the demonic fires of the tunnel. It is precisely this traditional
association of fire with hell and with purification that
Crane lays hold of in the image. Air, too, is an equivocal
symbol. It is used most extensively in the *Key West* poems,
where it is stifling and fetid, an extension of Crane's own
spiritual and creative lethargy. Although the wind (the hurricane) arrives and freshens things, and his poetic enterprise
which had flagged also revives, it unleashes an elating destruction. The wind listeth where it will. Occasionally, Crane will
unite both images, as in the concluding lines to "Possessions":
"The pure possession, the inclusive cloud/Whose heart is fire
shall come,—the white wind raze/All but bright stones
wherein our smiling plays."

4. TOWERS, BRIDGES, TUNNELS. Crane was ambiguously in-
trigued by the artifacts of technology. This attitude, as well as
his fluctuating moods, his emotional gyrations from the
heights to the depths and back again, and the restless rovings
of his mind, is mirrored in the building images that appear
frequently in his poems. The tower is just such an image, a
traditional symbol used by Milton in "Il Penseroso," but
taken over by such Romantic poets as Shelley, Keats, and
Yeats. A retreat for the contemplative man above the dins and
demands of daily life, the tower is a consecrated spot from
which he can look out over the land—it gives him a long view
—and even more from which he can "jacket heaven." In his
aerie the poet still observes and records reality, but from an
aesthetic distance; the tower thrusts proudly into space,

"launched above Mortality," unshackled: an assertion of the self's grazing the horizons. (Trees like the Royal Palm often are tower symbols.) The tower is really the meditating imagination, sheltered from the frigid blasts of disbelief, which is free to create an autonomous art that in its perception of transcendental truths both includes and rises above moral and emotional confusion. Unfortunately, Crane's tower was often a broken one; he did not deceive himself that his imagination was as solid as, say, Yeats', but in "The Broken Tower," his last, elegaic review of his poetic career, when he asks, "could blood hold such a lofty tower/As flings the question true?" his answer is a tentative yes, though the tower is not built of stone, but of "slip of pebbles." [49]

The bridge, Crane's most famous symbol, is another version of the tower. It is not merely an aesthetic and mechanical achievement, evidence that man can use space meaningfully, for in its sweep towards the heavens, in its function as a reconciler of contraries, the bridge is imbued with almost supernatural powers. As early as "The Bridge of Estador" in 1921, the bridge was conceived as a symbol of unity, a way out of his impasses through the mapping of uncharted areas of the imagination. The allure of the bridge of Estador is that "No one has ever walked there before." Though unsure what visions will come to him from this lofty vantage point, he is convinced that his pristine dreams will be consummated. In "Recitative," "The bridge swings over salvage, beyond wharves," is liberating.[50]

The opposite of the bridge is the tunnel, the hideous dungeon in which modern man is trapped. It is the absolute negation of the absolute good. The way up and the way down are not one and the same for Crane. The terrible pathos of his life, and the main subject of his verse, what indeed moves the reader is the strenuous effort to escape his heart's undoing and to cling to his faith in the coming of that permanent happiness he coveted and, at long intervals, got. He had touched bottom often enough to know the cruel disillusionments of yet another failed expedient. As with Othello, chaos came again and again. He improvised his life, but he never ceased the struggle to give his art graceful order and he never lost his remarkable quixoticism. The tunnel is his image of the harrowing of hell, the bridge, his image of a longed-for apotheosis.

5. THE CITY. Crane's feelings about the city and civilization ranged from enthusiastic love to bitter disgust and alienation. The American city he saw as a parody of a humane environment, created by a nasty pandering to debased taste, greedy speculation, and moral aimlessness. The city was a place of "brokenness" and spiritual squalor, and, ironically, the issue of the "nasal whine of power" which "whips a new universe." Men were walled into a "prison crypt/Of canyoned traffic" far worse than the grotesque imagination of Poe ever set down. It was at times a sanctuary, the place where Crane could find camaraderie, good music and art, and exciting conversation. Writing to William Sommer, he called New York "the center of the world today, as Alexandria became the nucleus of another older civilization. . . . Life is possible here at greater intensity than probably any other place in the world today. . . ." [51] Crane's solicitude for the artifacts of the imagination, for poetry and the arts, is a sign of his con-

cern to offer an alternative construct to the ugly buildings, the sooty inhuman artifacts that American capitalism had constructed, with the complicity of the people: "a doubly mocked confusion/Of apish nightmares into steel-strung stone." It is not accidental that Crane called his first published volume *White Buildings.* His vision is articulated in "Recitative": "Then watch/While darkness, like an ape's face, falls away,/ And gradually white buildings answer day." Crane wished to be the Daedalus of his generation, to lead America out of its labyrinth and put it back on the open road, but mostly, "In Bleecker Street, still trenchant in a void,/Wounded by apprehensions out of speech," the stones of the city were too heavy for him to lift, though at times he could build with words a poem "wherein our smiling plays." Crane fought with the artifices of his imagination against the mercenary ethos of the city, but he failed; for every Brooklyn Bridge, there are one hundred nondescript buildings.

6. MUSIC, WORDS, BELLS, AND VOICES. Not unexpectedly in a rhetorical poet like Crane, with his highly developed ear, his extravagant love of words and music, and his zeal to incarnate the word, music and words, bells and voices constitute a large segment of Crane's imagery. Crane was a passionate lover of music—he composed his poems while he played Wagner or jazz or Scriabin loudly on the phonograph —for whom music's "brazen hypnotics" served as an outlet for his exacerbated sensibility and gave him emotional satisfaction. It is little wonder, then, that Crane chose music as a symbol of the supreme good. An art that depended on sequential time, but resolved the parts into a unified and

harmonious whole, music had an architectural, as well as a colorful, design. The writing of poetry is often imaged as the writing of words (notes) on a musical stave: "Bright staves of flowers and quills" (characteristically, Crane blends musical and flower images).[52] "Faustus and Helen II," as we saw, was alive with the sounds of cornets and drums: a "crashing opera bouffe."

The references to words, idioms, and sentences are too numerous to list. Crane's preoccupation with the word is typically Romantic. The construction of a perfect poem is a simulacrum of a perfected consciousness. He invests the word with a heavy load of religious significance, although not a specifically Christian one, and with magical and supernatural powers; the word subdues chaos. He speaks of "creation's blithe and petalled word," and the one imaged word becomes the "One Song": the "white, pervasive Paradigm," "The vernal strophe chimes from deathless strings." In "Atlantis," with its incredible outpouring of song, all creation seems to be singing or talking; for Crane, nature speaks directly to him, and even silent and abstract things are given the gift of tongues.

He hears voices—and bells. The voices are sometimes sirens luring him to death, but most often they are comforting and prophetic. Bells are the most haunting image in Crane's poetry. They reverberate with melancholy, seldom pealing out in joy and cheer. They toll a hopeful message of faith in "Faustus and Helen III": "The lavish heart shall always have to leaven/And spread with bells and voices, and atone/ The abating shadows of our conscript dust." In "The Broken Tower," the bells swing aimlessly, but also represent the Angelus which summons him to a rededication to his muse and his spiritual self. In *Voyages*, the bells off San Salvador chime in homage to the stars, but other bells ring out a funereal tune whose burden is the end of love. The bells have a kind of obtrusive public power, announcing the time, as in "Recitative": "In alternating bells have you not heard/All hours clapped dense into a single stride?"

7. FLOWERS, TREES, PLANTS.   Crane is not pre-eminently a nature poet, but flowers and plants figure as symbols of ineffable beauty, erotic loveliness (as in *Voyages* with its profusion of flower and petal images), and unity (the bridge is "whitest Flower," an Anemone). Crocus or poinciana or poinsettia are used sometimes for their colors and sometimes for their status as symbols of innocence, fecundity, or the exfoliating self. But Crane is less interested in describing flowers than in describing his delighted response to them. The flowers, trees, and plants in the *Key West* poems are exotic and flamboyant, and represent a nature that is prodigal and morally neutral. Though he felt discomfited by the city, Crane was an urban, not a rural poet; every time he traveled from New York to the countryside, he felt freer and happier, until his compulsive nature drove him back to the city.

8. CIRCLES, ARCS, RINGS.   These elements of Crane's Platonic imagery almost always stand for completeness and concord. They turn up most frequently in such visionary poems as "Atlantis" ("One arc synoptic of all tides below—"), "Ave Maria" ("This turning rondure whole, this crescent ring/Sun-cusped and zoned with modulated fire"), "Lachrymae Christi" (the "perfect spheres" that "Lift up in lilac-emerald breath the grail

of earth again"), "Faustus and Helen I" the "glowing orb of praise"), and "At Melville's Tomb" ("the circuit calm of one vast coil"). The vortex, its parodic counterpart, stands for confusion, disintegration of self, and death, as in "Passage": "A serpent swam a vertex to the sun."

9. BODY IMAGES: HANDS, SHOULDERS, BELLY, FEET, HAIR.   Hands are especially important as tokens of fellowship and reciprocal love, or the tendering of love. This image recurs throughout *Voyages*. Hair is a sexual image, almost always linked to an adjective of praise: "bright hair" (*Voyages* V), "gold hair" ("Faustus and Helen III"), though it can have a pejorative connotation, as in "O merciless tidy hair! ("The Fernery") Crane personifies the sea as a woman in *Voyages* and the land as a woman in "The Dance," enumerating the different parts of her body. There is also the anthropomorphic image of Elohim's "sounding heel."

10. ANIMALS, INSECTS, AND BIRDS.   It was Crane's bestiary, populated by strange animals—dolphins, seals, terrapins, apes, a goose, grasshoppers, lizards—which warmed the cockles of Marianne Moore's editorial heart. The two poems of Crane's she printed in *The Dial*, rewriting them without apology, were "The Wine Menagerie" and "Repose of Rivers." The ape is repulsive, associated with nightmare in "Key West" and darkness in "Recitative." The terrapins and lizards are denizens of the tropics who bespeak lassitude and a particularly hideous (psychic) death. The proverbial golden goose appears in "Faustus and Helen III" as one of the "gold-shod prophecies of heaven." The dolphin and seal are sea-creatures, the former

in "Emblems of Conduct" playing in the water, "arching the horizons,/But only to build memories of spiritual gates," the latter in *Voyages II* casting its "wide spindrift gaze toward paradise." Birds appear less frequently in the poems, though we have noted the seagulls in the "Proem" to *The Bridge,* the sparrow's wing in "Faustus and Helen I" and the eagle throughout *The Bridge,* but especially in "The Dance" and "Atlantis." [53]

11. MINERALS AND CHEMICALS. Minerals have a magical, honorific sound for Crane. He is fond of using precious stones either for their color, beauty, and texture—the "marble clouds" of "Emblems of Conduct," the River's "basalt surface" and "ochreous" grace, "In sapphire arenas of the hills," in "Passage," and "I heard the wind flaking sapphire" in "Repose of Rivers." Occasionally, as with the "muffled/Bronze and brass" of "Pastorale" and the "mammoth turtles" of "Repose of Rivers" "climbing sulphur dreams," the citation suggests something poisonous that has seeped out of the earth.

12. GORGES, RAVINES, DELTAS, SAVANNAH. References to these massive geological formations are scattered throughout the poems. When they occur in *The Bridge,* they reflect Crane's love of the grandeur and immensity of the American continent, as in the jubilant moment the Mississippi meets the Gulf of Mexico, "hosannas silently below." In such quasi-autobiographical poems as "Repose of Rivers" and "Passage" Crane hints at critical revelations and profound emotional crises that took place during childhood in "the black gorge," while the monsoon cutting across "the delta/At gulf gates" brings him relief

from some mortifying memory. In "Passage" the ravine is mildly unpleasant. Perhaps Crane intended these geological images to represent the unconscious.

The groups of images I have catalogued are Crane's most important ones. They recur, in one form or another, with welcome regularity, so that the reader or critic who would unlock their meanings need only keep his eyes and ears and mind open and let the poetry work its spell on him. Besides its sensuous immediacy, Crane's imagery is forthright in its appeal to the mind. Though sometimes gauche and strained, it is orderly and accessible to the patient student.

CHAPTER 8

Syntax

When Hart Crane arrived in New York in 1917 carrying a small packet of poems and armed with the hope of becoming a good poet, he came under the tutelage of Carl Schmitt, a painter friend of the Crane family from Warren, Ohio. Schmitt recognized Crane's potential and generously spent much time poring over Crane's works. It was the first time his poems had been scrutinized by an intelligent and stringent mind. Because Schmitt believed that technical mastery was a requisite of poetic growth, he set his pupil exercises to develop rhythmic suppleness and greater metrical variety. As Philip Horton tells it:

> It was agreed that the latter [Crane] should compose a certain number of poems a week solely as technical exercises with the purpose of breaking down formal patterns. These he would bring to his critic as he wrote them, and the two would read them over together, Schmitt illustrating with pencil on paper the rising and falling of cadences, the dramatic effect of caesural breaks, and the general movement of the poem as a whole.[1]

This keen respect for formal discipline stood the young poet in good stead, and never left him throughout his life. Although his letters are sparse in detailed prosodic matters, Crane clearly labored long over and thought hard about the craft of poetry and about the verse forms that would best support his rhetorical style.[2]

It is a fascinating paradox that Crane, with a character that was attracted to extremes and living in an age in which poets experimented with all kinds and extremes of verse forms or discarded them altogether, should have remained a poetic conservative, even a tory. Some sound instinct seemed to guide him away from the dangers in free verse of formlessness and metrical slackness. While many of his contemporaries rushed to embrace free verse and hailed it as the emancipation of poetry from the fetters of form, Crane grudgingly held back. Undoubtedly he read the manifestoes and poems that accompanied each new attack on traditional forms and scanned them for hints he might use in his own compositions, but they were not very relevant to the "wistful indetermination"[3] of the early poems or the hard lyrical declamation of the mature ones. The centrifugal force of Crane's emotions needed to be counteracted by the centripetal force of established verse structures.[4] Indeed, the more he explored extreme states of being, the more he sought strictness of form. Crane rightly understood that his effusions required the curb of metrical regularity or at least of some recurring dominant beat, iambic line, or rhyming pattern. A study of Crane's prosody reveals that it underwent no startling changes; Crane kept to the practices and forms he grew comfortable with fairly early in his career. The *Key West* poems, for example, written mainly between 1926 and 1930, employ the quatrains used in his first efforts, though with obviously greater subtlety.

Crane is not the dazzling virtuoso Auden is; there are only two sonnets and no rondeaus, triolets, sestinas, and terza rimas in his *Complete Poems*; nor does Crane explore the possibilities of adapting Provençal or classical forms to modern poetry as Pound did. He is a sturdy craftsman who prefers working in Romantic lyrical modes or in the quatrain.[5]

The New Critics lavished most of their attention on the verbal structure of the poem in order to uncover irony, paradox, and functional ambiguity. To a lesser extent, they pointed to the ways in which meter could express or reinforce meaning. They tended to prefer a poem that embodied an argument or dramatic conflict to a poem that stated abstract, general, or universal principles, or that described, in a highly colored and emotional way, cosmic and personal passions. Surprisingly, they usually ignored the crucial role syntax played in creating poetic style. More recently, however, Donald Davie and Josephine Miles have shed light on the semantic and rhythmic importance of syntax and have undertaken historical surveys to provide us with a set of guidelines by which we can recognize and assess particular poems from different periods; they have given us a handle with which to grasp the ways syntax controls poetic utterance and accounts for divergencies in style.[6]

Traditionally, syntax in verse, as in prose, is the articulation of thought and feeling through the significant arrangement of words and groups of words. Syntax often defines the relationships among words in a line or within the verse paragraph. Sentences might, by their jagged, involuted, or straightforward structure, direct the reader, like a series of signposts, to the poet's feeling. Although syntax may serve simply as an aid to rhythm, its chief value to the poet lies in its efficient patterning of experiences that would otherwise remain amorphous and unintelligible. In this view, the conscious mind actively shapes its materials in accord with the many grammatical structures available to it.

"What is common to all modern poetry," Davie writes, "is the assertion or the assumption (most often the latter) that syntax in poetry is wholly different from syntax as understood by logicians and grammarians." [7] Though not invented by the Symbolist poets, this attitude toward syntax permeates Symbolist poems. Syntax is present as a ghost in the machine, not as the cogs and wheels that make it function well. In his desire to present his network of relations and his contradictory feelings, without the intrusion of editorial comment, the modern poet tends to create a novel structure for each poem. He is willing to allow a certain amount of blurring when it is the effect of other virtues—vividness, musical effects, and discontinuity, for example. If he deserts traditional syntax, or dislocates it, he is not necessarily being capricious, but rather, as Davie suggests, approximating the condensed and "alogical" syntax of dream.

Davie lists five kinds of poetic syntax: the subjective, the dramatic, the objective, the musical, and the mathematical. These differ in the degree to which they follow some specific form of thought, action, or feeling in the poet's mind, as in Wordsworth and Coleridge; in some other mind created by the poet, as in Shakespeare; in the "world at large," as in Blake; through the poet's mind but without defining the thought, as in Pound and Eliot; or by directing the form back to the poem itself, as in Mallarmé. [8] These categories cannot be assigned in a strict historical or chronological sequence, since an Elizabethan poet, say, might employ any of the first three syntaxes. Most modern and Symbolist poets fall into categories four and five.

Crane's poetry, I think, combines Davie's first and fourth categories: the subjective and the musical. Its syntactical idiosyncrasies are the result of strenuous efforts to give organic form to his agitated inner life. Its complexity is of the sort which acts out the winding and turning of mind and feeling in a highly charged and compressed (yet, paradoxically, expansive) structure, one whose order is sometimes akin to dream and daydream. In such poems as "The Air Plant" and "The Broken Tower" the syntax may be deliberately distorted to underline the curve of feeling; in *Voyages II* and *III*, as we have seen, the unpredicated sentence was exploited for the sake of theme and rhythm.

Yet it would be a mistake to conclude that because there are dream-like elements in his poems, his syntax is willful and random. Crane was generally conservative and cautious in prosodic matters, even after he adopted the Symbolist method. If "Rhetoric is traditionally the province of pseudo-syntax," [9] and Crane is pre-eminently a rhetorical poet, that does not mean the poet always suspends the "logic of consecutive statement." [10] Being a lyrical poet, Crane avoids conceptualization and hence a propositional syntax. His syntax, in Davie's terms, is like music which "presents human feelings as they are born, develop, gather momentum, branch, sub-divide, coalesce, dwindle, and die away." [11] When a poem is difficult, as "Lachrymae Christi" or "Recitative," it is not because the syntax is careless—the sentence appears to be conforming to grammatical law—but because the images are spaced and connected in a series of multiple associations.

Not surprisingly, the narrow, emotionally misty world of Crane's apprentice poems reveal little tinkering with conventional word order or altering of sentence structure for rhythmic effect. These poems are stodgy, excessively constrained; their movement is flaccid, with each stanza molded almost arithmetically to accord with the grammatical unit. Nevertheless, although the lyric and episodic structure of the great poems, with its concomitant rhythmic openness, is missing here, three typical devices which importantly influence the pace and tone of Crane's late poems can be discerned: a preponderance of phrases over clauses and a large sprinkling of adjectives, participles, and compounds; a preference for simple and compound declarative sentences; and the frequent use of the imperative sentence.

An early Imagist poem, "October-November," illustrates the first aspect of Crane's method:

> Indian-summer-sun
> With crimson feathers whips away the mists;
> Dives through the filter of trellises
> And gilds the silver on the blotched arbor-seats.
>
> Now gold and purple scintillate
> On trees that seem dancing
> In delirium;
> Then the moon
> In a mad orange flare
> Floods the grape-hung night.

Crane does not try to alter drastically or experiment with the usual word order of English; he stays with the loose sentence, and the sequence of subject, predicate, object, except for a tendency to supervene a prepositional phrase between subject and predicate or between predicate and object, as in the three sentences above. This clustering of phrases, this gathering up of modifiers, is in general a compulsive feature of Crane's syntax. It is appropriate for the effects he seeks: the isolation of pictorial elements and the quickening or slowing up of rhythm. In "October-November," the three grammatical sentences that divide the poem correspond to the three panels of the poem-painting. The first stanza is a simple sentence with subject and triple predicates, the four prepositional phrases being interspersed in different positions. The sun performs three actions in rapid order, each strung out in a poetic line. The dash after "mists" adds a momentary pause to the comma as the mist is lifted and the sun can dive unobstructed to gild the arbor-seats. The first sentence of the second stanza is a direct complex sentence: in the main clause, compound coloristic subject, verb, and prepositional phrase; in the subordinate clause, subject, verb, and prepositional phrase. The sentence is constructed in an open way to suggest the light delirious dance of the colors. The last sentence repeats the pattern of sentence one, conveying the swift wild spreading of orange light throughout the darkening sky; the stress falls primarily on moon, mad, and flood.

The adjective is typical of a phrasal poem—the clausal poem relies more on other parts of speech and on subordination— and functions in Crane's poetry not as mere ornamentation but as careful sensuous delineation. In "October-November" almost all the adjectives describe color (crimson, orange, grape-hung) or surface (blotched). Still, without taking exception to Crane's fondness for adjectives, and often for oddly attributive ones at that, I think that his choice and exploitation of verbs are even more expressive. Tremendous energy courses through Crane's poems, a thrust that springs from the vigorous verbs he uses and from their strategic placement in the sentence where the metrical stress falls on them. Crane's verbs differ somewhat from those of his contemporaries and seem to possess a taut and unusual strength; they are active and agile, jumping out at the reader from their place in the line. In "October-November" the six verbs—"whips," "dives," "gilds," "scintillate," "dance," and "flood"—all seem to release the momentum of the sentence and the thought. (This propulsion is accomplished in spectacular fashion in "Faustus and Helen II" and in "The Hurricane.") Moreover, Crane skillfully avoids excessive use of copulative verbs and the accompanying dependence on the passive voice.

One consequence of a phrasal sentence structure is that equal weight is more likely to be given to each of the shorter grammatical units and modifiers, even when the sentence occupies an entire stanza of four lines or more. That is why the potency of Crane's verbs looms so large: they prevent the sentence from becoming too static and balanced. The potential virtues of a cumulative construction can be seen in the banal poem "Postscript," written in 1918, which sounds the note of sundering and spiritual brokenness, one of Crane's major themes:

> Though now but marble are the marble urns,
> Though fountains droop in waning light and pain
> Glitters on the edge of wet ferns,
> I should not dare to let you in again.

Mine is a world foregone though not yet ended,—
An imagined garden grey with sundered boughs
And broken branches, wistful and unmended,
And mist that is more constant than your vows.

The syntax of both stanzas is based on the principle of parallelism. Stanza one catalogues images of loss in three subordinate clauses beginning "though" (the third "though" is
implied). The postponement of the main clause until line four
is logical because the meaning of the line: "I should not dare
to let you in again," reflects the poet's feeling of reluctance,
hurt, and timidity. Stanza two reverses the order. The first
line is a complex declarative sentence, but the next three lines
collect appositive nouns—"a world . . ." "An imagined garden . . ."—a set of trailing modifiers tacked onto "garden"
and a subordinate clause ending the poem with an announcement of the lover's unfaithfulness, the cause for the poet's
demure melancholy.

If the syntax of the apprentice poems is orthodox, it is still
designed with care to contribute to their thematic and affec-
tive meanings. If anything, the poems display too rigid an
attachment to the strict requirements of grammar. This con-
servatism was probably the result of a self-imposed discipline,
and in the long run it enabled Crane to write unified poems
with pleasing patterns of versification.

One other feature of the early poems, indeed of the *Complete Poems*, should be noted: the recurrence of apostrophe,
invocation, and the imperative sentence. It is often hard to
distinguish the Romantic and modern sources of these rhetorical devices in Crane's verse. In the matter of apostrophe, Crane
sometimes writes in the ironic vein of Pound's "Doria" and

sometimes in the rhapsodic vein of Keats and Shelley. An example of Poundean apostrophe is the line from Crane's translation of Laforgue's "Locution Des Pierrots": "O prodigal and wholly dilatory lady"; an example of Keatsean apostrophe are the lines, "O brother—thief of time, that we recall/Laugh out the meager penances of their days." Since Crane read Pound and Keats at the same time, and was influenced by both poets, we can probably date the decisive shift from one vein to the other at the time Crane was composing "Faustus and Helen." There is scarcely one poem that does not have at least one imperative sentence; this kind of sentence induces a special importunity and emotional fervor. Sometimes, as in "To portapovitch" and "Lachrymae Christi," the person addressed is specifically named, but more frequently, the poet is as much engaged in a dialogue with himself, musing or urging himself on to some action or feeling (as in *Voyages II*), as in talking to another person.

II

The Logic of Grammar

In his valuable book, *Sound and Form in Modern Poetry*, Harvey Gross remarks:

> The logic of grammar sets up a pattern of expectation, and the expressive delays, the departures from usual word order, and the surprising repetitions all form an articulating rhythm representing the liveliest intellectual activity.[12]

Crane was intensely conscious of the many effects that could be gained by exploiting the "logic of grammar," and as his poetic style matured, he developed a surer hand in making syntax dance to varied and expressive rhythmic measures. Since Crane, unlike Pound, was not particularly interested in breaking up either the iambic or the pentameter line, he did not see the need to tailor the grammatical sentence to the line of verse; rather, he could let it extend, in a straight and crooked path, beyond the line to include the larger verse paragraph.[13] Crane's neglect of Pound's prosodic innovation is doubtless due to his bent for a more elevated and formal poetic speech, one that strayed further from the prose base and conversational tone that Pound favored and that allowed for a mingling of a Pound-like intimacy with his own transcendental rhetoric. Crane might sacrifice some of the subtle plaintive nuances Pound is able to draw out of his versification —which is, strangely, sometimes more formal and elegant than Crane's—but he also avoids the monotony that enters into Pound's poems, especially the Chinese translations like the "Song of the Bowmen of Shu," because of the continual reiteration of the same syntactical pattern. (When Crane is monotonous and wearying it is not so much because of the rhythm as the strident tone and bombastic diction.) To study Crane's handling of syntax, then, is to gain an important clue to his habitual patterns of versification, and to watch Crane change from a minor poet to a poet of almost major proportions.

"In Shadow," a minor but formally harmonious poem written when Crane was only seventeen, is an exercise in chiaroscuro, faintly emblematic like recollected dream images. Its hushed, langorous mood is evoked by the adjectives (furtive, amber, pale, misty), but even more by the clever arrangement of syntax. The woman is passive, swathed in late afternoon shadow (and, presumably, mystery), and she is seen in a blurred fashion, as though she were a wraith. She has no existence at first apart from her parasol, "furtive lace," and "misty hair." A sense of expectancy is built up as first the green twilight and then the steps of the poet impinge upon the woman's consciousness. When the poet joins her, in the last stanza, it comes as a mild shock to hear her voice emerge from the shadows and shatter the still harmony of the "amber afternoon." The poet's frigid words in the last line, "But her own words are night's and mine," suggest some vaguely ambiguous discord, a heightening and disruption of the portentous mood: to risk together the light's decline seems to hint at the impending end of their love, which the night and the man seem to ratify.[14] The bluntness of the last line is due to its being a simple sentence, the only one in the poem which is measured to the line.

The syntax of the first stanza is shrewdly done:

> Out in the late amber afternoon,
> Confused among chrysanthemums,
> Her parasol, a pale balloon,
> Like a waiting moon, in shadow swims.

The sentence is periodic, with the same wavering, swimming movement as the shadows. After the two phrases of the first two lines, the parasol, by a synechdochal substitution the woman, is compared to a pale balloon (its shape and color) and a waiting moon; the verb hangs suspended "in shadow." This same syntactical trick is repeated effectively in lines 11–12:

> She hears my step behind the green
> Twilight, stiller than shadows, fall.

where the syntax imitates the long pause between the woman's first inkling of the footstep and its fall.[15] This use of the periodic sentence is found fairly frequently in Crane's poems.[16] In most English prose, even when sentences unfold over five or six lines, the verb is kept close to its subject. But Crane preferred the loose sentence which permits the accretion of qualifying and coordinate phrases and single modifiers.

As Crane's style evolved from early impressionistic poems like "In Shadow" to symbolist poems like "Faustus and Helen" and *Voyages*, his syntax underwent interesting modifications, mostly in the direction of greater complication and a variety of internal rhythms. Grammatical sentences were made to end in the middle of a line, as in "Lachrymae Christi," and short abrupt sentences were introduced to alter or reverse the rhythmic flow, as in "O Carib Isle!" or almost any other of the poems written after "Faustus and Helen." These changes were introduced mainly in passages which brought the poem down momentarily from its flights of rhetoric to a more conversational speech, that is, reduced the pitch of the verse and set a counter-rhythm going in the poem. What Crane clearly favored, however, was a syntax that coiled and uncoiled sinuously and that kept pace with the ascent to and descent from the visionary center. What happens in Crane's lyrics is that the pressure of expanding and dilating feeling, the invocations, imprecations, and hymns that are so characteristic of his verse, lead to a particular sentence pattern: strongly phrasal, incremental, participial, and compounding. A poem that is loaded down with epithets and elliptical constructions is bound to have a different sentence structure, and rhythm, than a poem relying primarily on statement and rational exposition. The music of such verse is perforce different from the music of an argumentative and clausal lyric, such as Donne's, or a discursive and clausal lyric, such as Wordsworth's. The heaping up of phrases is a useful mode for rendering discrete sensory perceptions or the spasmodic and regular pulse of emotional experience. When this method is joined to a penchant for imperative sentences, the result is the ecstasy of passages like the climax of "Faustus and Helen":

> Anchises' navel, dripping of the sea,—
> The hands Erasmus dipped in gleaming tides,
> Gathered the voltage of blown blood and vine;
> Delve upward for the new and scattered wine,
> O brother-thief of time, that we recall.
> Laugh out the meager penance of their days
> Who dare not share with us the breath released,
> The substance drilled and spent beyond repair
> For golden, or the shadow of gold hair.
>
> Distinctly praise the years, whose volatile
> Blamed bleeding hands extend and thresh the height
> The imagination spans beyond despair,
> Outpacing bargain, vocable and prayer.

This passage illustrates both the success and density of Crane's syntax. It announces the poet's creed: the imagination is capable, in its contemplation of beauty and truth, of transcending sufferings ("bleeding hands"), mendacities ("bargain"), conventional piety ("prayer"), and the stammerings of incomplete poems ("vocable").[17] The poet can find, in rounded and extravagant form, the "incognizable Word," some spiritual value by which to live amid the anxiety and pain of a fractious and atomized epoch. The passage, like the poem, is an exhortation to believe that the imagination can metamorphose exile and the past (Anchises), despair, and human mortality into a present and future community rooted in love, knowledge, and hope. The verse does not move lightly, because Crane is aware of the huge effort that must be undertaken to achieve his difficult goal. That is why the verbs he uses are exceptionally strong. The man who wishes to share in the vision and exaltation must *"Delve upward* [18] for the new and *scattered wine"* (my italics); that is, he must labor against the direction of his age and dig not in the earth but in the heavens for the new faith and a new poetry; the scattered leaves of the sybil need to be gathered. The breath (words, poetry) [19] must be released and "the substance *drilled* and *spent* beyond repair." There can be no half-hearted commitment to the quest for the gold hair (truth and wholeness), for when the "volatile/Blamed bleeding hands *extend* and *thresh* the height," obloquy will greet the searcher, a kind of crucifixion or harassment by a hostile, disbelieving culture. In the face of these obstacles, the poet (and everyman) must beat and shake the harvest of the imagination to separate the grains from the husk.

What Crane is calling for, then, is the creation of a new man. His references to Anchises and Erasmus are not historical fillers. Each is a founder of a new order. Anchises is herald of the Roman Empire, a man who left the ruins of the Trojan War to establish a new and flourishing civilization (this is an apt analogy, since in this section of "Faustus and Helen"

Crane is devoting himself to rousing modern man from his *acedia,* his grisly memories of the ravages of the First World War, and getting him to build a fresh world).[20] Erasmus, of course, was the prototype of the Renaissance humanist who, despite a sardonic view of human folly, had unlimited hope in man and saw him as the center of things. Crane is what Harold Bloom would call an apocalyptic humanist. This is not a shallow or Messianic creed. Crane was not an inane optimist denying the reality of evil and pain, but a man who tried to divert the thoughts and energies of his age to ways of reconciling the Faustian and Helenic elements of its character— and of his own.

The syntactical principle that governs this passage and most Crane poems is phrasal enumeration and spiraling development. The first two lines describe the two heroic men who had immersed themselves in the sea (flux) and thus could gather the voltage, like a spiritual conduit or conductor, of the "blown blood and vine." The syntax is approximately parallel; each noun has its participial and prepositional phrase, arranged in slightly different order, which come together in line three. Despite the semicolon after "vine," the transition from third to second-person point of view is rather abrupt, but it might be explained as an effort to represent, structurally, the difficulties of bridging the two disjunct periods and aims. Lines four and five consist of a complex sentence interrupted by the apostrophe "O brother-thief of time." The next four lines contain another complex sentence, which begins with an imperative verb, but it accumulates a load of paired requirements for the act of faith: "the breath released," "the substance drilled and spent," and "golden, or the shadow of gold hair."

The last stanza follows the same procedure, building up its praise from the initial imperative, in an outward looping cast, through compound verbs to the participial phrase ending the section and the poem. The heavily stressed and crowded second line conveys the tremendous resistance to reaching the heights. The passage's sonority, its end-rhymes—there are three couplets, two of which use the same rhyme: vine/wine; repair/hair; despair/prayer—and alliterations further help unify the statement and give it rhetorical sweep. Syntax is not a mere adjunct of poetic meaning; it is the complex source from which ramifications spring.

Crane's liking for compounds and paired words is best illustrated by two excerpts from *Voyages*:

> Past whirling pillars and lithe pediments,
> Light wrestling there incessantly with light,
> Star kissing star through wave on wave unto
> Your body rocking!
>
>   .   .   .
>
> All fragrance irrefragably, and claim
> Madly meeting logically in this hour
> And region that is ours to wreathe again,
> Portending eyes and lips and making told
> The chancel port and portion of our June—

The effect in the first excerpt (*Voyages III*) is to depict the powerful rush of the sea, the play of waves and light, the ecstatic rush of feeling, and the erotic movement of the poet to his lover.

The syntax in the second excerpt (*Voyages IV*) swirls and dances in a state of demoniac joy; it literally wreathes the love and joins the parts together—there are five compounds—in a frenzied but unbroken circle; the senses riot, the very sounds bang against each other yet make a harmonious melody: madness and logic are fused. And an undertone of desperate haste is heard, like a ground bass, for the poet already feels the presentiment of final estrangement. As can be seen in these two passages, the compounds take a strong metrical stress in the line, brace the line, and give it integrity in the larger, arching structure of the stanza. The cumulative power is at times overwhelming.[21] In fact, this syntactical device probably appealed to Crane precisely because it propels a rhythm forward and because it allows for the balancing of opposites, the pairing of likenesses, and the expression of tumultuous feelings. The poetic music he achieved is very much like the tonal voluptuousness, chromaticism, and harmonic timbres of Wagner and the other neo-Romantic composers whose music he enthusiastically advocated.[22]

One of the concomitants of a phrasal style, according to Josephine Miles, is a preponderance of nouns and adjectives over verbs. A study of Crane's verse, however, reveals that in spite of its inclination toward a phrasal rather than a clausal construction, it maintains a fairly even ratio between nouns and verbs, and that though the adjective figures largely in Crane's poetry, the verb remains the most remarkable armament in his poetic arsenal, "stronger and more structurally determining than [his] adjectives." [23] Crane's richly congested style is marked by the accretion and recurrence of key phrases and words: it is typical of the sublime mode, because it concentrates on sense experience and passion rather than on intellectual process, on what Miles calls "the whole ethos-pathos range of discernment; sweeping, lofty, harmonious, emotional." [24]

III

"Lachrymae Christi"

To conclude this survey of Crane's poetic syntax, I shall analyze the Symbolist poem "Lachrymae Christi" in order to demonstrate how its sentence structure, in conjunction with verse form, meter, and particularly imagery, both fosters and hampers communication of meaning. The difficulty of interpreting "Lachrymae Christi" lies not only in its knotty language, but also in its apparent lack of temporal order and sequence. More so than in any other Crane poem, words and images leap across the sentences in which they are found to link up daringly. Metrically, the verse slides unexpectedly from long lines to short lines, breaks lines in puzzling places, and while this, together with a highly irregular stanzaic patterning, is expected in an ode, there is no visible rising and falling action. Although a confessional lyric, the poem does not beat in the systole-diastole rhythm of such poems as "Possessions" and "The Wine Menagerie," yet it is not static. The poem does not move conventionally from a description of nature and the industrial environment (the light of the moon and the factory) to some controlling moment. The climax of the poem, with its beseeching of the god to lift up the grail of earth and his face, does not really coincide with the culmination of some dramatic episode or with the poet's quest for grace. Finally, since the syntax is often both elliptical and representative, one is ready to conclude with Davie that it is "something that may look like normal syntax but fulfills a quite different function." [25] A close reading of the poem will perhaps illustrate what that function is.

"Lachrymae Christi" is a canticle, quasi-religious in spirit,[26] which celebrates the mystery of death and rebirth. Crane takes the ancient myths of the crucified god as the deliverer of man from death and the pains of transience, and relates them to the cycles of nature and the seasons and his own "too well-known biography" of dissolute experiences that tainted his imagination. "The year's first blood," for example, the blossoming of flowers and plant life, is likened to Christ's wounds ("Twanged red perfidies of spring"). The poem testifies to the passion of all living things, as well as the passion of the gods, and to the sacrifice that inflames and waters all men and nature—the poem balances these two elemental forces, fire and water, in the imagery—and acts as both purgation and redemption.

> Whitely, while benzine
> Rinsings from the moon
> Dissolve all but the windows of the mills
> (Inside the sure machinery
> Is still
> And curdled only where a sill
> Sluices its one unyielding smile)
>
> Immaculate venom binds
> The fox's teeth, and swart
> Thorns freshen on the year's

First blood. From flanks unfended,
Twanged red perfidies of spring
Are trillion on the hill.

These two stanzas constitute the first movement of the poem. The grammatical order keeps to Crane's frequent practice of beginning with an adverb and subordinate clause (as "invariably when wine redeems the sight" in "The Wine Menagerie") that take the reader into the middle of an already started process, but the parenthetical insertion of a complex sentence with a clustering of adjectives interrupts the completion of the sentence, forcing the reader to focus on the machinery. This is partially justified because the poet wishes to play off the "one unyielding smile" of the "sure machinery" against Dionysus' "Unmangled target smile"; the one is incapable of saving man, the other, despite the "charred and riven stakes" of his crucifixion, is capable of doing so. The machinery is curdled (clotted) and still, unspeaking and unmoving to man, in contrast to Christ whose blood flows "Unstanched and luminous"; ironically, the sill sluices its smile, sluices denoting the pouring out of water to cleanse, but it is a futile cleansing for the machinery is outside the bounds of natural process, the "benzine/Rinsings from the moon," whereas the tears of Christ, the "Perpetual fountains" of his eyes, gush and his blood flows, thus offering mankind salvation.

The adverb "whitely" is isolated and delayed, since it modifies both "dissolves" in stanza one and "binds" in stanza two. In the first instance, it connotes the powerful light of the moon, and in the second, purity, which is reinforced by the word "immaculate." Benzine, an inflammable cleanser, connects up with Christ's "tinder" (tender) eyes and "un-dimmed lattices of flame" that bring light, grace, warmth, and renewal to man. This kind of imagistic trafficking creates some syntactical problems. The adverbial conjunction "while" leads one to expect some simultaneity of action in the two coordinate main clauses, but their connection seems tenuous. This much is clear: while the moonlight shines on the mills, nature is suffering the throes of rebirth. But in the creation of multiple images from the same words, the sense of the syntax and the sense of the image diverge. Similarly, the venom that binds the fox's teeth is contrasted with the "vermin and rod" (line 28) that Crane later tells us no longer bind, probably because Christ's sacrifice provides an escape from self-mortification. The "swart thorns" that "freshen on the year's/First blood" literally depicts the black thorns that grow on the boughs of spring's first flowers, and figuratively suggests Christ's crown of thorns that grows on the "sable, slender boughs" of his body and the crucifixion that must precede the resurrection. He is the "year's first blood." "Freshen" is a fine choice because it connotes innocence, spontaneity, and the vitality of pain involved in nature's cycle of death and rebirth. Crane transfers to rhyme, assonance, alliteration, and metrical stress some of the unifying tasks that traditionally belong to a syntax. One cannot help admiring the repetition of "s" and "l" sounds in stanza one and "f," "t," and "n" sounds in stanza two, or the three consecutive heavy stresses—swárt/Thórns fréshĕn" and "Twángĕd réd pérfĭdĭes."

The sentence that ends stanza two is a simple declarative one—indeed, the entire poem is studded with statements voiced in a factual tone—with a full complement of adjectives and prepositional phrases; its one deviation is the inverting of the adjective "unfended" to emphasize Christ's defenselessness on the cross. Literally, it pictures the burgeoning of innumerable red flowers from the sides of the earth; figuratively, it bodies forth Christ's betrayal on Calvary as the blood pours from his flanks. Yet the meaning of Easter is that from perfidy and death is twanged the tune of man's salvation. (Crane wittily puns on the trill in "trillion.") "Twanged" in fact introduces the music images—chimes, song, chant, and whistle—which are emblematic of the harmony that will come out of Christ-Dionysus' sacrifice and pervade the universe.

The syntax of the next two sections is complicated, but helps enact the poet's meaning:

> And the nights opening
> Chant pyramids,—
> Anoint with innocence,—recall
> To music and retrieve what perjuries
> Had galvanized the eyes.

> While chime
> Beneath and all around
> Distilling clemencies,—worms'
> Inaudible whistle, tunneling
> Not penitence
> But song, as these
> Perpetual fountains, vines,—

> Thy Nazarene and tinder eyes.

The first five lines consist of a complex sentence whose main clause contains a single subject ("nights") and a series of four verbs strung out either with an object or a prepositional phrase to the second of which is tacked on the subordinate clause. The mood of the passage being exuberant, the structure is expansive and incremental: the nights open out like the flowers opening in spring. We are meant to linger over the tranquil atmosphere and the awakening of nature after the long sleep of winter (the addition of the dash to the comma forces us to increase the length of the pause after each segment). The poet celebrates the return of his vision to its proper business—the pursuit of harmony and beauty—after its errant course and "perjuries," which, incidentally, recall Judas' perfidies. The syntax projects a parallelism of four verbs, four activities of the opening night, but they are only somewhat provisionally connected. "Chant pyramids" points forward to the "sphinxes" and "betrayed stones" of stanza five that "slowly speak," suggesting the freeing of Crane's imagination from its infatuation with death and self-deceit: his tongue is cleared to sing, that is, to write poems. "Anoint with innocence" pertains to this newfelt absolution, as though he were crowned with something more precious than the laurel—innocence and self-respect, balm to a spirit wounded by "swart thorns," the prickings of conscience. "Recall to music" continues the motif of poetic rededication, as does the final clause: his eyes, his faculty of perception, had been distorted by lies, false testimony, distracting stimulations. (Crane characteristically ties concrete verbs to abstract nouns like "innocence" and "perjuries.")

The music that has begun to sound soon fills the air, "distilling clemencies," and Crane traces its source to Christ's "Nazarene and tinder eyes." The mood is Blakean. As in the

"Book of Thel," all nature joins in the joyful song of praise of God's creation: even the worm, which usually devours corpses and is traditionally the macabre reminder of man's mortality, is heard "tunneling/Not penitence/But song." Christ's death is the reason for this outburst of cosmic delight; His tears and blood ("Perpetual fountains, vines"),[27] ordinarily emblems of sorrow, are here fruitful assurances of an inexhaustible forgiveness of man's sins. Christ solves the riddle of death for man (the sphinx is mentioned in the first line of the next stanza); He brings light and purity; and He kindles the fire of man's faith (again, the fusion of water and fire images) by His Passion and His tenderness (Crane puns brilliantly on the word "tinder"). By identifying his vision with Christ's (both stanzas end with "eyes"), Crane proclaims or reclaims his faith in his own creative powers.

The syntax of this stanza, despite its violation of grammatical rules (it is merely a sentence fragment—a subordinate clause without a main clause), helps along the meaning. By its circuitous unfolding it seems to imitate the tunneling of exquisite sounds that hover around the poet, while the interpolation set off by dashes serves to delay his ascription of the sounds to Christ, as though entranced by the songs of innocence he wished to draw them out as long as possible. The syntax enacts the process of Crane's retrieval of his fallen self. And it is also suitable for the delicate shuttling rhythms which lead to Christ's mercy.

Having confidently evoked the enchantment of a world participating in the spiritual amnesty bestowed by Christ, Crane moves on, in a parenthetical stanza, to declare his own release from the bondage of ignorance and abnegation:

> (Let sphinxes from the ripe
> Borage of death have cleared my tongue
> Once and again; vermin and rod
> No longer bind. Some sentient cloud
> Of tears flocks through the tendoned loam:
> Betrayed stones slowly speak.)

The passage is cryptic, taxing even Blackmur's considerable analytic powers, but it does repay persistent readings. The principal problem again is the relation of syntax and imagery. The stanza contains four simple declarative sentences that seem not to possess any consecutive logic. Even if the predication in one clause is understood, the intent of the whole or the movement between clauses can not necessarily be grasped. Why is the section put into parentheses? If it is not merely an interlude, but the heart of the poem, it should not be punctuated as an interruption. Since Crane chooses this point to inject himself into the poem and testify to the redemptive kindness of Christ, it was a mistake, I think, to set the stanza off by parentheses.

What should we make of the first clause? "Let" is apparently not in the imperative mode, but rather as Blackmur observes, "a somewhat homemade adjective." [28] Blackmur lists the meanings of the key words, "Let," "sphinxes," and "borage," and then ends up offering an educated guess that he calls ultimately worthless because, "with the defective syntax, the words do not verify it." [29]

It is true that the image of "sphinxes" literally being let out of the "ripe borage of death," is obscure. But the words do hold together. In part, Crane is rephrasing, in condensed form, his belief, already enunciated in "The Wine Menagerie," in the liberating power of alcohol. "Borage" is a cordial made from the perpetual vines, Christ's blood, and the reborn earth: hence its power as a restorative to comfort Crane and clear his tongue. It is also a demulcent, like olive oil, that perhaps "anoints with innocence." The sphinxes' riddle of life and death is solved; the answers are "let," that is, they are given up, released by the elixir he has drunk and given to him as a possession for use in his poems. The poet's perception of the meaning of Christ's sacrifice (he closely identifies himself with it) and the periodicity of nature's renewal have freed him from fearing death; he sees the bounds of mortality. The saint's practice of binding himself closely to Christ by mortifying the body with "vermin and rod" are rejected by Crane as a far lesser thing than love. The semicolon accurately marks the causal link between Christ's medicinal cure and Crane's change of heart. No longer shackled by guilt at his degradations, Crane can feel the "sentient cloud/Of tears" flow through his body ("tendoned loam"), just as the rain flocks through the earth and revivifies it: Christ's tears sustain him and the world. Crane describes a "pure possession," as if "the inclusive cloud/Whose heart is fire" has come and "Betrayed stones slowly speak." This last image alludes to the stone rolled away from the entrance to Christ's tomb and the "fixed stone of lust" [30] for which he had reproached himself and which had effectually cut him off from a finer vision, until the stones yield up their secret of resurrection. The syntax, of this stanza, then, has more than a modicum of plausibility and logic.

The next stanza mainly retreads old thematic ground, but it does exemplify Crane's intuition of the need for syntactical variety and his partiality for compounds and apostrophe:

> Names peeling from Thine eyes
> And their undimming lattices of flame,
> Spell out in palm and pain
> Compulsion of the year, O Nazarene.

Crane addresses Christ directly in a tone of affectionate certainty, as though Crane were a pupil repeating to himself the lesson he has learned from his savior-mentor. The names peeling from Christ's eyes, those "lattices of flame" which echo "tinder eyes," spell out the suffering and triumph, the rhythm of death and rebirth, that runs through all creation and that holds out a promise of eventual unity for Crane. Crane approaches hesitantly that state in which, in the words of "A Name For All," he would be "Struck free and holy in one Name always." [31] Where the previous stanza consisted of short declarative sentences, some of which began and ended in the middle of a line, this stanza consists of one simple sentence curving through its modifiers until finally reaching its object of address: the Nazarene:

> Lean long from sable, slender boughs,
> Unstanched and luminous. And as the nights
> Strike from Thee perfect spheres,
> Lift up in lilac-emerald breath the grail
> Of earth again—
>
> Thy face
> From charred and riven stakes, O
> Dionysus, Thy
> Unmangled target smile.

This last stanza is cast in the form of a prayer in which the petitioner asks the god for the preservation of grace (and creative inspiration) and the assurance that the seasons will continue to give their bounty to men. Although he is the object of derision and abuse ("target"), Christ-Dionysus is unmangled, and he is still able to work miraculous, life-enhancing acts, to "Lift up in lilac-emerald breath the grail/Of earth again." The syntactical principle governing the passage is the accumulation of parallels—phrases, the beseeching verbs "Lean" and "Lift up," the objects "Thy face" and "Thy smile," and the several adjectives (two in the first two lines and the last line, and one in lines three and four). This parallelism dovetails with the doubling of images here and rounds off images from earlier in the poem. Thus the "perfect spheres" are related to the "Unmangled *target* smile" (my italics) as symbols of an incorruptible and benign wholeness. Christ hanging on the cross and Dionysus tied to the "charred and riven stakes" are the center of the world from which emanates an ineffable cosmic harmony. The syntax presents, and realizes, the simultaneous acts that Crane requests of the gods with a mingling of awe and humble conviction (for the first time he shifts to the imperative). As the nights open again, this time striking up a music of the spheres,[32] the earth lifts up, a movement beautifully conceived by Crane as an exhalation of Christ's precious and perfumed sweet breath, as though embracing the heavens, and Dionysus raises his face and smile from the sacrificial boughs. This stanza has a majestic air and a music of restrained ardor that is matched in only a few of Crane's poems, particularly the third stanza of "At Melville's Tomb," and it reflects not only Crane's strong religious impulse, but his faith in the periodic healing of his divided self that will give him the power to depict, as he puts it in "Purgatorio," the "landscape of confession" and "absolution," both "the scents of Eden" and the "dangerous tree." The long cadence after the word "again" provided by the dash and line break recalls us to the earlier lines "(Let sphinxes from the ripe/Borage of death have cleared my tongue/Once and again . . .)."

The few minor flaws do not mar the stanza. Though Dionysus' name appears first in the end, the sense of Dionysus has existed from the start, hinted at in some images. The adjectives "Unstanched and luminous" are grammatically ambiguous, but I take it that they modify the implied subject, "You," Christ. The preponderance of adjectives in the stanza contributes to the stanza's stately pace, while the verb "Lift up" serves as the fulcrum of the passage.

As a general rule, Crane's practice in "Lachrymae Christi" applies as well to his other odes and Symbolist poems: he retains some of the traditional semantic functions of syntax, but primarily allies it with the inferential imagery for dramatic effect and rhythmic liveliness. In "Lachrymae Christi," for instance, the slant rhymes—"boughs"/"O"; "Smile"/"grail"; "nights"/"Thy"/"smile"—and the internal rhymes—"Dionysus, Thy"—do unify the irregularity of line lengths and in this way directs Crane's syntax toward an asymmetrical balance.

CHAPTER 9

Verse Forms

Crane relies on two verse forms, in early and late poems: the quatrain and a relatively stable yet varied Romantic odal stanza. Almost always these stanzas involve some rhyme or near rhyme, some chiming of sounds even if, as with his diction, they are spaced intermittently throughout the poem; a rhyme may be completed three stanzas later. For all his love of the Elizabethan poets and playwrights, Crane seems to have decided that blank verse would not be suitable for his rhetorical flights (their verbal richness would still be useful to him), perhaps because it demanded a firmer control of intellectual discourse and drama than he could manage, or perhaps because it carried such a heavy Elizabethan tone that it would submerge his contemporary statement. "Faustus and Helen" flirts with blank verse, but it is better seen as primarily odal. Of the more uniform stanzaic structures he tried, "Pastorale" and *Voyages II* are written in five line stanzas, "Garden Abstract" in a six-line stanza, and "Quaker Hill" and "Atlantis" in an eight-line stanza. Since these poems are sprinkled with rhymes, accidental as they may seem, and

do not hold steadily to an iambic pentameter line, they do
not give more than a faint whiff of blank verse.

The majority of Crane's poems were written in quatrains. At
first glance this seems odd, since the quatrain demands great
intellectual rigor and rational control from the poet, and a
regularity that would not seem to square well with Crane's
fondness for a musical speech that continually presses against
the limits of form. This, however, is precisely the source of
the stanza's attraction to Crane: he discerned that he could
create a formal pattern that would enclose the crescendo and
diminuendo of his feelings and perceptions. Since Crane's
poems typically do not present an intricate argument but
rather an outburst of emotion—they are almost exclusively
lyrics[1]—they are amenable to the stops and starts that the
quatrain enforces and to the piling up of descriptive phrases.

Crane's handling of the quatrain in his early poems suffers
from four-square rhythm; the poems are bulky and unwieldy
and slow, which is in keeping with their mood and slight subjects, but their very somnolence suggests an embryonic poetic
talent. An early poem, "To Portapovitch," catches this static
dream-like urgency:

> Vault on the opal carpet of the sun,
> Barbaric Prince Igor:—or, blind Pierrot,
> Despair until the moon by tears be won:—
> Or, Daphnis, move among the bees with Chloe.
>
> Release,—dismiss the passion from your arms.
> More real than life, the gestures you have spun
> Haunt the blank stage with lingering alarms,
> Though silent as your sandals, danced undone.

Written in 1919 as a tribute to his friend Portapovitch, a male dancer of the Ballet Russe, the poem breaks into two self-contained units. Most of the lines are end-stopped, which fixes the attention, especially in the first stanza, on the dancer posing in his most notable roles; a series of *tableaux vivants* is presented; the rigid parallelism of the imperative clauses reinforces the pictorial stateliness and the artifice of the poem (the dancer's art is "More real than life"). The poem is typical of early Crane in its regularized iambic pentameter line, its unvarying end rhymes, and its preference for the imperative mood, but its placement of caesuras does not interrupt the rhythmical monotony.

As a rule, Crane's poems in quatrains tend to be clearer in meaning than his odal poems. Their texture is leaner and their grammar easier to unravel; the metrical scheme is followed with a minimum of fuss and change and with few substitutions; the lengths of lines do not vary much, and a rhyme scheme once introduced is repeated. There are poems, of course, like "At Melville's Tomb," "Stark Major," and "Recitative" which adopt a freely improvised rhyme scheme, one that shifts from stanza to stanza, or which avoid rhyme altogether. But on the whole the quatrain afforded Crane a large measure of flexibility.

"Black Tambourine" is interesting as a transition from the stiff structure of the early quatrains to the more tractable structure of "The Air Plant" and "The Broken Tower":

> The interests of a black man in a cellar
> Mark tardy judgment on the world's closed door.
> Gnats toss in the shadow of a bottle,
> And a roach spans a crevice in the floor.

Aesop, driven to pondering, found
Heaven with the tortoise and the hare;
Fox brush and sow ear top his grave
And mingling incantations on the air.

The black man, forlorn in the cellar,
Wanders in some mid-kingdom, dark, that lies,
Between his tambourine, stuck on the wall,
And, in Africa, a carcass quick with flies.

The slight increase in run-on lines corresponds neatly with the uniformly declarative character of the syntax, but every two sentences the poem grinds to a halt and must begin again with a new subject. Only in the third stanza does the fitful movement, with its subordinate clauses and phrases, overcome the dull insistence of the meter and pairing of the lines. The gain in fluency is almost nullified by the ponderous steadiness of beat and by the absence, except in the last stanza and the first line of the second stanza, of caesuras. Nevertheless, Crane deliberately exploits the verse form and rhythms here to accentuate the theme of the poem, a practice at which he excels in this and later poems. The boxed-in sentences and sluggish rhythm of the first two stanzas characterize the Negro's impasse and "the world's closed door," while the syntax of the last stanza seems to wander aimlessly with the black man between the degrading alternatives of his life, only to come to rest in a psychic jail and emotional slavery.

In "Black Tambourine," restrained tension and careful moral analysis are heightened by Crane's treatment of the quatrain. Crane remarked to Gorham Munson that the poem is "a description and bundle of insinuations. . . . The value of the poem is only, to me, in what a painter would call its 'tactile'

quality—an entirely aesthetic feature." [2] Despite this dis-
claimer, Crane cleverly uses the tripartite structure almost
like a *da capo* aria. The first stanza describes uncompromis-
ingly the physical and spiritual squalor forced upon the black
men: the brutal facts of gnats, roaches, and bottle. The moral
comment is played down, but the circumscribed world insinu-
ates itself upon the reader. The second stanza goes outdoors
and back into history to meditate ironically on Aesop, another
slave, but one who at least achieved some literary fame, who
was able to convert his predicament into folk wisdom. The
"tardy judgment" reappears in the fable of the tortoise and
the hare mentioned in stanza two, but such slowness and patience are a way of keeping the Negro imprisoned. The "mingling incantations" suggest some superstitious rite and some
music to ease slavery's burden. The last stanza returns to the
plight of the Negro "forlorn in the cellar" and recalls Pip, the
"isolatoe" cabin-boy of *Moby Dick*,[3] who saw visions and
also wandered in a "mid-kingdom," possessed of a dark knowledge the white man would not heed. Pip, it will be remembered, played his tambourine in the rowdy dance on the quar-
ter-deck, but the black man's tambourine in Crane's poem
is stuck on the wall, unplayed. Bereft of his heritage, the
Negro is condemned to a spiritual death. The Negro's situation has worsened since Melville's time; Crane is not didactic
about it, he makes his point by indirection.

Crane's rapid stylistic development, his hard-earned profi-
ciency with the quatrain, is illustrated by "Praise for an Urn."
This poem, written less than a year after "Black Tambourine,"
is an elegy for Ernest Nelson, a painter-friend whom Crane
had briefly known in Cleveland. Technically the poem sur-

passes almost everything else Crane had written to this point (1922), and it deserves Monroe K. Spears' praise for its "moral and aesthetic poise" and "moral penetration and awareness." [4] Although Crane made use of lines from the earlier "The Bridge of Estador," the poem has an elegant, effortless, inevitable structure.[5] It is a simple, delicate tribute to Nelson, but in typical Cranesque fashion, it is also about his own poetry and its chances of survival in a hostile culture.

Crane had been a pallbearer at Nelson's funeral and thought the whole affair, especially the finale at the crematorium, was beautiful, even though it left him "emotionally bankrupt," [6] yet the poem has a richly controlled emotion, an emotion recollected in tranquility. Nelson was, in Crane's words:

> One of the best-read people I ever met, wonderful kindliness and tolerance and a true Nietzschean. He was one of many broken against the stupidity of American life in such places as here [Cleveland]. I think he has had a lasting influence on me.[7]

Nelson was probably one of Crane's surrogate fathers, but his benevolent, Old World wisdom must have struck Crane with great force as being out of place in America: the artist was an exile in his own country, and Crane faced the same destiny.

The power of "Praise for an Urn" derives from its mature observation, its quiet rueful tone, and its lovely symmetry. Of the six quatrains the first two and the last two are self-enclosed; only the middle two are joined together as a grammatical unit. The effect is of a slowing down of time, as Crane is assessing the meaning of his loss and of the ideas he had discussed with Nelson. The first quatrain is a daguerreotype, an attempt to fix Nelson's physical and spiritual features; its matter-of-factness and syntactical clarity are modified only by the inversion of the fourth line, which serves to emphasize Nelson's hearty humor, his "Nietzschean" force. Nelson's eyes expressed the pathos of the clown and the comic exuberance of Rabelais' prodigal hero. In the second quatrain, Crane sees himself as Nelson's spiritual heir, who understands now the significance of the older man's thoughts and the wisdom that enabled Nelson to ride out the storms and disappointments of his life; the syntax moves sinuously, emphasizing the key words "inheritances" and "storm." The next two quatrains form a movement of their own, beginning with the remembrance of a shared experience and knowledge that is brought up short by the aseptic chill of the "crematory lobby." The clock's tickings ironically undercut both the knowledge he and Nelson had got from the "presentiments/Of what the dead keep" and the mourners' "praise/Of glories proper to the time." The fifth quatrain is equivocal, terse, sorrowful, and despairing:

> Still, having in mind gold hair,
> I cannot see that broken brow
> And miss the dry sound of bees
> Stretching across a lucid space.

"Gold hair" refers to the imaginative truths and love (Nelson's legacies to him) that, in spite of the curt warnings of time, he cannot rid his mind of; yet Nelson's "broken brow" (death) reminds him ambiguously either of some kind of rational and "sweet" activity or of emptiness.[8] The last stanza, which is like an ironic inversion of Shelley's exultant invocation to the West Wind, ends with the scattering of Nelson's ashes and Crane's poem (both "well-meant idioms") in the suburbs "where they will be lost." They are not durable trophies of the imagination. Thus the poem ends in defeat: the lessons of Nelson's life and death seem forfeited, and the praise is for nothing more tangible and lasting than a cold urn (and how different from Keats' Urn!).

The impersonality of the poem owes something, I think, to Crane's artful manipulation of the quatrain. Crane looks at the face of death and at the question of immortality without self-pity and without averting his eye from the reality of death; it is a poem entirely lacking in illusions. One peculiarity of the quatrains that contributes to the compact statement of theme is the choice of an iambic tetrameter line. Crane's verse is never swift; it's major trait is a majestic solemnity and deliberateness, but the shorter lines restrain Crane from lingering sentimentally over the moral of Nelson's life or death (Crane is one of the least didactic of modern poets); he again relies on "insinuations."

Crane's cultivation of the quatrain led, as might be expected, to an ease in handling its difficult demands. Most of the poems in the *Key West* volume solve the problem of sustaining tension and shifting moods without constricting the verse or allowing it to become diffuse and baggy. (Except for "The Broken Tower," the poems do not run beyond three or four stanzas, which probably facilitates matters for Crane.) The *Key West* poems have generally been underrated; their impact derives from the formal perfection of the verses and the acuity of the vision.

When Crane went to the Isle of Pines in the spring of 1926, he was in the midst of a crisis in his creative life. Exhausted by his efforts to make headway with the intractable material of *The Bridge*, he sought rest and diversion in his tropical paradise. The strange opulent beauties of the island, its "sublime uneventfulness," stirred Crane and reminded him of Melville and Rimbaud, fellow artist-voyagers who had sought refuge from the corruption of civilization in faraway sensuous and primitive lands. At first Crane dwelled lovingly on the exotic fruits and plants that grow so profusely in the tropical climate. But at the same time that he responded to the heavy perfume of the South, he became aware that another, more terrible, almost antediluvian world existed under and around the luxuriant appearances: terrapins and crabs and insects. The ferocious sun baked the will out of him, shriveling up his creative vitality. In July, unable to scribble more than a few lines on *The Bridge*, he writes to a friend: "the mind is completely befogged by the heat and besides there is a strange challenge and combat in the air—offered by 'Nature' so monstrously alive in the tropics which drains the psychic energies . . . For I've lost all faith in my material—'human nature' or what you will." [9]

With his feeble will, Crane was no match for Nature's scorching power. Yet, paradoxically, in spite of his pessimism, he was able to write a series of harsh lyrics describing the pitiless landscape and the evisceration of his poetic self: a harvest of violently controlled poems wrung from the soil of his fierce uneasiness. For Crane's tropics are not the lazy, languorous, fecund tropics of Wallace Stevens' poems. For Stevens the imagination can leisurely transform the myriad colors of reality that shimmer so invitingly in the Gulf; he can strum on his blue guitar, and sing his meditative ditties, conjuring up a warm spacious landscape accessible to man. For Crane, however, the imagination is so inert that he can seldom unwind sufficiently to transform anything. The tropical abundance, "so monstrously alive," assaults him, taunts him like "the tossing of sand in his eyes" with signs of his impending death. Like the Air Plant, he thrives on "saline nothingness."

The existential dread that permeates the *Key West* poems gives them their undeniable grisly power. Crane does not attempt to affirm life; he succumbs, horrified, to a nihilistic view of things. It is to his credit that he does not spare himself as he records his own retreats and failures: his syllables want breath, his senses are mildewed, and he "Congeals by afternoon here, satin and vacant." In a way, the dry, impassive forces he describes make for a more infernal waste land than Eliot's, because it lacks any literary and historical or mythical references to a state of spiritual fertility and coherence. The complicated gestures of the quatrain are peculiarly suited to the themes and feelings of these poems. The bitter humor and the fatigued wonder, the meticulous drawing of ugly and sinister plants and animals, the discovery of death everywhere, and the stark neutrality of nature—all these press down against the sequential order of the quatrain and create a unique tension and an ominous calm. Syntax, rhythm, and rhyme are manipulated for the sake of rendering the literal yet spectral landscape.[10] The invoking *I*, the speculative boldness, is subdued, detached, impersonalized; indeed the *I* almost disappears completely, as though it were overwhelmed by the grotesque things the poet observes.

"The Idiot" is a modest, almost literal transcription of several encounters Crane had with an idiot boy in the Isle of

Pines,[11] with the addition of Crane's embarrassed and compassionate reaction:

> Sheer over to the other side,—for see
> That boy straggling under those mimosas, daft
> With squint lanterns in his head, and it's likely
> Fumbling his sex. That's why those children laughed
>
> In such infernal circles round his door
> Once when he shouted, stretched in ghastly shape.
> I hurried by. But back from the hot shore
> Passed him again . . . He was alone, agape;
>
> One hand dealt out a kite string, a tin can
> The other tilted, peeled end clapped to eye.
> That kite aloft—you should have watched him scan
> Its course, though he'd clamped midnight to noon sky!
>
> And since, through these hot barricades of green,
> A *Dios gracias, graç*—I've heard his song
> Above all reason lifting, halt serene—
> My trespass vision shrinks to face his wrong.

The genre of the poem is the familiar Wordsworthian one of the "halted traveller": the poet passing by stumbles upon a scene which brings about some recognition and internal change in him. What is striking about the poem is the way Crane has managed the conversational gait within the quatrains to build to the abruptly crestfallen climax. In contrast to the practice in early poems like "Black Tambourine," most of the lines here are enjambed and create a fluency despite the hesitations of the miscellaneous vignettes he recounts. The run-on movement within a stanza is paralleled by the liberty with which grammatical sentences and rhythmic phrases spill over from one stanza to the next. The verse seems to sway in an orderly fashion from the images of the idiot to the poet's interpretation of them. And the looping comely rhythms spin leisurely like the kite in the sky or straggle as if in imitation of the idiot boy's walk and mind. This last effect is achieved by letting sentences begin and end in the middle of a line, the caesuras thereby falling anywhere and everywere in the stanza. The alternating masculine rhymes and the frequent alliteration hold the stanzas together, while the variety of sentences Crane employs, from the simple declarative to the compound-complex, establishes pleasing departures from the metrical norm. The shy, imperturbable song of the idiot therefore rises and halts, and the poet's "trespass vision" rounds off the poem in the falling cadence of a perfect iambic line (the only regular one in the poem), as if the squint-eyed vision of the idiot, fixed on the sky, can penetrate higher and deeper than the poet's. The quatrains unify the anecdotal moments and pictorial fragments into an expressive whole.

Crane found the young royal palms growing on the Isle of Pines "perfect delights" due to their "ornamentation, stateliness and open-airiness," [12] but the fine poem he composed about them, quiet and cool in demeanor, partakes of the ambiguity toward nature and himself mentioned earlier. The quatrains are carefully wrought, the idiom is chaster than in Crane's more odal poems, as though the majestic dignity of the palm imposed a restraint upon the utterance; the quatrain afforded Crane a disciplined freedom which he exploited subtly:

> Green rustlings, more-than-regal charities
> Drift coolly from that tower of whispered light.

Amid the noontide's blazed asperities
I watched the sun's most gracious anchorite

Climb up as by communings, year on year
Uneaten of the earth or aught earth holds,
And the grey trunk, that's elephantine, rear
Its frondings sighing in aethereal folds.

Forever fruitless, and beyond that yield
Of sweat the jungle presses with hot love
And tendril till our deathward breath is sealed—
It grazes the horizons, launched above

Mortality—ascending emerald-bright,
A fountain at salute, a crown in view—
Unshackled, casual of its azured height
As though it soared suchwise through heaven too.

On first reading, "Royal Palm" seems merely stylized conventional description, heavy decoration like Victorian furniture, but further inspection reveals a close relation between
syntax, stanzaic structure, and rhythm: they enact the theme,
so to speak. The poem moves unhurriedly in an ascending arc,
without the tense swooping motions of Crane's habitual
rhythms; its sequence of images unfurls with a grave impersonality that is in keeping with the formal coherence of the
quatrain itself. There are only three grammatical sentences
for the entire poem, and the last two are specifically patterned
to suggest the audacity of the tree, its upward thrust to
heaven, free equally of the hot sexual importunity and the
death that afflict mankind. The palm, which bestows comfort
by its coolness, shelters the poet from the "blazed asperities"
of the noonday sun (reality); (the tree is likened to a tower,
and towers almost always symbolize unviolated selfhood,

imagination, and spiritual purity in Crane's poems). The palm becomes a paradigm of the grace of a life unassailed by the dividing passions "earth holds." Yet the tree is a holy eunuch; it can soar, "forever fruitless," "unshackled, casual of its azured height," precisely because it is an anchorite.[13]

The quatrains have an openness which insures that the rhythmic flow will be parallel with the eye traveling up the tree and watching the tree graze the horizon. The calm pauses of the ascent are duplicated by the slowly unwinding clauses of the sentences and the uncluttered passage from stanza to stanza, best illustrated by stanzas two and four.[14] Each interruption is calculated, as when the palm is imaged first as "A fountain at salute" and then as "a crown in view." The poem as a whole seems to "Climb up as by communings," its flights spreading from a thick base. The poem, in short, compensates in poise for its lack of emotional fervor.

"The Broken Tower," Crane's last masterpiece, does not always adhere to the practices in the other quatrains, mainly because it closely resembles the odal poems in emotion and lyrical intensity, but it adroitly maneuvers pitch and cadence and makes the given verse form work against the curve of the emotion which rises and falls precipitously. Everything follows the poet's dramatic moods, from feverish prostration through self-perplexity to exultant joy and tenuous harmony. "The Broken Tower" is a poem of difficult questions and brusque exclamations, smooth and abrupt, which convey almost simultaneously a sense of termination and beginning. The quatrains mirror the poet's struggles against despair, his flickering poetic creativity, and his lapses into the darkness of defeat and imperfection until his vision lifts him to the faith that the imagination will endure all. Thus within each stanza of the first movement (stanzas 1–4) there is little end-stopping; the self-reproaches that pour freely out of him always end in an abrasive assertion of self-doubt or in sorrowful self-interrogation. The second movement (stanzas 5–7) continues to be punctuated by questions as Crane tests and probes the worth of his creative efforts; he wonders whether or not he has betrayed his poetic gifts, whether or not his word was adequate to incarnate his visions. Enjambment within each stanza again is forced to stop at the end of the stanza. But in the third movement of the poem (stanzas 8–10), the poet's growing conviction that he can build by his own powers a poetry that is grounded in imaginative truth, strength, and love is emphasized by the mounting tension of the sentence that sweeps over three stanzas. The "visible wings of silence" that "lift down" are suggested by the internal complications of the syntax,[15] while the love that "lifts up" is suggested by the fluidity and levitation of the sentence.

The deviations from grammatical norms reflect, not incoherence or a breakdown in structure, but a conscious artistic device. The sentence fragments of the fourth stanza are part of a catalogue of poetic failures—the circle of the perfected poem is still eluding Crane—since the bells in breaking down their tower also break down the syntax. This is not a fanciful rationalization, for Crane uses punctuation and grammar to heighten the inner drama of breaking and healing. The bells which peal rebukingly to the poet wake him from lethargy and become an Annunciation, a reminder of the times he had entered, quietly and gently, "the broken world/To trace the visionary company of love."

By placing caesuras at the point in a line or stanza where they can be most dramatic, and by interrupting long declarative and complex sentences with short expletives, Crane succeeds in involving the reader in the poet's crisis and in marking the contrapuntal voices of the suppliant and the frenzied self. The third stanza is a good example of this skill:

> The bells, I say, the bells break down their tower;
> And swing I know not where. Their tongues engrave
> Membrane through marrow, my long-scattered score
> Of broken intervals . . . And I, their sexton slave!

Strictly speaking, there should be no semicolon after "tower," since the governing rule is that a compound predicate should not be separated by any punctuation: the bells break down and swing.[16] But this violation of grammar does two things: it suggests, onomatopoeically, the repetition of the bells, and it hems the sound inside the tower and then releases it to swing aimlessly for the moment. As Marius Bewley remarks, Crane has no supporting faith, and his poetic voice threatens to crush his poetic vision.[17] In a like manner, the three dots after "broken intervals" simulate the musical interval he has just mentioned and suggest as well the sporadic creative moments to which he is enslaved; and parentheses throughout the poem serve to heighten the poet's uncertainties, since they almost always make a qualifying negative statement. The total effect of the quatrain in "The Broken Tower," then, is to catch the reversals of thought and feeling within its enveloping structure. In this his last great poem, Crane marshals grammar, meter, and verse structure to create a marvelous valedictory.

II

The Odal Poems

The second dominant verse form Crane employs is some version of the Romantic ode. The attractions of the ode were manifold. First of all, it suits Crane's bias for the sublime, for oracular utterance, since its structure allows for the deployment of thought in an irregular fashion. Second, especially as developed by the Romantic poets, the ode is a flexible instrument for voicing the waywardness of the emotions, the gropings of the mind for illumination, and, most importantly, the bending back of feeling upon itself and its sudden release to fill the poet with joy and hope. The lyric, as A. Alvarez observes, "rises from a single, intense moment of perception and concerns the poet's reactions to the object rather than the object itself." [18] The ode is just such a lyrical self-dramatization; it proceeds not in a linear or circular pattern, but in a crisscrossing pattern; the linear and the circular bisect each other and then go their own ways. Third, since the stanzaic form of the ode is uneven (not lawless),[19] the poet can experiment with rhythms that convey the ebb and flow of feeling, with transitions being smooth or disjointed, depending upon the effect sought.

The large pattern of the ode, with its modulations from bold extroverted passion to confessional intimacy, allows an "admixture of reflection, question, invocation, petition, and praise." [20] The rules of versification which enforce a fairly strict continuity in the quatrain are modified in the ode. Keats, for example, worked out a compromise between the rigor of the sonnet and the expansiveness of the dramatic lyric which could bring out the emotional "turn and counterturn" [21] of his experience. The result was the rich music of the great odes; Crane, desiring something similar and personal, devised a stanza which could slide back and forth from a regular quatrain to a five, six, seven, or eight line stanza. The length of the stanza or even of a line would be determined by the pressure of feeling. For example, rapture might be sustained for a few lines and then trail off into bemusement. The verse would be prevented from disintegrating into fragments by the occasional rhymes or slant rhymes, the alliteration and assonance, the governing syntax, and the overarching pattern of tentative passionate approach to a visionary center, a moment of revelation or confession, and the subsequent retreat from it. This is the pattern of poems like "Lachrymae Christi," "The Wine Menagerie," "Possessions," "Faustus and Helen," and *Voyages*.

It is not easy to determine exactly the models of Crane's odal stanzas. Generically, they belong with the Romantics', though it is doubtful that Crane consciously set out to adapt their style. Although Wordsworth is not mentioned once in Crane's Letters, Keats, Coleridge and Shelley are cited, enthusiastically,[22] and since there is common ground in language and imagery between Crane and the Romantic poets it is logical to assume that it extends as well to verse forms and prosody. Crane also learned much from T. S. Eliot's artistry in "Preludes" and *The Waste Land*, since in both poems Eliot resorts to a flexible stanza with a fortuitous rhyme scheme and a shifting number of lines. Eliot's poems, however, do not conform much to the movement I have outlined above; they are more linear and informal than Crane's, as well as being alien to Crane's outlook.

On the whole the odal poems are opaque and difficult. "The Wine Menagerie," for instance, verges on obscurity and taxes the reader's skill at engineering the associative movement of images, but the shape of the poet's experience and the theme dictate the form. The poem is an odal hymn to the intoxicating visions wine brings and to the liberating of the empathic imagination, though the momentary flaring up of insight is extinguished by a dark sense of dissociation and exile, of pursuit by the ruddy "tooth implicit of the world." The vision and the divine afflatus that accompanies it exact a price in anguish afterwards for their fugitive presence. Alcohol can stimulate a state wherein the imagination can "travel in a tear/Sparkling alone, within another's will," but it cannot last long.

The poem renders, both in its diction and its verse form, the interplay between the finite, occasionally deceiving realities of the external world and the transforming perceptual powers of the imagination. Ordinarily the poet's gaze is blurred or he squints, sees dimly, but wine awakens him to notice each man's struggle to overcome his limits and the gap between his earthly nature ("the heap of time") and his spiritual aspiration ("the arrow shot into the feathered sky"), the effort to snare "new purities." This struggle, like the creative process itself, involves failed metamorphoses (unmaking, unskeining, severing) and successful ones (wreathing, building, inventing). But although "New thresholds" open out to "new anatomies," self-mistrust and exhaustion overtake the poet and close the doors of perception.

The structure of the poem is neither haphazard nor mystifying. The stanzas are broken up into groups of 4,4,5, 5,5,5, 4, 5, 6, 4, 2, the tension building slowly to the climactic statement of his joyous creed in stanza seven, which, however, barely lasts through the next stanza. The final three stanzas, which form a unit of their own as a self-colloquy—the poet's wit speaking to himself—return to the slightly stupefied tone of the early stanzas. The numerous five-line stanzas are marked by the signs of the quatrain, but their mood is odal and the rhyming is fairly irregular: mostly *a-b-c-b*, but with couplet lines ("shell/hell") and *a-b-a-c-a*. In addition there are several off-rhymes, like "eyes/gaze," "wills/repeals," and "brow/snow," and the reiteration of certain basic or triple rhymes such as "slow/glow," "snow/brow," "know/snow," "eyes/gaze," "eyes/pries/skies," and "distill/will/skill" which contribute to the poem's bounded wildness. The rhymes are obsessive, as if they were infected by the intoxication the poet feels, and aptly fit the subject of the poem: perception, art, and knowledge.

Rhythmically, the poem moves at a lumbering gait. There is scarcely any continuity between one stanza and the next, although the percentage of enjambed lines within a stanza is high. This is due, I think, to the pairing of opposed states of being throughout the poem or even within one line, as, for instance, the leopard in the brow (power) and August in the child's brow (innocence) or the image "Between black tusks the roses shine!" Crane cannot shake off his torpor, so that time moves slowly, concentratedly, inexorably; there are few intemperate outbursts, but much arduous self-consciousness; sensation is intensified. The metrical and syntactical complexity of the poem leads to the clustering of images and rhythms. The direction is from wantonness to control, from the periphery to the center of consciousness. The rhetorical emphasis falls on the excited announcement of new insights (the word "new" is repeated three times in six lines) in stanza seven after the somewhat plodding ascent through the clotted five-line stanzas; the poet cannot lose his sense of the equivocal nature of the world, which is probably why there is no free movement between stanza and stanza. The odal strophes of poems like "The Wine Menagerie" and "Lachrymae Christi" are complicated partly because the poet is so psychologically blocked that he cannot find the proper form to unveil his feelings, and partly because he wishes to let the stanza represent the pattern of befuddlement and sudden illumination. In other poems, especially in the *Voyages* sequence, the stanzaic structure, while still odal, is rational.

Voyages I is divided into three parts of unequal length; a stanza of five lines is followed by a four-line stanza and one of seven lines. This division corresponds to the contrasting movement of the poem, involving the children, the elements, and the poet. The first stanza simply describes the children at play. The brevity of the second stanza is admirably suited to the terse mention of nature's menacing indifference to the children. The inevitability of nature's processes is paralleled by the urgency of the poet to warn the "brilliant kids" of their danger: the first and the fourth lines both begin with *and*, thereby ironically linking the two answers to the kids' "treble interjections." The last stanza directly addressing the children spells out the cruelty of the sea, and since the poet is also talking to himself, the children and he are bound together against the common enemy: death. The poem has no loose ends; what might have been an arbitrary structural division is justified by the triadic arrangement.

The pattern of *Voyages II* is much more complicated because of its emotional import and its lyrical evocation of the sea's presence. The poem is divided into five stanzas of five lines each, which immediately suggests some formal harmony and evenness. Though aware of doom and transiency, the poet is serene and confident in his love. The urgency to hurry is somehow muted by the unhurried flow of the verse, just as the spontaneity is balanced by order, and the sea's "sceptered terror" is balanced by its good nature (implied by its "great wink"). The poem blends measured and ecstatic utterance. Each of the stanzas is end-stopped, like a musical motif that closes one bar in one key and begins the next bar in another yet related key. The syntax represents the rolling sea itself, its tidal ebb and flow. The care Crane takes to make the structure of emotion conform to the poem's pictorial and rhetorical structure is further shown by the beginnings of the stanzas. Stanzas one and three begin with "And," as if to characterize the infinite flow of the sea; the lack of grammatical predication in stanza one reinforces this apprehension. Stanzas two, four, and five begin in the imperative mood, those chaste imperious commands that the poet, conscious of his impending death, speaks to himself and his lover.

Where *Voyages I* made its effect without rhyme, its absence stressing the poet's unheard or unheeded communication, *Voyages II* uses rhyme unobtrusively and sparsely, but subtly. Like the five-fold stanzaic structure, there are five pairs of rhymes,[23] only one of which appears in the same stanza. The rhyming is not accidental, because each pair logically incorporates a theme or paradox. The rich and royal nature of the sea as pictured in the first stanza culminates in a sort of ritualistic worship: the sea harmoniously *bends* to the moon. The image of the sea in stanza two is of a magistrate; laughter has turned to a "sceptred terror" that *rends*, estranges, and although at this point in the sequence the lovers seem exempt from the sentence of death, the pairing of "bends/ rends" conveys this dual nature of the sea. The next coupling of rhymes, "knells/spells," links stanzas two and three. The diapason (the concord) of the sea knells its funereal summons but along the way it mingles the more charming bells off San Salvador which salute the stars as before the sea saluted the moon. The echo of knells is delayed as the lovers dally in the alluring "poinsettia meadows of her tides," but they must "Complete the dark confessions her veins spell." This is a complex and beautiful resolution of several strands of imagery. The diapason writes "snowy sentences," that is, both poems and the judge's doom, so that the "dark confessions" she spells is death. Spell continues the writing image and suggests the spell of the music, the glimpses or sounds of harmony they had.

The third pair of rhymes, "hours/flower," appears in stanza four. It concentrates on the dominant theme of the stanza: the poet's love can come into being and can flower because it is rooted in the flux of time—its ephemerality makes it both precious and desirable—a flux that will also eventually destory it. (With this perception of the intertwining of love and death, the poet begins the next stanza by invoking the seasons to "Bind [him] in time.") The last two stanzas are joined together by two pairs of rhymes. The first and least significant pair, "desire/fire," recalls perhaps the poet's association of his desire with the warmth of the Caribbean voyage. "Wave/grave" points to the inescapable identification of the sea as the burial ground of the poet's love.

Crane's exquisite art here is proof of his consciousness of the ways rhythm, rhyme, stanzaic sequence, assonance, consonance,[24] punctuation, etc., all must combine to convey meaning. Having abandoned the guide of traditional forms, the modern poet must invent other semantic and formal devices to insure the integrity of his poem; he must give extra weight to such matters as line breaking, line and stanza length, repetition, rhetorical emphasis. Crane, as noted previously, was more reluctant than his contemporaries to lose the benefits of the older patterns of organizing feeling. Nevertheless, since his poetry is not engaged in logical argument, but in lyrical declamation and apostrophe, he creates conventions proper to the emotional burden and gravity of his song. Form, as in *Voyages II*, is adapted to feeling and thought.

In his book *Poetic Meter and Poetic Form*, Paul Fussell, Jr., commenting on the obstacles modern poets have to overcome in order to construct a well-made poem, even a short one, says:

> the poem generally tends toward a greater density the closer the number of stanzas accords with the number of divisions of action or intellection which the poem enacts. That is, the number of stanzas into which the poem is divided should itself express something; the number must not give the impression of being accidental. Just as in, say, a successful Petrarchan sonnet the sestet offers a different kind of material from that presented in the octave because its shape and

rhyme structure are different, so in poems written in either fixed and nonce stanzas separate and different shapes should embody separate and different things. . . . The white space between stanzas means something. If nothing is conceived to be taking place within it, if no kind of silent pressure or advance or reconsideration or illumination or perception seems to be going on in that white space, the reader has a legitimate question to ask: Why is that white space there, and what am I supposed to do with it? [25]

If Fussell's strictures are applied to Crane's poems, Crane's skill as a prosodist is further verified. The generally felicitous conformity of sense and feeling, tension and perception, in Crane's quatrains, and the delicate way he shaped the experience of love and sea to the structure of the stanzas in *Voyages II* have already been discussed. That Crane solves the problem of "white space" is demonstrated, I think, by *Voyages III*. The poem's structure is bipartite, although there is a slight rhythmic and grammatical pause before the last line and a brief break in the middle of the second stanza. The poem, both a dirge and a prayer, depicts through its syntax and its arching rhythm the motions of the sea and the play of light on waves, and subtly weaves them into the unfolding drama. Two themes are enacted by the poem: the "infinite consanguinity" of sea and lovers, sea and sky, lover and lover; and "The silken skilled transmemberment of song." The first theme is placed in stanza one and the second in stanza two, with the sea flowing throughout the poem as a unifying force.

The first stanza is beautifully contrived. The opening line announces the theme, and then proceeds without pause to the end of line four where the light that is retrieved from "sea plains" is returned and "enthroned." The poet's voyage, too, is uninterrupted, admits no impediments, and because he cleaves to his beloved, the sea in homage "lifts, also, reliquary hands." It is a devotional gesture of blessing, in keeping with the richly ceremonial and religious feeling of the love. The "white space" between the stanzas is alive with meaningful silence, a silence that contains the poet's poised recognition of what he is about to pass through. It prepares him, so to speak, for his immersion in the death which will lead to transfiguration. It is as if the black swollen gates swing slowly open and the poet enters. The "And so" imparts a feeling of logical necessity and consequentiality; the poet is caught in the rushing intensity of the waves, as the rhythms quicken and the syntax, as in the opening stanza of *Voyages II,* sweeps on without any predication, by a series of compounds that indicate structurally and rhythmically the union of the lovers and of the poet and the sea:[26]

> Light wrestling there incessantly with light,
> Star kissing star through wave on wave unto
> Your body rocking!
>   and where death, if shed,
> Presumes no carnage, but this single change,—
> Upon the steep floor flung from dawn to dawn
> The silken skilled transmemberment of song;

Punctuation makes the emphasis fall on light, rocking, death, and change; the long curve of the sentence ends, despite the syntactical check at "single change," only with the completion of the transmemberment of the song. A second pause follows during which the poet turns to his love and chastely beseeches him: "Permit me voyage, love, into your hands . . ." There is a fine symmetry between this line that ends the poem (and its gesture) and the line that ends stanza one (and the sea's movement of hands).[27]

In his best poems, Crane creates a verse structure that is a sturdy vehicle for his meaning, that is in some way the meaning itself, and that fuses the conceptual and the emotional harmoniously. "Rhythmic structures," Harvey Gross remarks, "are expressive forms, cognitive elements, communicating those experiences which rhythmic consciousness can alone communicate: empathic human responses to time in its passage."[28] Crane achieved this formal prosodic perfection more often than not, and this is an ineradicable sign of his poetic skill.

CHAPTER 10

Metrics

The early decades of the twentieth century witnessed many experiments in versification; they were a veritable hurly-burly of metrical activity. Suddenly poets and critics were alive to a need to overhaul traditional prosodic practices, or so it seemed, to throw out the *ancien régime* of Romantic poets and epigoni, and to substitute a prosodic government responsive to modern rhythms of speech and motion. The air was filled with accusations as partisans argued and propagandized for their favorite cause; manifestoes were issued, poems written, derided, defended; revolutions and counterrevolutions followed swiftly upon each other. The clashes sometimes seemed as much political as aesthetic, but they were reflective of radical departures in poetry and when the air cleared Pound and Eliot had altered poetic taste.

The rallying cries were, of course, Imagism and *vers libre,* though not necessarily in that order. To confuse matters, devotees of Imagism might at times be vocal critics of free verse, while, conversely, an admirer of free verse might be disdainful of Imagism or Amygism, in Ezra Pound's witty term.[1] The impetus for these controversies came from many hands—and it was not entirely unexpected. The French Symbolists, for one, iconoclastic continuers of the Romantic movement, had broken with many traditional usages, and had introduced along with their recondite and exotic vocabulary, new and daring rhythms. English poetry had reached the point where the lyrical insipidities of the post-Tennysonian generations, whether the vagueness of Swinburne or the predictable posturings of the minor lyricists, so nostalgically lampooned by Pound in "Mauberley," had engendered a strong desire for sparer verse, a new metric—or none at all. The Georgian poets made some modest prosodic reforms, but they reacted to the First World War by reaffirming traditional English values and by clinging to the solaces of a pastoral world. Unlike Pound, Eliot, Hulme, and Wyndham Lewis they were not in determined opposition to the vast body of nineteenth-century verse or its prosody.

Crane came of age poetically while the disputes raged [2] and the new poems were being printed in the little magazines. In a sense, he went to school to these magazines for his stylistic education; he read them avidly and thereby kept abreast of the latest technical discoveries. Yet the important thing is that though the early stages of his career coincided with these wars and experiments, and though he was eclectic by temperament, Crane kept himself aloof. He did not enlist under the banner of the *vers libre* movement, nor did he join the Imagist's crusade to oust the nineties versifiers from their places of eminence. Despite his unstable, enthusiastic character, when it came to poetic matters Crane was invariably a traditional craftsman. If he occasionally flirted with these movements, it was in a spirit of bemused caution.

Crane had a good ear, although he was not a virtuoso metrist. He could not compare with the indefatigable Pound as an inventive experimenter or as an adapter of rhythms from foreign languages and from antiquity.[3] He did not possess the "unified vision" or disciplined rhythms that Eliot commanded in his poems.[4] Nor did he renovate blank verse, as Wallace Stevens did (in poems like "Sunday Morning" "The Comedian as the Letter C," and "Le Monocle de Mon Oncle," to take three well known examples). Yet Crane's metric, conservative as it generally was, is interesting for several reasons.

First of all, it attempted to fuse Romantic and modern rhythms into a new rhetoric. It is helpful to compare him to Blake and Shelley, two of his favorite poets. A visionary poet who stays within the bounds of conventional metrics, Crane is unlike Blake, for example, who contrived a loose-jointed line which could, in the Prophetic books, combine narrative and apocalyptic preaching. Crane's visions are not anecdotal; they are closer to the lyrical Blake of "Songs of Innocence" and "Songs of Experience," and his line tends to be balanced, lush, and violent. He is closer to Shelley. Both are rhapsodes, but because Crane's language is more forceful than Shelley's, his poems do not dissolve into the urbane and smooth rhythms of Shelley's verse (of "Epipsychidion," "The Witch of Atlas," and "Prometheus Unbound," for example). Crane made use of jazz rhythms and "machine" rhythms, though not to the extent that he himself called for. These rhythms, whether jackhammer or ragtime, are often singled out as Crane's main contribution to modern poetry, but I believe that they constitute a minor motif, a snatch of melody in the overall symphonic form. The rhythmic life of his verse does not depend

on mechanics. Taken together, his poems yield three characteristic rhetorical lines: one emphatic, one nervous, and one re-
poseful. Crane restored to American poetry, and this is his
greatest contribution, the strong rhetorical surge; though he
used rhymed stanzas, he caught the feel of blank verse, which
he had admired in his beloved Elizabethan playwrights.
Crane's swollen line is Marlovian in sound and intensity; it is
loaded with a rich music; yet it is unmistakably very much
of its age.

Crane's rhetoric raises several questions about the Americanness of his metric, the direction it took, and its validity—and
its connection with Whitman's. Crane is usually cited together
with Whitman as a vatic poet, but there are few *prosodic*
resemblances between their poems; their music is altogether
different. Although Crane's syntax, as was stated previously,
is based in part on the principle of parallelism, it does not
rely for stanzaic organization, as Whitman's does, on the reiteration of sentences that begin with the same words or groups
of words. Crane is seldom operatic. His compositions resemble, if anything, tone-poems. Moreover, Crane almost never
writes the long prosy Whitmanesque line; as a rule, he writes
in iambics, and quite often in iambic pentameter. Crane's line
bends in upon itself in the middle much more than Whitman's,
which is almost exclusively expansive. This difference is due
primarily to their syntax. Crane's sentences are heavily qualified and often move in a twisting way over two or three lines,
whereas Whitman's sentences, even when qualified, follow a
deliberately repetitive pattern: several consecutive lines move
outward from the initial few words until the statement is
concluded, usually in the same line. Crane's rhythms are gen-

erally tenser than Whitman's. Crane's poems tend to be strophic, Whitman's not. In other words, each uses rhetoric in opposite ways. And while it would be misleading to deny Whitman as an influence on Crane's verse, he was considerably less important than Marlowe, Webster, Eliot, and Pound, among other poets.[5]

Rhetoric has been unpopular with modern critics, though some of the best poets, Yeats and Stevens foremost among them, have been able practitioners of it. "Rhetoric," Harvey Gross warns:

> . . . can only be sustained by consummate rhythmic control. . . . Rhetoric is language with more sensuous surface than conceptual substance; it becomes the job of prosody, then, to keep rhetoric from flowing into pure sound or dissolving into pure image. Rhythm, the container in which time is contained, tells us how an idea feels; rhythm will rescue for cognition what may never receive articulate verbal expression, what rhetoric may overstate or conceal.[6]

Gross's definition of rhetoric is a good one, but he has been churlish in dismissing the bulk of Crane's poetry as jejune and "self-defeating." He gives Crane fairly low grades as a metrist, claiming that Crane is restricted to only "a few octaves of feeling," and that only in a few poems, such as *Voyages*, the "Proem" to *The Bridge*, and parts of "The River," does his meter satisfactorily express his subject in a varied and subtle way. Crane perhaps achieved the highest metrical discipline in a handful of poems—this could be said about most good poets—but he was an able craftsman in most of the poems. This point cannot be too much stressed, since critics still carp at him for being an indiscriminate tumbler of words.[7] Yet he clearly labored over prosody and phonetics in order to avoid crude rhythms. If his work is uneven in quality, that derives usually from the perils of a declamatory style and his adventurous themes, not from technical uncertainty. A study of Crane's stylistic evolution indicates a constant refining of technique for expressive and cognitive ends. The meter in "The Broken Tower," his last poem, is handled with consummate skill, and breaks new metrical ground.

II

Early Experiments with Rhythms

The metrics of Crane's early verse can be divided into two stages. The first is marked by a rather conventional and earnest languor; there are few signs of the opulent sonorities, the gaiety and vehemence, that reverberate in his later poems. These first poems owe much to the metrics of Swinburne, Wilde, Dowson, and early Yeats, so that it is not surprising that Crane did not participate in the wranglings over free verse and Imagism or write many poems in those manners ("Pastorale," "North Labrador," and "My Grandmother's Love Letters" are organized on a very loose rhythmic basis, while "October-November" and "In Shadow" qualify as Imagist poems). From the outset, recognizing that he needed to attain control over his materials, Crane worked alone and with Carl Schmitt to master traditional metrical forms and variations. In a strict sense, his early poems are études designed to secure an unerring sovereignty over rhythm, sound, pitch, and cadence. Most of these apprentice poems are written in iambic tetrameter and iambic pentameter. Indeed the majority

of Crane's verse, early and late, is written in iambic pentameter. The evolution of his style must be studied in light of
his growing artfulness in handling the line, the most durable
in English poetry, and in making it both undulant and strong.
The vice of these early poems is their excessive regularity.
That they are pretty, sedate, and unexceptional rhythms, in
most cases, is beside the point. What matters is the diligent
effort to avoid monotony. Crane was, after all, very young and
untutored, and the astonishing fact is that he could so soon
strike out on his own and secure a technical competence. He
would have to wait upon "Faustus and Helen" to find his subject matter and his style.

Nevertheless, these poems are instructive. Certain metrical
idiosyncrasies that begin to appear in embryonic form indicate Crane's talent. "Forgetfulness," an uncollected poem
written in 1919, is representative of Crane's initial faults and
aims:

> Forgetfulness is like a song
> That, freed from beat and measure, wanders.
> Forgetfulness is like a bird whose wings are reconciled,
> Outspread and motionless,—
> A bird that coasts the wind unwearyingly.
>
> Forgetfulness is rain at night,
> Or an old house in a forest,—or a child.
> Forgetfulness is white,—white as a blasted tree,
> And it may stun the sybil into prophecy,
> Or bury the Gods.
>
> I can remember much forgetfulness.[8]

This poem achieves its limited variety, not so much through substitution as through alternation of long and short lines and through syntactical rhythms: the recurrence of "Forgetfulness" in the initial place in four lines and its emphatic shift to the last word of the single-line last stanza. The meter is clearly iambic even though Crane does not establish a metrical norm for line length and hence for departures from it. It is possible that Crane wished to convey the dazed forgetfulness through this straggling structure. The iambic beat that is felt from the first line on reinforces the feeling of numbed remoteness, as though the poet were droning absent-mindedly his remembrance of "much forgetfulness."

The poem is curiously flat, its effects overcalculated. The rhythms are like a child counting on his fingers. There are only two pauses, in the second and seventh lines; the first one at least partially succeeds in imitating musically the wandering song (the sense of the simile). Crane's liking for a phrasal syntax, discussed in a previous chapter, is responsible for another metrical trait: the preponderance of unbroken (unpunctuated) lines which ascend in slow and majestic pace to a climax and then die away. The rhythmic momentum is retarded, if at all, by pauses at the ends of lines, not by internal caesuras. This device seems to me crucial also to the attainment of a formal, rather than a plain, style. An abundance of interrupters can more closely catch conversational speech, and although Crane could at times achieve a colloquial cadence, his gifts were not essentially mimetic; fragments of dialogue are infrequent or stylized. There is only one enjambed line in the poem. For the most part, the early poems are free of run-on lines. No foot is prominently substituted for the iamb for variation.

"Fear," a two-quatrain poem, illustrates other typical metrical devices and shortcomings. Its bathos stems in part from the contrived fear of the thumping iambs, and in part from the embarrassing refrain:

> The host, he says that all is well,
> And the fire-wood glow is bright;
> The food has a warm and tempting smell,—
> But on the window licks the night.
>
> Pile on the logs. . . . Give me your hands,
> Friends! No,—it is not fright. . . .
> But hold me. . . . somewhere I heard demands. . . .
> And on the window licks the night.[9]

The poem is trite, but beneath the surface melodrama, a sense of genuine disquiet is felt, mainly in the clause "somewhere I heard demands" (though even this fear of obligation is vague), but it is undercut by the mawkish language and the long gaping pauses of the second stanza. The first stanza maintains a relatively steady iambic beat—lines one and four are entirely regular—inducing a lulling feeling of security, like the bright fire, warm food, and reassuring words of the host, but the fourth line, because of its ordinariness, does not convey menace. There is more metrical substitution in the second stanza, but it is too obvious. The shift to the imperative necessitates some trochees and spondees (lines five and six), but the pleas for help are neither forceful nor credible. The various internal pauses are inserted to indicate the grip of fear and the effort to control it. Still, even though the poem is almost hackneyed, and its meter undermines feeling, it does show Crane trying to exploit meter for the sake of characterization.

"In Shadow," that slight cameo written when Crane was only seventeen, manipulates sound and meter as well as syntax[10] for expressive purposes. It is one of the most regular and disciplined of Crane's early poems. The basic meter is iambic tetrameter—half the lines are perfectly regular—yet Crane avoids monotony by the judicious use of two metrical variants: trochees and pyrrhics, and by the tactful deployment of iambs. For example, the first line of the last stanza, when the woman speaks for the first time, scans this way:

$$\text{Cóme, ĭ ĭs tŏŏ láte,—tŏŏ láte}$$

The first foot is a catalexis; the stress communicates the woman's beseeching urgency. The next foot, a pyrrhic, frequent with Crane, aptly fits the murmuring tone and together with the iambic repetition of "too late" conveys the mood of hushed foreboding.[11] (Pyrrhic feet are generally found neighboring a spondee or in a polysyllabic word; I shall examine this point more fully later.) Crane's sensitivity to vowel and consonant sounds is also well illustrated by the poem: the assonance of "amber afternoon," "parasol," and "balloon"; the slant rhyme "chrysanthemums/swims"; and especially the subtle, liquid dispersal of the letter *l*.

During this first stage of self-instruction Crane also wrote a few poems that lack a set meter and that rely for organization on unity of point of view and theme rather than on syntax and meter. These poems can be predominantly imagistic

("October-November"), spare and nihilistic ("North Labrador"), or sentimentally ruminative ("My Grandmother's Love Letters"), but the rhythmic modulations, the unaccountable shifting from long lines to short ones within a stanza, do not necessarily destroy the integrity of the poem. In "October-November," for example, the meter of the second stanza lightens and quickens in order to suggest the lively play of color in the autumn twilight:

> Now gold and purple scintillate
> On trees that seem dancing
> In delirium;
> Then the moon
> In a mad orange flare
> Floods the grape-hung night.

What Crane accomplishes is a weaving of a visual spell through rhythmic means, especially anapestic substitution, and a highlighting of colors through spondaic stress. The stanza is organized rhythmically around the three heavy beats on "trees," "moon," and "flood." The lightness is struck off against the pressure of the vowel sounds, which seem to be held for a long time, like rubato in music. Crane works with great precision and subtlety with vowel sounds. Since the poem is brief, one does not miss a dominant beat.

"North Labrador," too, displays some cunning metrical substitution. The trochaic stress that falls on the verb "Flings" in line three seems to push the glacier into eternity. By its shuffling movement and its blending of spondees and pyrrhics, the meter of line nine conveys "the shifting of moments/ That journey toward no Spring." And the solemn, excruciatingly slow unfolding of line eleven ("Nŏ bírth, nŏ déath, nŏ tíme nŏr sún"), with its row of iambs, verging on spondees, and its punctuation, gives the feeling of bleak finality and unending process.

III

The Forging of the Iambic Pentameter Line

The second stage of Crane's development as a metrist is the crucial one. It extends from 1920 to the early part of 1923 when Crane completed "Faustus and Helen" and sketched out the first lines of the "Atlantis" section of *The Bridge*. He had fallen under the spell of T. S. Eliot, and through him of the Elizabethan and Jacobean dramatists,[12] and he had to make a strong effort to break out of the Eliotic mode and launch out on his own: to discover "new timbres." This was a period of study and experimentation, a transition from a genteel, *fin-de-siècle* Romanticism to a richly daring (if imperfect) Romanticism infused with the nervous spirit of modernity. There is, curiously, a relative paucity of poems; Crane's most prolific period came between 1923 and 1926.

What Crane took from Eliot, I think, was a toughening and tempering of the iambic line that went along with a toughening and deepening of vision. Eliot's ironic disenchantment with a faithless age and his distrust of certain emotions were, to be sure, ultimately uncongenial to a man of Crane's temperament.[13] But being impressionable and, in one side of his poetic nature, rational, Crane could respond favorably to, that is, assimilate, Eliot's rigorous technique. Specifically, this meant two things: learning how to express vital emotion and finding the proper metrical equivalents for these emotions. This explains why the dry, pointillistic method of Imagism would be useless to Crane: Imagism restrained emotion and concentrated on painting external realities. Crane wished to express his subjectivity fully in his poems. Eliot, therefore, would be the logical model to imitate, since, in Harvey Gross' words, "No modern poet has so effectively used rhythm to evoke a 'knowledge of how feelings go'; no rhythms have shown such power to summon emotion to the forefront of consciousness." [14] Eliot, with incomparable astuteness, knew the advantages of traditional forms and consequently did not ride with the free verse and Imagist hounds after their favorite hares. Most important, his prosody was flexible and defined by "the evasion and approximation of iambic pentameter." [15] Since this was Crane's habitual line, he could only stand to benefit from a close reading of Eliot. Crane's technical advance waited only upon a certain amount of maturing, which soon took place.

The Eliot influence quickly made itself felt in the two impromptu tirades Crane wrote in 1921, "The Bridge of Estador" and "Porphyro in Akron," [16] though neither poem fits into the iambic pentameter pattern I have been discussing. In both poems, romantic dreaming is deflated by mordant observation of harsh realities: "the dun/Bellies and estuaries of warehouses,/Tied bundle-wise with cords of smoke." The following stanza is a direct echo of "Prufrock":

> I will whisper words to myself
> And put them in my pockets.

> I will go and pitch quoits with old men
> In the dust of a road.

This is not just fashionable despair or flattering imitation. Crane is consciously testing his poetic resources, stretching his imagination by coarsening his lyrical impulse; this prosiness is a step away from sentimentality toward flexibility. The tirades are directed against himself, as he debates how to reconcile Romantic and ironic modes. To his credit, he soon realized that he did not want to be, and could not be, a faithful follower of Eliot's style.

Not the least of Eliot's valuable aids to Crane was putting him in the way of the Elizabethan and Jacobean poets. Crane's immediate response to Jonson, Webster, Marlowe, and Donne was wholehearted enthusiasm. In a series of letters to William Wright and Gorham Munson in October and November of 1921, he set down the reasons for their great appeal for him.[17] He mentions first their "verbal richness, irony, and *emotion*" [18] (my italics), and notes Eliot's successful adaptation of these virtues in his verse, in "Gerontion" in particular. He confesses to Munson:

> I have never, so far, been able to present a vital, living, and tangible,—a positive emotion to my satisfaction. For as soon as I attempt such an act I either grow obvious or ordinary, and abandon the thing at the second line. Oh! it is hard! One must be drenched in words, literally soaked with them to have the right ones form themselves into the proper pattern at the right moment.[19]

He is impatient to be about the Muse's business and to write poetry that, like Donne's, is a "dark musky, brooding, speculative vintage, at once sensual and spiritual, and singing rather the beauty of experience than innocence." [20]

These clearheaded statements shed light on Crane's wrestlings with the problem of form and his confidence in his possession of "gigantic assimilative capacities." [21] They indicate his ambitious program for poetic self-improvement. And they account for his petulant dismissal of forms as strict as the ballade, which, he says, can "be used satisfactorily for only very artificial subjects, or abstract themes." He does not approve of "the slouchy vers libre work" but he likes even less the "mechanical insistence of certain formal patterns." [22] He is chastising himself for the thinness of his previous work (only "Black Tambourine" escapes his condemnation). Crane does not specifically refer to the versification of his Elizabethan and Jacobean models, but as the letters hint and "Faustus and Helen" shows, he fastened eagerly on their spacious rhetoric.[23] Their poetic line was both weighty and delicate and it served as a *vehicle of emotion*. From them he learned how to animate the line with lyrical passion, to make it dextrous, ample, abrasive, and colorful. Crane's success in constructing the unabashedly rhetorical textures of "Faustus and Helen" emboldened him to declare his independence from T. S. Eliot. As 1923 began, while he was preoccupied with the last part of "Faustus and Helen," Crane could write about his mentor:

There is no one writing in English who can command so much respect, to my mind, as Eliot. However, I take Eliot as a point of departure toward an almost complete reverse of direction. His pessimism is amply justified, in his own case. But I would apply as much of his erudition and technique as I can absorb and assemble toward a more positive, or (if [I] must put it so in a sceptical age) ecstatic goal. I should not think of this if a kind of rhythm and ecstasy were not (at odd moments, and rare!) a very real thing to me.[24]

"Faustus and Helen," then, is the turning point in Crane's career. If it is perhaps somewhat uneven in quality, it compensates for its lapses by its range: from orphic song to catchy jive. The poem is a synthesis of Crane's Faustian (modern) and Helenic (Romantic) sources, a wedding of the masculine and feminine parts of his self. There are traces of the Elizabethans and Eliot, who pried open his sensibility, but the poem is a unified work of art. And just as the poem heralded the appearance of a new diction,[25] so it signaled the arrival of the metrical idiom that, with slight modifications, was to be the hallmark of Crane's style for the rest of his life.

Crane's description of the form of "Faustus and Helen III" as symphonic, by which he meant its organization and rhythm, covers Part I too. The style of both sections is lyrical declamation; rhythm and syntax are governed by the pressures of rising and falling emotion and by trance-like meditations; only occasionally does a conversational cadence intrude upon a line. What makes the poem symphonic is the weaving together of rhythmic motifs in one stanza and the carrying over and modulating of them in subsequent stanzas. The basic iambic meter is introduced right away and recurs, with a sort of courtly intensity, so frequently as to impose an almost metronomic beat. The opening lines of stanzas I, II, IV, and probably V start as tetrameter and then expand to pentameter.[26] Irregularity, the unexpected prosodic detail that provides the freedom within discipline, is a welcome wrenching of order that enlivens the poem. The syntax, which is heavily phrasal

and spiraling, further enforces a slow tempo. The incantatory
meter of "Faustus and Helen" is, of course, consonant with
its ceremonial nature, but it does not permit quite enough
diverting variation from the norm. Nevertheless, much of the
regularity is deliberate.

The first stanza, for instance, sets down the average dull-
ness of the mass mind occupied with quotidian details. The
meter is similarly ordinary and sluggish:

> The mind has shown itself at times
> Too much the baked and labeled dough
> Divided by accepted multitudes.

When Crane wishes to create a startling reversal of this level-
ing rhythm, he drops a trochee and a spondee into the line,
which forcefully rouses the mind from its torpor and makes it
aware of an ambiguous possibility for a higher communion:
"Smutty wings flash out equivocations." [27] The only exceptions
to the iambic pattern before the last line of the stanza (just
quoted) are the polysyllabic words which result in three or
four consecutive unstressed syllables and a slackening of intensity—"Across the memoranda," for example.[28] The consequence of a vocabulary such as Crane's, which is well
stocked with polysyllabic words, is that it may overload the
line and force it to collapse; it may become limp, afflicted with
a broken spine. This does not happen too often in Crane's
poetry, since he is alert to setting the long word in a context
of stressed monosyllabic words.

The options for metrical change and hence for variety are
numerous, but at this stage in his writing, Crane is still a bit

cautious and often returns in the very next foot to the metrical pulse he has just left. This makes for symmetry and for tension. There are indeed few lines that depart from the metrical figure that do not seek to return to the status quo. Thus, an initial trochee—and the most frequent variation occurs in the initial foot—is often immediately reversed in the next foot:

> Táke thĕm ăwáy . . .
> Númbĕrs, rĕbúffed bў ásphălt, crówd . . .

The same impulse is true of an initial dactyl: "Vírginăl pĕrháps, lĕss frágmĕntăry, cóol" or "Ímmĭnĕnt ĭn hĭs dréam."

Another device that contributes to the feeling of metrical stability is the even spacing of caesuras within a line; most caesuras fall, in a pentameter or eleven-syllabled line, in a medial position. Moreover, there are almost no stops in the middle of a line and almost twenty full stops at the end of a line (there are few unstressed endings). In poems like *Voyages,* with their more dramatic and unpredictable inversions, even when the metrical variation falls on the first foot, the line is weighted in an unequal and unbalanced way. In "Faustus and Helen," however, the curve of the syntax over the entire verse paragraph shapes the rhythm, and slows down or accelerates the particular iambic pentameter line. It must be remembered that Crane did not follow Ezra Pound in destroying the pentameter line. Where Pound let each sentence comprise one verse line and got his rhythmic variety through subtle shifts in grammar and punctuation, Crane did not care or need to defend the integrity of the single line, since the line was patterned in a larger arching phrase.

The metrical problem facing Crane in Part II of "Faustus and Helen" was, simply, how to strike up rhythms that would approximate jazz dance steps, how to achieve a change of pace. He needed a meter that would be sprightly, humorous, and metallic but would skirt banal tripping (anapestic) measures. What he hit upon, logically enough, was iambic tetrameter,[29] which he had used successfully before in poems of a serious sort, "In Shadow," "Praise for an Urn" and "Stark Major," but handled in a specially felicitous way. Since the poem has very few broken lines, he could suggest the smooth loping gait of the dance with comparative ease, and since there are few run-on lines, he could convey the stops and starts of the dance. And, in order to evoke the antic grace and alternating dips and scurryings, he inserted many metrical substitutions, especially trochees and spondees and three stresses in a row, in the first three feet. When the poem switches from descriptions of the sensuous rompings to a didactic summary of the dance's meaning, the meter, as it were, reluctantly lengthens to iambic pentameter.

The meter is not forced. It has bite and "rhythmic ellipses" to please the reader and give him the illusion he is tapping his foot or actually gliding breathlessly around the speakeasy roof garden. Consider the following passage:

> Brazen hypnotics glitter here;
> Glee shifts from foot to foot,
> Magnetic to their tremolo.
> This crashing opera bouffe,
> Blest excursion! this ricochet
> From roof to roof—

The trochees in lines one and five and the spondee that opens line two are set off against the predominantly rocking iambic motion of the rest. The meter imitates the ricochet and the shift from foot to foot and the modulations from tetrameter to trimeter to dimeter suggest the skittish movement of the dance:

> A thousand light shrugs balance us
> Through snarling hails of melody.
> White shadows slip across the floor
> Splayed like cards from a loose hand;
> Rhythmic ellipses lead into canters
> Until somewhere a rooster banters.

Though only the last two lines rhyme, the entire passage gives the feel of couplets, and the fairly parallel syntax creates an additional balance. To thwart the danger of sameness, Crane increases the number of inverted feet and places them in such a way as to produce a slightly syncopated beat. Thus in the first line three sharp stresses follow each other, the last wittily landing on balance and pointing up the difficulty of keeping one's precarious balance. The snarling hails of melody are regular when irregularity would be expected—another shrewd reversal. The third line begins with a spondee and then slips back into iambs. Line four begins with a catalectic foot, emphasizing the odd word "Splayed," and then like the cards spreads out with an iamb, a pyrrhic, and a spondee. Line five encloses the two middle iambic feet with trochees, though perhaps Crane might have gotten a more striking "rhythmic ellipse" here.[30]

In sum, Crane was capable of shaping the meter of the poem to fit his goals. A line like "With perfect grace and equanimity" does what it says. I do not want to exaggerate Crane's skill as a metrist at this stage in his stylistic development—it is more than adequate—but it is clear that in "Faustus and Helen" he transformed himself into a poet capable of a richly fluent line "striated with nuances, nervosities." "Faustus and Helen" occupies a place in Crane's *oeuvre* roughly analagous to "Hyperion" in Keats'. And though the poem can be criticized, particularly Part III, for being overblown and sing-songish, Crane's successful struggle to overcome mawkish and crude rhythms should be applauded. He found his style. In future poems, he would be able to hazard more personal themes and present vital emotion as excitingly at times as John Webster.

IV

"The silken skilled transmemberment of song"

The years from 1923 to 1926 saw a blossoming of Crane's talent. He had progressed steadily toward a mastery of craft and consolidated his metrical gains in some of his finest poems —"At Melville's Tomb," "Possessions," *Voyages,* "O Carib Isle!," and from *The Bridge,* the "Proem," "The River," and "The Tunnel." [31]

The rhythms of the *Voyages* poems are exquisite.* The sequence as a whole is composed with extraordinary finesse,

---

* Since I have written at length on the *Voyages* poems in other chapters, I shall confine my illustrations to three or four passages.

unerring ear, and structural incisiveness. The pace of the poem, as is usual in Crane's best work, is regal and unhurried. The iambic pentameter of *Voyages II, III, IV,* and *V* is stately, luxuriant, and sensuous.[32] There is no lack of emotional force, but it is chastened by the contrapuntality of the writing and by the skill with which onamatopoeic effects are earned. *Voyages I,* for instance, is buoyed by internal consonant rhymes ("processioned," "sessions"); the tolling of funeral bells is echoed in the mournful repetition of *l* sounds, while the menace and shimmering beauty of the sea are limpidly evoked by the subtle use of *s* sounds. In addition, the meter represents the flow of the sea, its changeableness and processional "unfettered leewardings." The clustering of polysyllabic words also contributes to the rhythmic compulsions of the poem in two ways. First, it sets up phrasing which alternates strong stresses with three or four consecutive unstressed syllables. In a terminal position this leads to a trailing off, a dying out of sound, as in "unfettered leewardings." In a medial or initial position this takes the form of a dactyl followed by an anapest, as in "Infinite consanguinity it bears" or "All bright insinuations that my years have caught." [33]

Even more marked is the effective use of spondees in initial or terminal position to heighten the intensity and excitement of the love:

> Mark how her turning shoulders wind the hours,
> And hasten while her penniless rich palms
> Pass superscription of bent foam and wave,—
> Hasten, while they are true,—sleep, death, desire,
> Close round one instant in one floating flower.

The heavily stressed first foot is proper to the imperative syntax and the knowledge Crane is communicating of time's irresistible doom: it seizes the emotions and rivets the attention on the key words of the stanza, and it serves as a rhythmic contrast to the looser pulse of line five and the steady pulse of line one, where one can hear, metrically, the ticking of the sea's time. The haste he is urging is beautifully conveyed by the four swift unaccented syllables between "Hasten and true"; three heavy stresses then fall on the crucial words of the line, "sleep," "death," "desire." The musical energy that charges these lines is present also in the following examples from *Voyages III* and *IV*:

> Past whirling pillars and lithe pediments,
> Light wrestling there incessantly with light
> Star kissing star through wave on wave unto
> Your body rocking! . . .
> Upon the steep floor flung from dawn to dawn

In this passage the momentum is set going in the first foot and gradually modulates into regularity, like the agitation of the sea when some object is thrown into it and the water ripples most calmly in the farthest concentric circle. This rhythmic motif is aided by the strongly alliterative character of the verse—the *l*'s and *p*'s in line one, the compounds in lines two and three, and the arresting violence of line five, which in turn is followed by the incandescent penultimate line of the poem: "The silken skilled transmemberment of song":

All fragrance irrefragibly, and claim
Madly meeting logically in this hour
And region that is ours to wreathe again,
Portending eyes and lips and making told
The chancel port and portion of our June—[34]

The eloquence of this passage is due to the wreathing syntactical rhythms and to the irregularity and clangor of the first two lines with their spondees and trochees; the iambs seem to emerge from the logical madness of the ecstatic moment. The lines are overloaded yet preserve a lovely precariousness. Syntactically, the verse has no predication; it really needs none, since the poet is experiencing an unduplicable voluptuous magic sensation; but the intimations of metrical regularity give credence to the logical claim of the mad surrender. The sounds jostle each other, but there is breathing space between word and word. The poet's irresistible passion carries down to the very bedrock of language, the syllables, the alliterations and consonances: the *f's*, *r's*, and *g's* in line one and the *m's* and *l's* of line two; the repetition of "*Port*ending," "*port* and *port*ion"; the assonance of "irref*ragibly*," "*Madly* meeting logica*lly*," "*region*" and "*wreathe*."

What Crane has learned to do is to forestall monotony and pedestrian rhythms by introducing some slight metrical divergence so that the heavily accented line will not disfigure the texture of the verse. This care is necessary because Crane's rhythms are relatively unencumbered and because he does not employ many caesuras, thereby losing a valuable chance to fashion an asymmetrical line. Crane was unable to sustain this functional metric in all his poems. When his poems fail it is not because he is a faulty technician, but because he has nothing to say; he relies too much on his own subjectivity. All Romantic poets are solipsists, but those who incorporate the external world into their poems stand a better chance of circumventing the dangers of a purely rhetorical line. Nonetheless, it is unjust to ask of Crane that he be some other kind of poet, since he is so good as a rhetorical poet.

V

The "trespass vision"

There is little discrepancy between the metrical practices of Crane's odal poems and his quatrains. In both, the iambic pentameter is the underlying inflectional line. Yet as early as "O Carib Isle!" (1925), that extraordinary tour de force, Crane was experimenting with a more open and pungent metric which was not to appear again until his last great poem, "The Broken Tower." Both are the outstanding poems of the *Key West* volume. Though similar in mood and language to Crane's other poems, they break new rhythmic ground. Thematically, the two poems are unalike, since "O Carib Isle!" is probably Crane's most grimly pessimistic poem, whereas "The Broken Tower" reaches a tentative beatitude and a consoling faith in self and in the poetic imagination. Metrically, they are alike and unalike. Where "O Carib Isle!" either conceals or suspends the iambic pentameter line, "The Broken Tower" retains and transforms it. Both, however, introduce angular and short rhythms in juxtaposition with elegant and long ones.

To summarize the prosodic features of "O Carib Isle!" requires extensive demonstration, so I shall quote the poem entire:

1 The tarantula rattling at the lily's foot

2 Across the feet of the dead, laid in white sand

3 Near the coral beach—nor zigzag fiddle crabs

4 Side-stilting from the path (that shift, subvert

5 And anagrammatize your name)—No, nothing here

6 Below the palsy that one eucalyptus lifts

7 In wrinkled shadows—mourns.

                           And yet suppose

8 I count these nacreous frames of tropic death,

9 Brutal necklaces of shells around each grave

10 Squared off so carefully. Then

11 To the white sand I may speak a name, fertile

12 Albeit in a stranger tongue. Tree names, flower names

13 Deliberate, gainsay death's brittle crypt. Meanwhile

14 The wind that knots itself in one great death—

15 Coils and withdraws. So syllables want breath.

16 But where is the Captain of the doubloon isle

17 Without a turnstile? Who but catchword crabs

18 Patrols the dry groins of the underbrush?

19 What man, or What

20 Is Commissioner of the mildew throughout the ambushed
    senses?

21 His Carib mathematics web the eyes' baked lenses!

22 Under the poinciana, of a noon or afternoon

23 Let fiery blossoms clot the light, render my ghost

24 Sieved upward, white and black along the air

25 Until it meets the blue's comedian host.

26 Let not the pilgrim see himself again

27 For slow evisceration bound like those huge terrapin

28 Each daybreak on the wharf, their brine-caked eyes;

29 —Spiked, overturned; such thunder in their strain!

30 Slagged on the hurricane—I, cast within its flow,

31 Congeal by afternoons here, satin and vacant.

32 You have given me the shell, Satan,—carbonic amulet

33 Sere of the sun exploded in the sea.[35]

The poem is many things. It is a tragic document in which
Crane expresses his extreme nausea for life; a stark landscape
painting; a pitiless self-exposure of his failure to find and
sustain an identity as man and poet (contradicted by the brilliance of the poem); a moral confrontation of evil and death;
and a metaphysical inquiry into the nature of a meaningless
and brutal universe. There is no self-pity. Crane is mercilessly
lucid. His loss of faith is delivered in a voice of sour humor,
but he is not playing the village atheist. The poem assaults
and unsettles the reader because Crane has succeeded in
universalizing his stricken sensibility; he is in the poem not

only as participant and spectator, but also as the impersonal chronicler, doggedly and courageously venturing to the edge of consciousness to face ugly truths.

Radical changes in the prosody were necessary if Crane were to present the jagged, ambushed rhythms of the tropic hell he inhabited. Some of the metrical shifts resulted from syntactical shifts. What the reader first notices is the tremendous decrease in the number of unbroken lines. There are only fourteen such lines in the poem. This naturally causes a redistribution of pauses, a pushing of cadences into any place in the sentence where the sense logically or the emotions unconsciously demand that they go. A freer rhythm is created, and since there is a high percentage of enjambed lines in the poem, the effect is a more flexible opening and closing of musical phrases. Crane adds another strong new effect: as many full medial stops as full final stops. This is brought about by letting a sentence begin or end anywhere in the line, quite frequently in the middle. This device is used in stanzas two, three, and four in particular, and produces an abrupt and unexpectedly simple cadence, as in "So syllables want breath," and sets polyrhythms going in counterpoint to the iambic measure. This recurring periodicity is a welcome roughening of the meter and of the poetic texture.

The other changes are more modest but no less important and effective. The iambic pentameter loses its commanding position and is demoted to first among equals. This means two things: the poem can vary from lines of six to lines of sixteen syllables, the majority being of ten, eleven, and twelve syllables; and it can modulate its stresses from seven to two, with the majority falling on five, six, or seven. These statistics indicate that the poem is weighty, which is true, but also acute, like a knife cutting through the lethargy that grips Crane on the Carib isle and reduces him to bestiality. So many stresses also lead inevitably to more spondees and trochees either spread out evenly or compressed tightly into one segment of the sentence: lines three and twenty-two are examples of the first type, and lines five, thirteen, and thirty examples of the second type.

The first stanza presents with fascinated horror the ghastly spectacle of all creation supine, scarcely able to rouse itself from inertia. There is nothing but ponderous instinctual movement.[36] Death pervades all. Crane sees the lowest forms of creation not only as indifferent parts of an empty cosmos, but as desecrators of life; "The tarantula rattling at the lily's foot," like the dog digging up the corpse in the garden in *The Waste Land*, is an emblem of gratuitous cruelty, of a world without sacrament. The first line is metrically irregular; the first two feet are anapests which convey the rattling movement. The paradox of beauty and evil coexisting is not resolved in the poem. The stanza is built syntactically in three tiers, each one leading to the appalling conclusion that no one mourns the anonymous dead (Everyman?) buried in the sand.

Line two begins with two iambs and an anapest, and then, after the caesura, ends with a trochee and a spondee. The heavy stresses and the consonantal *d*'s convey the torpor and the finality of death. Line three begins with yet another anapest, and the frequency with which this foot is substituted is proof of the poem's unusual metric; the line halts in the middle, as the poet musters the will to describe the fiddler crabs sidling out into view. Line four balances line two: the regular iambic pulse in the later feet rather than in the first few. The parenthesis further delays the momentum. Naming is a primary act for Crane, associated with a unified self, but here the crabs scramble ("anagrammatize") a name, confuse an identity. The third section announces in a melancholy tone that nothing mourns on the isle; the double accenting of "no" makes the discouraging fact irrevocable. Even the eucalyptus tree is palsied. The withholding of the verb "mourns" to the end of the stanza is effective. To counteract the freer rhythms and restore some stability to the stanza, Crane beautifully balances repeated vowel sounds:

> The tar*a*ntula r*a*ttling *a*t the *li*ly's foot
> Side-st*i*lting from the p*a*th (that sh*i*ft, subvert

The next two stanzas constitute a single logical and semantic unit, since they put forward a syllogistic proposition that ends, so to speak, in the non sequitur of death. The poet stirs himself from his stupor and seeks to find order and meaning in the carefully circular ("necklace") arrangement of shells that decorate the graves (in contrast to the anagrammatized name); they are "brutal" aesthetic memorials because they are out of place amid the parched signs of a "tropic death." The meter in stanza two is fairly regular in keeping with Crane's counting of the neat pile of shells. The only variants are the anapest of "nacreous frames" and the two trochees and anapest of "Brutal necklaces of shells" which emphasize the harsh beauty.

Having forced himself to count the shells, a ritualistic gesture like telling his beads, he then may be able to overcome his alienation and speak some fertile name to the barren land and to his own barren self. He has a momentary hope that he can regain his poetic tongue and become a second Adam conferring names and identity on flowers and trees. This primary act, the poetic process, is an affirming of life, a gainsaying of "death's brittle crypt." Crane's revived faith is short-lived. He becomes aware of the feeble wind (his spirit) that "knots itself in one great death—/Coils and withdraws." The air is enervating. "So syllables want breath," that is, wish for the animating breath of life and lack it. As Crane tries to throw off his lethargy, the meter undergoes a number of interesting changes. The first line begins with a pyrrhic and thus throws the stress on the next spondee "white sand" (an echo of the dead buried in the beach), follows with an iamb, and ends with a trochee on "fertile," which enunciates his longing to write, even in a "stranger tongue." Line three is the most heavily accented in the poem, with four consecutive stresses, as Crane strives to "gainsay death's brittle crypt."

The fourth stanza consists of three sardonic questions and a grisly fatalistic answer. Crane is searching for a clue to the riddle of this tropic inferno. Who is responsible for the existence of this sterile world ("dry groins")? No one seems to run this inhospitable island in which the senses are mildewed and the imagination prostrated by the extreme heat of the Carib sun. Only the "catchword crabs"[37] militantly occupy and patrol the island (presumably they can survive the ambush), but by whose orders (Captain or Commissioner) is not clear.[38] All he knows is that his "eyes" are covered with a film that prevents vision ("web" recalls the tarantula, the poisonous spider). He can only wonder at the anonymous overseer's inscrutable calculations which cast the horrible pall on man. Metrically, what is noteworthy in the stanza are the accents on *Who, What man,* and *What,* the short fourth line which precedes the deliberately slack fifth line that represents the vitiated senses: it is a sixteener, whose stressed feet seem to labor painfully to be born. The clever repetition of the ugly sound *k* adds to the sense of a hostile environment.

Stanza five continues the mood of jocose resignation. The poet imagines himself lolling under a poinciana tree seeking relief from the sun's ambushing glare. He apostrophizes the tree to render his ghost "sieved upward," separated into a wispy substance and rising, like a genie from a bottle, to mingle with "the blue's comedian host," that is, the clouds, or since Crane is punning on the word "host," the god who plays comical games with, and practical jokes on, men. The poem drops into regular quatrain form, with an *a-b-c-b* rhyme scheme, and a fairly regular meter, the only substitutions being one anapest in line one and the trochees that stress the verbs in the sentence.

Crane has all along identified himself with the primitive creatures that crawl on the island: they are a symbol of his own paralyzed will and immobilized intelligence, his passive infatuation with death. Now, in stanza six, he admonishes himself, and others who have undertaken a similar pilgrimage to find themselves, to be wary of allowing an indifferent world to cast him and others aside to die. He is transfixed by the disemboweled "huge terrapins" who are bound on the docks "Spiked, overturned," and awed by the power and endurance they project even in death.[39] Like his, their eyes are "brine-caked," closed. The stanza is again a quatrain, but this time there are three slant rhymes: "again/terrapin/strain." The second line is especially brilliant. It is a fourteener, which mimics the "slow evisceration" it mentions. The punctuation, for the first time in the poem, is anomalous; grammatically, "their brine-caked eyes" is not in apposition to anything in the sentence before it; but the strong emphasis on "brine-caked eyes" conveys the chilling terror of the scene. And the chopped-up syntax of line four, together with the inversions of "Spiked, overturned," graphically depict the gruesome sight of the dying terrapins.

The poem ends on a note of weary bitterness, self-condemnation, and submission to death. His pilgrimage a failure, the poet sees himself as slag, as refuse that has been separated by the smelting process (again extreme heat) and thrown into the water, thus polluting it. The poet betrays himself, since he is utterly passive; the spiked terrapins at least "thunder in their strain" to escape the burning out. He only appears to be "sieved upwards," for adrift and melted, he paradoxically also "congeals by afternoons." The adjectives "satin and vacant" are interestingly paired. "Vacant" refers to the existential emptiness he has powerfully etched. "Satin" suggests some rich smooth fabric, as if Crane were luxuriating in his sloth and loss of will. "Satin" is an odd antithesis to "Satan," who is addressed in the next line. Satan is assigned the captaincy of the isle. He has given Crane the shell, a carbonic amulet of the explosive sun, a withered inefficacious talisman, the emblem of death. The rhythms are not exceptional here, though meaning is again enacted by alliteration, the hissing *s's* of the last line, and by assonance and consonance—satin, vacant, amulet, Satan. The first two lines of the quatrain peter out like Crane's hope, while the last line explodes, like the sun in the sea.

A remarkable, harrowing poem, "O Carib Isle!" is one of the central documents of Crane's biography and poetic development. It marshals all the potential advantages of prosody —meter, sound, and syntax—as well as a terse, menacing imagery to present an experience of morbid despair, black humor, and moral acuteness.[40]

VI

"the visionary company of love"

The tragic circumstances surrounding the composition of "The Broken Tower" imbue it with a poignancy independent of its many artistic merits. When he started writing the poem in Mexico near the end of his life, Crane seems to have lost faith in his poetic gifts; in sober moments he regretted having wasted them. "The Broken Tower" is therefore about poetry and his whole life. It combines a confessional intimacy with a haunting elegaic disquietude; its melancholy lyricism is pierced by extremes of joy and agony until it ends in quiet self-acceptance and love. In beauty and range it is one of Crane's most finely wrought poems. The fluctuations of emotion are handled with firm rhythmic control. Its rhetoric is sensuous and nuanced. The poem is moving proof that Crane had not forfeited his art.

The metrical tension of the poem is between a fairly consistent iambic pentameter line and a syntactical rhythm that requires numerous stops. Its novelty in Crane's work lies in this difficult harmony of regularity and spasmodic measure.

For the first time in a predominantly iambic pentameter poem —"O Carib Isle!" was metrically free-wheeling—there is a fantastic decrease in unbroken lines (only twelve of forty-four). And because there is a high percentage of run-on lines (twenty-five of forty-four), the music of the verse is also irregular. As in the "Proem," "O Carib Isle," and *Voyages V*, sentences begin and end anywhere in the line; the cadence is therefore more various than we would suppose. It is through these rhythms that Crane conveys the uncertainties he feels and tries to reconstruct his tower: to strengthen the imagination and to bring it once again into fruitful interplay with reality. The poem is, after all, about a broken tower, and the broken rhythms have an appropriate relevance to the subject, just as the rhymed quatrains, in their formal congruity, embody the idea of resolution and oneness.

Crane's handling of the meter is subtle and unobtrusive and functions as a major characterizing force. Bells echo throughout the poem as they did in *Voyages II*, and they ring a compelling reiterative time—regular yet occasionally fitful and off-beat. In the first three stanzas, when his disbelief oscillates most wildly, like the fast beating of his heart and a kind of frozen despair, the iambic pulse sways "Antiphonal carillons":

> The bell-rope that gathers God at dawn
> Dispatches me as though I dropped down the knell
> Of a spent day—to wander the cathedral lawn
> From pit to crucifix, feet chill on steps from hell.
>
> Have you not heard, have you not seen that corps
> Of shadows in the tower, whose shoulders sway

Antiphonal carillons launched before
The stars are caught and hived in the sun's ray?

The bells, I say, the bells break down their tower;
And swing I know not where. Their tongues engrave
Membrane through marrow, my long-scattered score
Of broken intervals . . . And I, their sexton slave!

It makes no difference whether Crane is exclaiming or questioning; the meter governs the feeling. Thus in stanza one, the only interruptions are trochees and spondees that fall on key words and stress his spiritual limbo: "bell-rope," "dropped down," "spent day," and "feet chill." For the rest, one feels in the rhythm the poet's painful steps as he wanders to the doleful music of the bell summoning people to worship and him to death. The mood is supported by the alliterations—the *g*'s of line one and the *d*'s—and the consonance—*p*'s, *g*'s, *d*'s, *f*'s, and *l*'s. In stanza two, the syntactic repetition coincides well with the iambic uniformity. Indeed the only variation is "in the sun's ray," but once again alliteration binds the images, and the rhythm, by its delicate placement of caesura and its ascending movement, matches the swaying of the "corps of shadows." The insistence of line nine is rendered by the iambic pattern. It is again the third line of the quatrain that turns the meter around and introduces the initial trochee, the pyrrhic in the third foot, and the important spondee on "long-scattered." The punctuation rather than the meter of line twelve expresses the feeling of "broken intervals." The alliteration becomes almost compulsive; lines eleven and twelve sound like Hopkins, though the stresses do not stray far from the metrical mean.[41]

The rest of the poem follows the metrical configurations of the first three stanzas. Only in the highly grandiloquent fourth stanza, with its attempt to fill the stanza with sound as the bells fill the poet's consciousness ("heaping/The impasse high with choir"), is there much active variation. Every time the meter verges on it, Crane deftly avoids monotony. It should be noted that the iambic foot, being essentially a rising one, is rhythmically apt for the building of the tower which occupies the poet in the last two stanzas.

Thus Crane's valediction is, prosodically, evidence of a new beginning: "new inklings, new verities"; "new thresholds, new anatomies." The tower is not patchwork or gimcrackery. It is a superbly florid and chaste edifice. Its rhythms live in the imagination.

Crane's Views on Poetry
and the Machine

Crane devotes the bulk of his essay "Modern Poetry," written in 1929, to a consideration of the uneasy relations of poetry and technology in an era in which the latter increasingly dominated the thoughts of men. Throughout the nineteenth century and the first three decades of the twentieth century, poets usually viewed the progress of technology with alarm and dismay. Though some artists accepted the challenge of the machine with buoyancy and equanimity, there was a surprising near-unanimity of distaste for the world science had brought into being. Technology was both cause and symptom of moral chaos, loss of feeling, and spiritual shallowness; modern man, in the words of "Gerontion," is "whirled/Beyond the circuit of the shuddering Bear/In fractured atoms." T. S. Eliot, in poem after poem, registered his nausea at the barrenness and *anomie* that science and its pesky child, technology, had visited upon men and society. The Waste Land is the horrible "Unreal City" of "trams and dusty trees," gashouses, oil barges, litter, and throbbing taxis.[1] (The First World War doubtless reinforced this horror, since the machines of de-

struction made this war seem more monstrous than other
wars.)

It is against this background of profound discomfort with
the machine that Crane's comments about the role poetry had
to play in a Machine Age should be viewed. By temperament
he was uniquely fitted to speak about these issues: his sensibility was marvelously attuned to the shocks and sensations,
the nervous rhythms, and, as A. Alvarez says, "the inner
disturbance"[2] of his day. Though not equipped with a deep
or special knowledge of science, Crane, almost alone among
his contemporaries, enthusiastically accepted the fact that
science was "the uncanonized Deity of the times."[3] He was
not gloomy about the prospects for poetry in an Einsteinean
world; the influence of machinery need not be pernicious or
unduly alarming; indeed, the possibility of it being so might
not even exist. Buoyed by Waldo Frank's praise of "Faustus
and Helen," he wrote to Gorham Munson, "Potentially I feel
myself quite fit to become a suitable Pindar for the dawn of
the machine age."[4] That the machine age had created a
strange new psychic environment and that its artifacts affected
men's emotions were undeniable *facts,* and led Crane to conclude, sensibly, that the poet must be in the vanguard of these
changes ("Power's script"), recording, analyzing, and interpreting them. The machine, like the camera in the hands of
Alfred Stieglitz, could stimulate or become an instrument of
vital "apprehension," affording the opportunity of making the
moment eternal, of extending personal perception into previously unexplored regions: "Seeing himself an atom in a shroud
—/Man hears himself an engine in a cloud." Far from being
diminished by the machine, man was capable of being set

free by it. It conferred new visionary powers on those who were not daunted by it, leading them, in Blake's words, "in at Heaven's gate,/Built in Jerusalem's wall." Crane justly invoked Pindar. Like the Greek odist, he wished to celebrate and affirm in his poems the heroic spirit of his world and the romance and adventure, manifest, for example, in the uncanny speed of airplanes and the shutter of a camera.

The poet translated these new forces into "positive terms." (Whitman had cheered "Hurrah for positive science!") Critics have frequently assailed Crane for this belief, charging him with facile optimism and woolly-mindedness, just as they have misunderstood his remark that the modern poet needs an "extraordinary capacity for surrender, at least temporarily, to the sensations of urban life." [5] Crane does not mean abandoning all intellectual control in quest of sensation, glorifying the irrational, or even deranging the senses to heighten one's perceptions. He means simply that the poet must involve himself fully in the pluralist emotional life around him, "carrying sensation into the midst of the objects of science itself":[6]

> The function of poetry in a Machine Age is identical to its function in any other age; and its capacities for presenting the most complete synthesis of human values remain essentially immune from any of the so-called inroads of science. The emotional stimulus of machinery is of an entirely different psychic plane from that of poetry. Its only menace lies in its capacities for facile entertainment, so easily accessible as to arrest the development of any but the most negligible esthetic responses. The ultimate influence of machinery in this respect remains to be seen, but its firm entrenchment in our lives has already produced a series of challenging new responsibilities for the poet.[7]

Crane was too much of a realist to delude himself that simple quotation of the nomenclature or objects of science would suffice, but he firmly held that the poet could not default on his responsibility to his people and his own imagination to incorporate the most important spiritual and material event of his time into his verse. His esthetic responses are not negligible.

Crane thought that the modern poet should exploit science and the machine in two ways: as "religious dogma" and as metaphor. That is, science might be used to support the poet's vision as Milton used the myth of the Fall of Man in *Paradise Lost,* and radios, derricks, automobiles, and telegraph wires might be integrated into the poem as casually as the pulley was in George Herbert's poem. In his own poetry Crane, much as Whitman had before him, found the second goal easier of attainment than the first. The reason is not hard to find:

> The most typical and valid expression of the American *psychosis* seems to me still to be found in Whitman. His faults as a technician and his clumsy indiscriminate enthusiasm are somewhat beside the point. He, better than any other, was able to coordinate those forces in America which seem most intractable, fusing them into a universal vision which takes on additional significance as time goes on.[8]

Crane knew that coordinating the intractable forces, accommodating the facts of the machine with the humanist values of poetry, was hard to achieve. Even Whitman, who lived when the machine was not nearly as complex and all-impinging as in the 1920s, could not manage the synthesis, not because of "clumsy and indiscriminate enthusiasm" but because of the "American psychosis," by which Crane means a divided consciousness.

Inevitably, this "American psychosis" found its way into Crane's poetry, and Crane responds ambiguously to the sensations of New York life. *The Bridge* blends the vibrancy and raw power of technology with its bruising destructive force. The bridge itself is imagined as a lovely symbol of spiritual aspiration and unity:

> And Thee, across the harbor, silver-paced
> As though the sun took step of thee, yet left
> Some motion ever unspent in thy stride,—
> Implicitly thy freedom staying thee!

but its serenity is set off by the remorseless activity of machine and men; nature itself is infected by the motion, as in this image of a jagged shaft of light:

> Down Wall, from girder into street noon leaks,
> A rip-tooth of the sky's acetylene;
> All afternoon the cloud-flown derricks turn . . .
> Thy cables breathe the North Atlantic still.

Moreover, the railroad in "The River" and the subway in "The Tunnel" are images of a brutally splintering dynamism, "interborough fissures of the mind." Most explicitly in "The Tunnel," but also in the "Proem" and in "Harbor Dawn," the sensations of city life and the emotional tumult are presented in a negative fashion. The bridge may rise stilly and sensuously above the bay, but the civilization of steel and stone that surrounds it assaults the men who live and work in it and who pass through its "iron year." In fact, the city is most pleasant when the machines are just starting to whir or have just shut down for the night, when the power is felt from the distance: "It is particularly fine to feel the greatest city in the world from enough distance, as I do here, to see its larger proportions. When you are actually in it you are often too distracted to realize its better and more imposing aspects" [9]

> The city's fiery parcels all undone,
> Already snow submerges an iron year . . .

or:

> And then a truck will lumber past the wharves
> As winch engines begin throbbing on some deck;
> Or a drunken stevedore's howl and thud below
> Comes echoing alley-upward through dim snow.

Crane did accomplish his more modest proposal to add the language of science and the machine to the traditional linguistic resources of poetry. He nearly always fulfills his program enunciated in "Modern Poetry" to create a diction that will convey the racy feel of the new technological environment:

For unless poetry can absorb the machine, i.e., *acclimatize* it as naturally and casually as trees, cattle, galleons, castles and all other human associations of the past, then poetry has failed of its full contemporary function. This process does not infer any program of lyrical pandering to the taste of those obsessed by the importance of machinery; nor does it essentially involve even the specific mention of a single mechanical contrivance. It demands, however, along with the traditional qualifications of the poet, an extraordinary capacity for surrender, at least temporarily, to the sensations of urban life. This presupposes, of course, that the poet possesses sufficient spontaneity and gusto to convert this experience into positive terms. Machinery will tend to lose its sensational glamour and appear in its true subsidiary order in human life as use and continual poetic allusion subdue its novelty. For, contrary to general prejudice, the wonderment experienced in watching nose dives is of less immediate creative promise to poetry than the familiar gesture of a motorist in the modest act of shifting gears. I mean to say that mere romantic speculation on the power and beauty of machinery keeps it at a continual remove; it cannot act creatively in our lives until, like the unconscious nervous responses of our bodies, its connotations emanate from within—forming as spontaneous a terminology of poetic reference as the bucolic world of pasture, plow and barn.[10]

Crane's language does two things exceptionally well: it presents a sense of space, that is, movement within space and the dizzying power of men conquering that space, and it evokes the emotional ambience of the world of airplanes, derricks, winches, etc., and the vibrant humming of the senses in response to this force. In both instances, Crane seeks to obey his injunction to shape a language that can refer unself-consciously to these things, a language that is not merely referential but also vividly encompassing. For the most part he has succeeded.

For all its bombastic passages and fulsome praise of Walt Whitman, "Cape Hatteras" is an imaginative grasping of the physical and spiritual experience of space. In "Faustus and Helen III" Crane had presented the exhilarating movement of planes cutting through the air. Here, in "Cape Hatteras," he returns to this image to body forth, like Shelley with his spatial images, the adventure of consciousness as it "conjugates infinity's dim marge":

> But that star-glistered salver of infinity,
> The circle, blind crucible of endless space,
> Is sluiced by motion,—subjugated never.[11]

As Crane himself suggested in "Modern Poetry," the mere mention of a machine does not guarantee its casual absorption into the texture of the poem. When Crane wishes to convey the cyclonic force of the machines, his language can fall into self-parody and a ridiculous huffing and puffing:

> The nasal whine of power whips a new universe . . .
> Where spouting pillars spoor the evening sky,
> Under the looming stacks of the gigantic power house
> Stars prick the eyes with sharp ammoniac proverbs,
> New verities, new inklings in the velvet hummed
> Of dynamos, where hearing's leash is strummed . . .
> Power's script,—wound, bobbin-bound, refined—
> Is stropped to the slap of belts on booming spools, spurred
> Into the bulging bouillon, harnessed jelly of the stars. . . .

We are reminded of Henry Adams' bemused despair at the demonic potency of the dynamo. The onomatopoeic tricks that seem to mimic the driving energy of the machine do not quite conceal the embarrassing failure of the passage. Elsewhere, however, Crane beautifully evokes "cupolas of space," "Easters of speeding light," and "Vast engines outward veering with seraphic grace," imbuing the machines with a religious aura.

Notes

CHAPTER 1: LIFE AND CRITICISM

1. Grunberg made this comment on a television program "In Search of Hart Crane."

2. Letter to his mother, May 30, 1919. *The Letters of Hart Crane 1916–1932*, edited by Brom Weber, p. 18.

3. Letter to Gorham Munson, June 18, 1922. *Letters*, 92.

4. *Partisan Review* (vol. XX, 6, November–December, 1953), p. 695. Miss Hardwick's judgment seems based entirely on the letters. "Reading these letters it is hard to remember the withered and anesthetized tragedy we thought Crane had become. Yet you cannot easily account for the amount of joy you receive from getting close again to Crane's life. Perhaps it is his magical freedom from true *disgust* which makes you think this 'doomed' poet was, after all, under the protection of a 'charm.' " *Ibid.*, 696.

5. See Malcolm Cowley's affectionate reminiscence, *Exile's Return*, pp. 232–33.

6. Letter of December 23, 1923. *Letters*, 163–64.

7. Waldo Frank, *Our America*, p. 229.

8. Letter to Allen Tate, June 12, 1922. *Letters*, 90.

9. Thomas frequently included a Crane poem in his public readings, as, for example, to the English Club at Cambridge University in December 1939. Dylan Thomas, *Letters to Vernon Watkins*, edited by Vernon Watkins, p. 75. In a letter to his friend Henry Treece, dated May 16, 1938, Thomas promised to "try to write something about Crane" for Treece's literary magazine. Thomas probably dropped the project. *Selected Letters of Dylan Thomas*, edited by Constantine Fitzgibbon, p. 220. Thomas denied any overt influence by Crane on his

own poetry, though he saw resemblances in "identical bits of phrasing" and the "actual sound." *Ibid.,* 197.

10. Louis Simpson, "Dead Horses and Live Issues," *The Nation* (CCIV, #17, April 24, 1967), pp. 521–22, lists Crane as one of the "native masters" who would be useful instructors to today's young poets. Simpson praises the Russian poet Andrei Voznesensky for his "involvement with the subject" and his "unashamed tenderness." These qualities are conspicuous features of Crane's poetry, too.

11. Robert Lowell, "An Interview with Robert Lowell," *The Paris Review,* xxv (Spring 1961), p. 89.

12. R. P. Blackmur's severe yet just appraisal of Crane's poetic methods appear in "New Thresholds, New Anatomies," *Form and Value in Modern Poetry,* pp. 269–86. Tate's assessments can be found in two essays in *Collected Essays,* pp. 225–37, 528–32. Yvor Winters' characteristically dogmatic discussion appears in *In Defense of Reason,* pp. 575–603.

13. Winters and Tate stress Crane's mystical proclivities. Louis Dembo, *Hart Crane's Sanskrit Charge,* and Sister Bernetta Quinn, *The Metamorphic Tradition in Modern Poetry,* are concerned with searching out and expounding Crane's myth in *The Bridge.*

14. Winters has made all of these charges against Crane's verse, while Blackmur and Tate object to Crane's obscurity, confused idealism, and irrationality. "He falls back on the intensity of consciousness, rather than the clarity, for his center of vision. And that is romanticism," Tate remarks, *Essays,* 235. In fairness to Blackmur it should be pointed out that he also criticized Pound and Eliot for poetic defects, even though they were strictly not Romantics.

15. T. E. Hulme, "Romanticism and Classicism," *Speculations,* edited by Herbert Read, p. 118.

16. In a lecture at Hunter College, March 1964.

17. Wallace Stevens, "Adagia," *Opus Posthumous,* p. 160.

18. *Ibid.,* 171.

19. Winters, *Reason,* 578.

20. *Ibid.,* 596.

21. *Ibid.,* 583.

22. *Ibid.,* 602.

23. Ralph Waldo Emerson, "The Poet," *The Complete Essays and Other Writings of Ralph Waldo Emerson,* edited by Brooks Atkinson, p. 323.

24. Stevens, *Opus Posthumous,* 162.

25. George Santayana, *Three Philosophical Poets,* p. 90.

26. *Ibid.*, p. 92.

27. Frank, *Our America*, 202. See also Robert L. Perry, *The Shared Vision of Waldo Frank and Hart Crane*. University of Nebraska Studies, #33. This pedestrian study repeats the old line that Crane was a mystic. Perry's use of psychological terms is crude, and he seems unaware of Crane's exceptional intelligence.

28. Letter to Yvor Winters, May 29, 1927. *Letters*, 301–2. This long letter is not only an extraordinarily rich document of Crane's aesthetic views, it is immensely revealing of his candor, warmth, disinterestedness, and fairness.

29. Letter of August 25, 1923. *Letters*, p. 145.

30. Letter of July 4, 1923. *Letters*, 138–39.

31. T. S. Eliot, "Blake," *Selected Essays*, pp. 279–80.

32. Letter to Waldo Frank, June 20, 1926. *Letters*, 260.

33. Emerson, "The Poet," 322.

34. *Letters*, 261.

35. The influence of Crane's rhetoric can be seen in Robert Lowell's *Lord Weary's Castle*, John Berryman's *Homage to Mistress Bradstreet*, and Sylvia Plath's *Ariel*.

36. T. S. Eliot, "Dante," *Essays*, 200.

37. I have concentrated on the lyrics from *White Buildings* and *Key West* because they are more accessible to the reader and a preparation for *The Bridge*, and because the bulk of Crane criticism deals with *The Bridge*. There is no fundamental discrepancy in style between the lyrics and the lyrical epic, though the problems of design and content differ.

38. Emerson, "The Poet," 324.

CHAPTER 2: EARLY POEMS

1. This imaginative procedure, it should be stressed, does not do away with rigorous control; it is not an indiscriminate method. Quite the contrary, it is purposive, directed by the poet's need to describe his experience faithfully. Accordingly, a particular poem will be more or less associative depending on the nature of the experience, the poet's sensibility, and the status and conventions of language at a particular historical period.

2. R. P. Blackmur, "New Thresholds, New Anatomies," *Form and Value in Modern Poetry*, p. 283.

3. R. W. B. Lewis, "Hart Crane and the Clown Tradition," *The Massachusetts Review*, pp. 745–67.

4. Letter to William Wright, October 17, 1921. *The Letters of Hart Crane 1916–1932, edited by Brom Weber,* p. 67.

CHAPTER 3: THE SINGING MASTERS

1. Letter to Allen Tate, June 12, 1922. *The Letters of Hart Crane 1916–1932,* edited by Brom Weber, p. 90.

2. Letter to Gorham Munson, November 20, 1922. *Ibid.,* 105.

3. *Ibid.,* 90.

4. Letter to Allen Tate, May 16, 1922. *Ibid.,* 89.

5. Letter to Gorham Munson, June 4, 1922. *Ibid.*

6. Letter to Gorham Munson, March 2, 1923. *Ibid.,* 129.

7. Malcolm Cowley relates that Crane frequently shouted that he was Christopher Marlowe. *Exile's Return,* p. 231.

8. *Letters,* 71.

9. Ralph Waldo Emerson, *The Complete Essays and Other Writings of Ralph Waldo Emerson,* edited by Brooks Atkinson, p. 320.

10. IV, iv, 114–32. Christopher Marlowe, *Five Plays,* edited by Havelock Ellis.

11. Letter of June 12, 1922. *Letters,* 90. Besides the above quotation from the "Duchess of Malfi," Crane copied into his notebooks the following passages from "The White Devil": l, i, 2–9; IV, iii, 119–30; V, iii, 68–76, and Cornelia's exquisite dirge "Call for the Robin-Red-brest," V, iv, 89–98.

12. John Webster, *The Complete Works of John Webster,* edited by F. L. Lucas, I, 36.

13. *Ibid.,* 30.

14. *Ibid.,* 23.

15. Letter to William Wright, October 17, 1921. *Letters,* 67.

16. Letter of January 10, 1922. *Letters,* 77.

17. "John Donne," *The Nation and Athenaeum,* xxxiii, 1923, pp. 331–32. Quoted in A. Alvarez, *The School of Donne,* pp. xii-xiii.

18. T. E. Hulme's contemptuous phrase for Romantic poems in "Romanticism and Classicism," *Speculations,* edited by Herbert Read, p. 120.

19. Crane also copied into his notebooks two other Donne poems—"The Apparition" and "The Prohibition," and from "The Progress of the Soule," lines 51–60.

20. *Letters,* 67.

21. Letter to Allen Tate, July 13, 1930. *Letters,* 353.

22. *Ibid.,* 354.

CHAPTER 4: "FAUSTUS AND HELEN"

1. Vincent Quinn, *Hart Crane*, p. 69.

2. Letter to Gorham Munson, January 14, 1923. *The Letters of Hart Crane*, edited by Brom Weber, p. 116.

3. *Ibid.*

4. Brom Weber, *Hart Crane: A Biographical and Critical Study*, p. 180.

5. Letter to Waldo Frank, February 7, 1923. *Letters*, 120.

6. Ralph Waldo Emerson, *The Complete Essays and Other Writings of Ralph Waldo Emerson*, edited by Brooks Atkinson, p. 331.

7. *Ibid.*, 325.

8. T. E. Hulme, *Speculations*, edited by Herbert Read, p. 126.

9. Crane may have been thinking of Keats' epithet in "The Eve of St. Agnes": "silver-snarling trumpets."

10. Weber, *Hart Crane*, 182.

11. Quinn, *Hart Crane*, 65.

12. Weber, *Hart Crane*, 182.

13. Letter to Waldo Frank, February 7, 1923. *Letters*, 121.

14. *The Notebook of Hart Crane*. Hart Crane Collection. Columbia University Library.

15. *Letters*, 121.

16. *White Buildings*—Manuscript: Hart Crane Collection. Columbia University Library. Ca. 1922.

17. Even after we understand what Crane was seeking to do in "Corymbulous formations of mechanics," we should still criticize the phrase for being stilted. It is possible Crane intended us to hear the sound-effects of "corymmulous" echoed in "nimble blue."

18. "Teeth unjubilant" is another striking inversion.

19. R. P. Blackmur, *Form and Value in Modern Poetry*, passim.

20. Letter to Waldo Frank, February 27, 1923. *Letters*, p. 128.

CHAPTER 5: VOYAGES

1. Letter to Gorham Munson, dated Monday (1923). *The Letters of Hart Crane*, edited by Brom Weber, p. 99.

2. Metamorphosis is also central to Ezra Pound. It is hard to pinpoint Pound's direct influence on Crane. Crane read him assiduously, and memorized some poems—he misquotes the lines from "A Virginal," "No, no! Go from me. I have left her lately./I will not spoil my sheath

with lesser brightness," omitting one "no" and substituting "shield" for "sheath"—and planned an essay on Pound he never wrote. Pound was a favorite poet, but references to him in the *Letters* stop in the middle of 1922, while Crane was writing "Faustus and Helen." "Garden Abstract" is very Poundean and the mellifluous language of early Pound, not the language of "Propertius," "Mauberley," and *The Cantos*, made an impact on Crane's early style. There is little of Pound in "Faustus and Helen" or in *Voyages*. As we have seen, for Crane Eliot was *the* dominant force in contemporary poetry. Pound contemptuously dismissed Crane's verse as adolescent rant. See letters of February 24, 1921, July 8, 1921, October 17, 1921. *Letters*, 54, 60–61, 67.

3. *Voyages II*,—Manuscript: Hart Crane Collection. Columbia University Library. Ca. 1923–24, dated Brooklyn.

4. *Ibid.* Another draft of the manuscript, ca. 1923–24.

5. In the margins of early drafts and in the texts themselves, Crane scrawled such words as "aureate," "lambience," "vermiculate," and "labial." Later, he crossed them out.

6. In a letter to Charmion von Wiegand, dated May 6, 1922, Crane mentions Melville in a list of his beloved Elizabethans he had just been reading. The high esteem in which he held *Moby Dick* is evident in this remark to Waldo Frank, in a letter of June 19, 1926, *Letters*, 260: "I read *Moby Dick* between gasps down in Cayman—my third time— and found it more superb than ever. How much that man makes you love him!" And, of course, Crane paid homage to Melville in "At Melville's Tomb."

7. Herman Melville, *Moby Dick*, p. 623.

8. .*Ibid.*, 711.

9. *Ibid.*, 309. Crane's love of the sea naturally played a large part in the selection of words.

10. The "steep floor" and "black swollen gates" of *Voyages III* echo Melville's "swallowed down to living gulfs of doom." Crane is transfigured; the *Pequod* is not. *Ibid.*, 79.

11. *Ibid.*

12. Cf. "And heaved and heaved, still unresting heaved the black sea, as if its vast tides were a conscience." *Ibid.*, 312.

13. "Dark," "grave," and "knells" are not, of course, Latinate words.

14. Hart Crane, "General Aims and Theories," *The Complete Poems and Selected Letters and Prose of Hart Crane*, edited by Brom Weber, p. 327.

15. Phillip Horton, *Hart Crane: The Life of An American Poet*, p. 310.

16. See *Voyages IV* and the first stanza of *Voyages V.*

17. Letter to Wilbur Underwood, July 27, 1922. *Letters,* 94.

18. Letter to Gorham Munson, dated Thursday (1922). *Letters,* 99.

19. James Joyce, *Ulysses,* p. 346.

20. *Ibid.,* 86.

21. *Ibid.,* 71–72.

22. *Ibid.,* 9.

CHAPTER 6: DICTION

1. C. S. Lewis, *Studies in Words,* p. 218.

2. Paul Valéry, "Preamble," *The Art of Poetry,* translated by Denise Folliot, p. 5.

3. See Yvor Winters, *In Defense of Reason,* pp. 575–603, Allen Tate, *Collected Essays,* pp. 225–37, 528–32. Tate says that since Romanticism aimed at "intensity of consciousness," rather than at "clarity of consciousness," Crane was prone to rhetorical muddle. Monroe K. Spears agrees with Tate and Winters, although he concludes that Crane's poetry "has a directness and immediacy, a haunting intensity and candor that are unlike anything else in English poetry." *Hart Crane,* p. 46.

4. Wallace Stevens, *Opus Posthumous,* p. 169.

5. Letter to Yvor Winters, May 29, 1927. *The Letters of Hart Crane 1916–1932,* edited by Brom Weber, p. 302.

6. Robert Lowell, "An Interview with Robert Lowell," *The Paris Review,* p. 89.

7. Letter to Harriet Monroe, *Letters,* 239.

8. For a brilliant explication of "The Broken Tower" see Marius Bewley, "Hart Crane's Last Poem," *Accent,* pp. 75–85.

9. Josephine Miles, "The Sublime Poem," *Eras and Modes in English Poetry,* p. 57.

10. See "The Poetry of Praise," 224–48, esp. 244, 248 *Ibid.*

CHAPTER 7: IMAGERY

1. David R. Clark, "Hart Crane's Technique," *Texas Studies in Literature and Language,* p. 389.

2. Crane had a darting and omnivorous mind, one that made up in an intuition of fundamental issues what it lacked in systematic training. Since he was largely self-educated and philosophically untutored, as he freely admitted to Yvor Winters (Letter of May 29, 1927. *The Letters*

of Hart Crane 1916–1932, edited by Brom Weber, p. 301), we should not expect an absolutely self-consistent theory of poetry, or the same compact elegance and lucidity that we find, say, in Eliot's or Valéry's essays. Crane's ideas, however, were not, as R. P. Blackmur has it ("New Thresholds, New Anatomies," *Form and Value in Modern Poetry,* p. 276), confused rationalizations of his weaknesses as a poet; rather, in spite of occasional turgidity and hasty terminology, they are thoughtful, acute, and speculative, and they provide us with valuable information for interpreting the poems.

3. See the following letters: December 13, 1919; March 6, 1920; October 13, 1920; November 26, 1921; and especially the letters to Allen Tate of May 16, 1922, and June 12, 1922. *Letters,* 26, 34, 44, 71, 88–89, 90–91.

4. *The Autobiography of William Carlos Williams,* p. 146.

5. *Letters,* 114–15. Crane never completely escaped Eliot's influence. In "The Tunnel" he depicts the squalor and phantasmagoria of the city in images that would not be out of place in "Prufrock" or "Gerontion." F. W. Dupee points out to me that only Crane would think of using the somewhat humorous word "skating" in the image: "A burnt match skating in a urinal."

6. It should be remarked that whereas Crane's rationale has been attacked as obfuscation, T. S. Eliot's defense along similar lines has generally been accepted. Graham Hough, however, in an incisive passage of *Image and Experience,* pp. 18–20, analyzes Eliot's argument in his introduction to St. John Perse's *Anabase* and shows that it is predicated on a contradiction. Eliot claims that Perse's (and his own) imagery falls into the memory successively with no question of reasonableness, of resultant obscurity. He presents two justifications of this method: first, that any obscurity is due to the suppression of connective matter and the logic is like the logic of any other kind of discourse, only more concentrated; and second, that the "logic of imagination" *differs* from ordinary logic. Hough is in the delicate position of recognizing the genius of the Symbolist poets in France, America, and England, while deploring the loss of "the most important tradition of all, that of a natural community of understanding between poet and reader." Hough does not mention Crane at all, but undoubtedly would include him in the list of those who drove away the common reader.

7. "General Aims and Theories," reprinted in Weber, *The Complete Poems and Selected Letters and Prose of Hart Crane,* edited by Brom Weber, p. 220.

8. "General Aims and Theories," reprinted in *The Complete Poems*, 220–21.

9. Letter to Gorham Munson, March 17, 1926. *Letters*, 239.

10. *Ibid.*

11. "General Aims and Theories," 219.

12. *Ibid.*, 222.

13. "A Letter to Harriet Monroe," in *The Complete Poems*, 234.

14. Letter to Gorham Munson, dated Friday (between May 21, 1921 and June 12, 1921), *Letters*, 58.

15. "A Letter to Harriet Monroe," 236.

16. *Ibid.*, 234.

17. *Ibid.*, 235.

18. *Ibid.*

19. *Ibid.* It is possible that Crane is restating here, in his own terminology, Eliot's theory of the "objective correlative": "The only way of expressing emotion in the form of art is finding an 'objective correlative'; in other words, a set of objects, a situation, a chain of events which shall be the formula of that *particular* emotion; such that when the external facts, which must terminate in sensory experience, are given, the emotion is immediately evoked." T. S. Eliot, *The Sacred Wood*, p. 100. Crane had read *The Sacred Wood* (mistakenly calling it *The Sacred Grove*) and thought it a "great study." See Letter to Gorham Munson, November 26, 1921. *Letters*, 71.

20. *Letters*, 176.

21. See pp. 93–95.

22. Herman Melville, *Moby Dick*, edited by Charles Feidelson, 25.

23. "A Letter to Harriet Monroe," 238.

24. *Ibid.*, 239.

25. *Ibid.*

26. *Ibid.*

27. R. W. B. Lewis, "Crane's Visionary Lyric: The Way to *The Bridge*," *The Massachusetts Review*, 246.

28. William Butler Yeats, "Symbolism in Painting," *Essays and Introductions*, 149.

29. "A Letter to Harriet Monroe," 239.

30. *Ibid.*

31. Wallace Stevens, "Adagia," *Opus Posthumous*, 162.

32. Harvey Gross, *Sound and Form in Modern Poetry*, p. 124.

33. In the "Immortality Ode," whenever Wordsworth wishes to represent his disordered, malfunctioning imagination, he suggests a separa-

tion of the senses of sight and hearing; whenever he represents an integrated consciousness, his senses are harmoniously blended. The great Romantic exponent of synaesthetic imagery is, of course, Keats. Crane was an enthusiastic reader of Keats; the affinity between their styles is large, though Crane probably arrived at synaesthesia independently of any of Keats' sources.

34. Apollo, the "tribunal monarch of the air/Whose thigh embronzes earth, strikes crystal Word/In wounds pledged once to hope— cleft to despair," is the god of poetry and that rational faculty which Crane lacked. See Marius Bewley, "Hart Crane's Last Poem," *Accent*, p. 80.

35. Crane may be punning on the word "corpse."

36. Crane may have picked up the image of the loom of time from his reading of *Moby Dick*.

37. Crane's mastery of sound—internal and final rhyme, alliteration, consonance, and assonance—is brilliantly demonstrated in these stanzas.

38. The frequent interchange of parts of speech, nouns made into verbs and verbs into nouns, is the grammatical cognate of imagistic synaesthesia.

39. Crane was a little uncertain about this line. When Caresse Crosby was seeing the Paris edition of *The Bridge* through the press, Crane wrote to her: "I have an idea for a change in one line of the dedication 'To B. Bridge.' If you don't like it, don't change it. But I feel that it is more logical, even if no more suggestive. Instead of:

    —And elevators heave us to our day

I suggest

    —Till elevators drop us from our day.

I'll leave the choice to you."

It seems to me that "heave" is less suggestive and less rhythmically exciting than "drop," and that it is not more logical. Letter to Caresse Crosby, December 26, 1929. *Letters*, 347.

40. John Unterecker, "The Architecture of *The Bridge*," *Wisconsin Studies in Contemporary Literature*, p. 11.

41. This detail is based on fact. Soon after the bridge was completed, several people were crushed to death when they panicked at a rumor that the bridge was collapsing. The bridge has also attracted its share of suicides. See Alan Trachtenberg, *Brooklyn Bridge, Fact and Symbol*.

42. Jewish doctrine is rather vague and indefinite about immortality. What Crane had in mind in his image of the Jew's heaven is a bit

obscure, though I think my interpretation of the quatrain substantially correct.

43. Compare these lines from "Possessions": "turning on smoked forking spires,/The city's stubborn lives, desires."

44. Unterecker, "The Architecture of *The Bridge*," 11.

45. Edward Dahlberg, "A Review of Hart Crane's *Letters*," *The New York Review of Books*, p. 22.

46. "Wide," another of Crane's favorite words, attests to his desire for a hospitable world whose boundaries encompass the universe. The poles often appear in Crane's imagery.

47. Crane's fascination with minerals and stones, words like "basalt" and "ochreous" may derive from Emily Dickinson. Appropriately, in his sonnet of tribute to her, he has the line "Leaves Ormus rubyless, and Ophir chill."

48. This image, though primarily of the Mississippi, also illustrates my point.

49. Yeats, even in his tower, hewed closer to the grain of reality. In "The Tower" he says:

> I mock Plotinus' thought
> And cry in Plato's teeth,
> Death and life were not
> Till man made up the whole,
> Made lock, stock and barrel
> Out of his bitter soul,
> Aye, sun and moon and star, all,
> And further add to that
> That, being dead, we rise,
> Dream and so create
> Translunar Paradise.

The tower is also a phallic symbol, and the broken tower an expression of a fear of castration.

50. "Faustus and Helen III" mentions "the sixteen thrifty bridges of the city." See also the first stanza of *Voyages IV*.

51. Letter of May 9, 1923. *Letters*, 134.

52. "Stave" also means a verse of poetry or music.

53. For a discussion of Crane's use of the eagle and the serpent as symbols of space and time, see Unterecker, "The Architecture of *The Bridge*," pp. 15–17, and L. S. Dembo, *Hart Crane's Sanskrit Charge: A Study of The Bridge*, 76, 110, 113.

CHAPTER 8: SYNTAX

1. Philip Horton. *Hart Crane,* p. 47.

2. Crane's manuscripts are proof that he struggled over each poem to perfect its form. There are twelve different sheets of *Voyages II* in the Columbia University Library Special Collections alone.

3. Letter to Gorham Munson, December 13, 1919. *The Letters of Hart Crane 1916–1932,* edited by Brom Weber, p. 27.

4. From an early age Crane was unusually aware of his grave need for psychic balance. One of the first letters he wrote to his father after settling in New York, an astonishing document of his moral precocity, sheds light on the connection between his emotional life and his poetry: "I realize more entirely every day, that I am preparing for a fine life: that I have powers, which, if correctly balanced, will enable me to mount to extraordinary latitudes. There is constantly an inward struggle, but the time to worry is only when there is no inward debate, and consequently there is smooth sliding to the devil. There is only one harmony, that is the equilibrium maintained by two opposite forces, equally strong. When I perceive one emotion growing overpowering to a fact, or statement of reason, then the only manly, worthy, sensible thing to do, is build up the logical side, and attain balance, and in art,—formal expression." Letter to his father, January 5, 1917. *Ibid.,* 5.

5. Crane wrote a few free verse poems, mainly when he wanted an anecdotal effect, as in the meandering fugal structure of "Cutty Sark." Crane wrote three prose poems, "The Mango Tree," "Lenses," and "Havana Rose." All are competent handlings of this difficult form.

6. See Donald Davie, *Articulate Energy* and Josephine Miles, *Eras and Modes in English Poetry.* I am indebted to these seminal books in my discussion of poetic syntax. The New Critics were lukewarm about Wordsworth's poetry, which depends for its meaning mainly on syntax (and rhythm) rather than on irony and wit.

7. Davie, *Articulate Energy,* 148.

8. *Ibid.,* 68–92.

9. *Ibid.,* 51.

10. *Ibid.,* 149.

11. *Ibid.,* 85.

12. Harvey Gross, *Sound and Form in Modern Poetry,* pp. 13–14.

13. Needless to say, Pound could and did write poems, "Near Perigord III," among others, whose syntactical unit was the verse paragraph. Pound had an amazing facility to compose well in any poetic

form, but his most important prosodic breakthrough was his discarding of the iambic pentameter line. For a thorough discussion of Pound's prosody, see Donald Davie, *Ezra Pound, Poet as Sculptor*.

14. The repetition of the words "too late" underlines the woman's trance-like urgency.

15. The lines contain an interesting and possibly deliberate syntactic ambiguity. If one reads the line aloud, the listener hears something like shadows' fall. It is also uncertain whether "stiller" modifies "she" or "step." The sense hovers between the two readings, accepting a little of each.

16. See, for example, the first stanza of "O Carib Isle!" where the verb "mourn" is withheld to the end of the stanza.

17. The imagination is, in Crane's most central image, a bridge that unifies the separateness of men. The last line recalls Faustus' bargain with the devil, his prayers, and his spells. Here he is redeemed.

18. "Delve upward" derives from Keats' phrase in the "Ode to a Nightingale": "deep-delved earth."

19. In "O Carib Isle!" the phrase "So syllables want breath" refers to his inability to write poetry.

20. "Anchises' navel" suggests the Omphalos, the sacred stone in the Temple of Apollo that was reputed to mark the central point of the earth. Anchises' partly divine kinship (he fathered Aeneas on Venus) accords with the transcendental orientation of the poem, and of course with the creation and worship of beauty. Finally, Anchises reminds one of Troy's ultimate nemesis, Helen, who becomes here the bride of Faustus in a quirky symbolic marriage.

21. The compounds can be of any part of speech: nouns, verbs, adjectives, participles, phrases, and clauses.

22. "Modern music almost drives me crazy! I went to hear D'Indy's *II Symphony* last night and my hair stood on end at its revelations. To get those, and others of men like Strauss, Ravel, Scriabin, and Bloch into *words*, one needs to *ransack* the vocabularies of Shakespeare, Jonson, Webster. . . ." Letter to Gorham Munson, March 2, 1923. *Letters*, 128–29. Crane loved Wagner, and often played the Prelude to *Meistersinger* on the phonograph while he wrote poetry. There is great need of a detailed study of Crane's life-long involvement with Impressionist and Post-Romantic music. It is possible that he took some of his aesthetic aims and methods from it.

23. Miles, *Eras and Modes*, 121.

24. *Ibid.*, 56.

25. Davie, *Articulate Energy*, 149.

26. I say "quasi-religious" because there is, besides the Christian imagery, a large strain of pagan and naturalistic imagery in the poem.

27. There is a famous Italian white wine, called "Lachryma Christi," made from grapes grown on the slopes of Mt. Vesuvius, near Naples. It is pale gold in color, aromatic, and delicate in taste. Frank Schoonmaker, in the *Encyclopedia of Wine* recounts a charming story of the origin of Lachryma Christi's name: "The lovely Bay of Naples country has been called a 'fragment of paradise,' and, according to one account, the Lord, returning to earth, found this heavenly corner of the world 'inhabited by demons' (presumably the Neapolitans); touched and distressed, He wept, and where His tears fell there sprung up green vines— the vines of Lachryma Christi vineyards" (p. 189). It is doubtful that Crane had this legend in mind but he probably meant to imply the wine of communion. Christ also distills clemencies from His tears and blood (vines).

28. R. P. Blackmur, "New Thresholds, New Anatomies," *Form and Value in Modern Poetry*, p. 282.

29. *Ibid.*, 282–83.

30. "Lachrymae Christi" should be read closely with "Possessions." Compare these lines: ". . .sifting/One moment in sacrifice (the direst)/Through a thousand nights the flesh/Assaults outright for bolts that linger/Hidden,—O undirected as the sky/That through its black foam has no eyes/For this fixed stone of lust. . . ." and "And I, entering, take up the stone/As quiet as you can make a man." Like Melville, Crane was fascinated by Egyptian religion. One of the chapters in *Moby Dick* is titled The Sphynx. See Crane's poems "Reliquary" and "By Nilus Once I Knew."

31. Compare these lines from "A Name For All:": "Names we have, even, to clap on the wind,/But we must die, as you, to understand."

32. This striking of the "perfect spheres" echoes and cancels out the "twanged red perfidies of spring."

CHAPTER 9: VERSE FORMS

1. Crane could not write narrative poetry, ballads, or even dramatic monologues (Columbus in "Ave Maria" sounds like Crane). His main subject was himself. As he wrote to his mother, March 19, 1927, ". . . I've never been able to think of things with plots to them." *The Letters of Hart Crane 1916–1932*, edited by Brom Weber, p. 293.

2. Letter to Gorham Munson, dated Friday (between May 21, 1921 and June 12, 1921). *Letters*, 58.

3. This image also anticipates Ralph Ellison's *Invisible Man.*

4. Monroe K. Spears, *Hart Crane,* p. 19.

5. Crane frequently transposed lines from one poem to another.

6. Letter to Gorham Munson, December 25, 1921. *Letters,* p. 75.

7. Letter to Wilbur Underwood, July 4, 1922. *Ibid.,* p. 93.

8. The syntax is difficult to paraphrase. It runs something like this: Because I can still recall Nelson's gold hair, I cannot be disturbed by the disfigured dead face (Nelson was killed by a hit-and-run driver). Nor can I really miss the golden (honey-colored, as bees) "conversation" of the lucid (because related to brows) time and place of our acquaintance. The syntax may also mean: "I do miss the dry sound" which would make the statement despairing and bleak. Our interpretation also depends on how we read "dry sound of bees" and "lucid space."

9. Letter to Wilber Underwood, dated July (1926). *Letters,* 264.

10. "O Carib Isle," one of Crane's most remarkable poems, presents the parched, hallucinatory atmosphere most vividly, but it uses quatrains sparingly.

11. See the prose poem "Lenses" and Letter to Waldo Frank, August 19, 1926. *Letters,* 273.

12. Letter to his Mother, June 1, 1926. *Letters,* 256.

13. The imagery, which mixes religious and royal words—regal, charities, crown, anchorite, communings, aethereal—reinforces the idea that the imagination is timeless, unravaged by mortality; sex is equated with death in the poem.

14. A steady iambic pulse is felt throughout the poem despite many spondaic and trochaic substitutions; the rhyme scheme is a regular abab, with only one feminine rhyme "charities/asperities."

15. The syntax unfolds in much the same way as section nine of Wordsworth's *Immortality Ode.*

16. A dash would be legitimate in this situation. Crane frequently substitutes a semicolon for a dash.

17. Marius Bewley, "Hart Crane's Last Poem," *Accent,* pp. 75–85.

18. A. Alvarez, *The Shaping Spirit,* p. 110.

19. The ode permits the choice of a stanza of fixed or shifting length, sometimes a tercet, as in Shelley's "Ode to the West Wind," sometimes a ten line stanza, as in several of Keats' odes, and sometimes in stanzas of indeterminate length, as in Wordsworth's "Immortality Ode."

20. Geoffrey Hartman, *Wordsworth's Poetry 1787–1814,* pp. 273–74. Professor Hartman's suggestive remarks on all aspects of the Romantic poetic are very useful to the student of Crane's poetry.

21. *Ibid.*, 27.

22. Letter to William Wright, October 17, 1921. *Letters*, 67.

23. There are two slant rhymes: "ill/Prodigal" and "awe/San Salvador."

24. The *s* sound predominates throughout, alternately as a harsh sibilant and a smooth sensuous note, to contrast the sea's conflicting roles as destroyer and preserver.

25. Paul Fussell, Jr., *Poetic Meter and Poetic Form*, pp. 167–68.

26. The meter becomes a steady iambic pentameter in the second stanza (it varied from pentameter to tetrameter in the first stanza), though many trochaic and spondaic substitutions are made to stress key words. The poem also coheres feeling and form through the deft use of alliteration and assonance. Sound and meaning are seldom separable in Crane's poetry. He had a fine ear.

27. The last three of the *Voyages* set are as carefully constructed as the three I have analyzed, but they do not present any new prosodic material. *Voyages IV* and *V* are divided into unfixed stanzas, the formal division corresponding to the poet's changes in mood (ecstacy in *IV*, despair and resignation in *V*) and his perception of the impending irrevocable estrangement. *Voyages VI*, which resolves the dramatic and thematic tensions of the sequence, is written in quatrains. The formal rigor is appropriate, since the content of the poem is the defeat of time and death and the apotheosis of love by "Creation's blithe and petalled word."

28. Harvey Gross, *Sound and Form in Modern Poetry*, p. 12.

CHAPTER 10: METRICS

1. These debates generated as much heat as the agitation for Free Silver did. Pound, of course, early in his career was much influenced by Imagism. His early poetry contained many features of Imagism, but he never went to the extremes of Amy Lowell and her followers either in theory or in practice. For a thorough study of these matters, see Donald Davie, *Ezra Pound, Poet as Sculptor*, *passim*.

2. For a brief survey of these arguments, see Harvey Gross, *Sound and Form in Modern Poetry*, pp. 100–29; Horace Gregory and Marya Zaturenska, *A History of American Poetry 1900–1940*, pp. 141–212, *passim* and Louise Bogan, *Achievement in American Poetry 1900–1950*, pp. 39–41, 53–54, 66.

3. Crane did not read French well, though he did translate Laforgue; he read the French poets with the aid of a dictionary. He did

not have a gift for foreign languages, but he knew which French Symbolist poets were being read and why. The little magazines were again his primer. For an assessment of Pound's prosodic achievements, see Gross, *Sound and Form in Modern Poetry*, pp. 130–68, and Donald Davie, *Ezra Pound, Poet as Sculptor*.

4. Eliot's greatness as a metrist has been overshadowed by Pound's reputation as a prosodist. Pound's cultural salesmanship, his catholicity, have been invaluable in making us aware of previously unfamiliar poetry. In poetic practice, however, I believe that Eliot, the student, surpassed his putative master. See Gross, *Sound and Form in Modern Poetry*, pp. 169–214.

5. In his essay "Modern Poetry," in 1929, Crane had harsh things to say about Whitman's clumsy faulty technique. Appendix to *The Complete Poems and Selected Letters and Prose of Hart Crane*, edited by Brom Weber, p. 263.

6. Gross, *Sound and Form in Modern Poetry*, p. 216.

7. See, for example, Edward Dahlberg's review of Crane's *Letters* in *The New York Review of Books*, January 20, 1966, pp. 19–22. Dahlberg, with poker face, recites the old tale about Crane's "bacchic orgy" language, while he indulges in an orgy of words that would have made Crane blush.

8. I shall adhere to the traditional method of scansion and shall mark unstressed syllables ⌣ and stressed syllables ∕ . In some cases, of course, a half stress is felt, but it would unduly complicate the system to mark every one.

9. Line six may be a deliberately intricate rhythm, with "not fright" scanned as a spondee. Lines four and eight, the refrain, might be scanned ⌣⌣∕⌣∕⌣∕ since the "on" is lightly accented.

10. See my discussion in Chapters 2 and 8, pp. 31–32, 173–75.

11. "Too late" can also be scanned as a spondee.

12. Crane was also reading and translating Laforgue at this time—Eliot's and Pound's doing.

13. Eliot's animus against romanticism does not negate the large streak of romantic pessimism in his verse.

14. Gross, *Sound and Form in Modern Poetry*, p. 169.

15. *Ibid.*, p. 177.

16. The subtitle an "Impromptu Tirade" was applied just to "The Bridge of Estador," but it applies equally well to "Porphyro in Akron."

17. *Letters*, 66–72.

18. Letter to Gorham Munson, November 26, 1921. *The Letters of Hart Crane*, edited by Brom Weber, p. 71.

19. *Ibid.*

20. Letter to William Wright, October 17, 1921. *Ibid.*, 67.

21. Letter to Gorham Munson, March 2, 1923. *Ibid.*, 129.

22. Letter to William Wright, March 2, 1922. *Ibid.*, 81.

23. The epigraph to "Faustus and Helen," it should be remembered, is taken from Ben Jonson's "The Alchemist."

24. Letter to Gorham Munson, January 5, 1923. *Letters*, 114–15.

25. See my discussion in Chapter 3, pp. 59–79.

26. The first three lines are nine-syllabled, but four-stressed.

27. "flash out" could also be a spondee.

28. "Divided by accepted multitudes" may be scanned differently.

29. Crane employs calculated deviations into dimeter and trimeter, too.

30. Alliteration and consonance are particularly enticing, possessing a tongue-in-cheek humor: "O, I have known metallic paradises/Where cuckoos clucked to finches/Above the deft catastrophe of drums."

31. Crane also wrote some middling and weak poems during this time; his poetic vices and poetic virtues are inextricably intertwined.

32. *Voyages I* is largely tetrameter with several pentameter lines and one trimeter line. *Voyages VI* is in iambic tetrameter.

33. "Infinite consanguinity it bears" is a tetrameter line, though it is possible Crane intended a stress on "con." It is easier to recite it as I scan it. There may be an accent on "sin" in the second foot of "all bright insinuations that my years have caught" but again, the spoken rhythm is more natural, I think, as I have scanned it.

34. Crane possibly accented the "ir" of "irrefragibly" in line one and the "in" of the penultimate foot in line two.

35. The following statistics may be helpful:

Number of Syllables	Number of Lines	Stresses Per Line	Number of Lines
4	1	3	1
7	1	4	1
10	12	5	4
11	6	6	11
12	6	7	10
13	2	8	6
14	4		
16	1		

36. The only work in American literature that rivals "O Carib Isle!" in rendering this kind of horrible physical atmosphere, so evilly exhaust-

ing, is Melville's *The Encantadas*. Crane may have been familiar with Melville's sketches. Many of the details of the poem are similar to Melville's descriptions: the extreme desolation; the "everlasting drought beneath a torrid sky"; the reptilian life, especially the giant tortoises who seemed to Melville "newly crawled forth from beneath the foundations of the world"; the terrifying sense of a place to which change never comes and in which the passions are perforce defunct. In the first sketch Melville writes: ". . . when leaving the crowded city to wander out July and August among the Adirondack Mountains, far from the influence of towns and proportionately night to the mysterious ones of Nature; when at such times I sit me down the mossy head of some *deep-wooded gorge,* surrounded by *prostrate trunks of blasted pines,* and recall as in a *dream* my other and far-distant rovings in the *baked heart* of the charmed isles; and remember the sudden glimpses of *dusky shells,* and long languid necks protruded from the *leafless thickets;* and again have beheld the *vitreous inland rocks* worn down and grooved into deep ruts by ages and ages of the slow *draggings of tortoises* in quest of *pools of scanty water;* I can hardly resist the feeling that in my time I have indeed slept upon evilly enchanted ground." (My italics.) This imagery found its way into "Repose of Rivers" as well as "O Carib Isle!" The two poems should be read together. The air of foreboding and the writers' tone of almost lunatic, or sun-struck, humor in front of such awesome reality seem further to connect the Galapagos with Crane's Carib isle.

37. "Catchword" is a droll adjective to apply to crabs; it signifies either the word at the bottom of a page which is the first word of the next page, or a slogan in general use. In this poem, the crabs anagrammatize the "incognizable Word," and are the only "speakers" of it.

38. Melville recounts a superstition that sailors cherished about the tortoises found in the Galapagos. "All wicked sea-officers, especially *commodores and captains,* are at death (and, in some cases, before death) transformed into tortoises; thenceforth dwelling upon these hot aridities, sole solitary lords of Asphaltum." (My italics.)

39. Were one so inclined, one could find many images of castration: "dry groins," "Evisceration," "spiked," etc. Compare these lines from "Repose of Rivers": "And mammoth turtles climbing sulphur dreams/ yielded, while sun-silt rippled them/Asunder. . . ."

40. It is interesting to note that in Waldo Frank's edition of the poems the remorseless vision of "O Carib Isle" immediately follows the more hopeful view of "Key West." Perhaps the distance he traveled from Key West to the Isle of Pines should be measured as a nightmarish

journey backward in time, a regression into chaos. In Key West he had found momentary ease in the very moral neutrality of nature he found so unbearable on the Carib isle, in the "skies impartial, that do not disown me/Nor claim me, either, by Adam's spine—nor rib."

41. Crane probably did not read Hopkins until 1928 when, on a trip to California, Yvor Winters read some Hopkins poems with him. "The Hurricane" is often cited as an imitation of Hopkins' sprung rhythm, but I am skeptical of the affinity. The evidence is skimpy, and Crane was sufficiently innovating to come upon the stress-line himself. Besides, he did not, to my knowledge, write any other poems in this manner. Given Crane's eclecticism and enthusiasm, this is surprising. The spirit of "The Broken Tower" is similar to Hopkins' "terrible sonnets" (but also to Keats' "Nightingale" poem). The following lines from Hopkins' sonnet "As King-fishers catch fire" may have been in Crane's mind when he composed "The Broken Tower":

> . . . ; like each tucked string tells, each hung bell's
> Bow swing finds tongue to fling out broad its name;
> Each mortal thing does one thing and the same:
> Deals out that being indoors each one dwells;
> Selves—goes itself; *myself* it speaks and spells;
> Crying *What I do is me: for that I came.*

APPENDIX: CRANE'S VIEWS ON POETRY AND THE MACHINE

1. Eliot attacks evolutionary theory in *Four Quartets,* and refers negatively in numerous poems to astronomy, physiology, anthropology, etc. For an extended discussion of the subject, see Hyatt Howe Waggoner's *The Heel of Elohim: Science and Values in Modern American Poetry.*

2. Letter of March 2, 1923. *The Letters of Hart Crane 1916–1932,* edited by Brom Weber, p. 129.

3. A. Alvarez, *The Shaping Spirit,* p. 112.

4. Hart Crane, "Modern Poetry" in *The Complete Poems and Selected Letters and Prose of Hart Crane,* edited by Brom Weber, p. 263.

5. *Ibid.,* 262.

6. William Wordsworth, "Preface to *Lyrical Ballads,*" *Selected Poetry,* edited by Mark Van Doren, p. 688.

7. "Modern Poetry," 261.

8. *Ibid.,* 263.

9. Letter to his Mother and Grandmother, May 11, 1924. *Letters*, 183.

10. *Ibid.*, 261–62.

11. Crane does not restrict himself to images drawn from aerodynamics, but also alludes to geological science and mineralogy, since they provide him with an opportunity to paint the grandeur and immensity of the American continent.

Bibliography

I. BY HART CRANE

The Bridge. Paris: Black Sun Press, 1930.

The Bridge. New York: Liveright, 1930.

The Collected Poems of Hart Crane. Edited with an Introduction by Waldo Frank. New York: Liveright, 1933. Includes the essay "Modern Poetry."

The Collected Poems of Hart Crane. Edited with an Introduction by Waldo Frank. Garden City: Anchor Books, 1958.

The Complete Poems and Selected Letters and Prose of Hart Crane. Edited by Brom Weber. New York: Liveright Publishing Corporation, 1966.

The Complete Poems and Selected Letters and Prose of Hart Crane. Edited by Brom Weber. Garden City: Anchor Books, 1966.

The Letters of Hart Crane, 1916–1932. Edited by Brom Weber. New York: Hermitage House, 1952.

The Letters of Hart Crane, 1916–1932. Edited by Brom Weber. Berkeley and Los Angeles: University of California Press, 1965.

The Notebook of Hart Crane. Hart Crane Collection. Columbia University Library. New York.

White Buildings: Poems by Hart Crane. Foreword by Allen Tate. New York: Boni and Liveright, 1926.

White Buildings (manuscript). Hart Crane Collection. Columbia University Library. New York.

II. BY OTHERS

Abrams, M. H. *A Glossary of Literary Terms*. New York: Holt, Rinehart & Winston, 1957.

Allen, Gay Wilson. *American Prosody*. New York: American Book Company, 1935.

Alvarez, A. *The School of Donne*. New York: Mentor Books, 1967.
—— *Stewards of Excellence*. New York: Charles Scribner's Sons, 1958. Published in England as *The Shaping Spirit*. London: Chatto & Windus, 1958.

Barfield, Owen. *Poetic Diction: A Study in Meaning*. New York: McGraw-Hill Paperbacks, 1964.

Bate, Walter Jackson. *The Stylistic Development of Keats*. New York: The Humanities Press, 1958.

Bateson, F. W. *English Poetry and the English Language*. New York: Russell and Russell, 1961.

Beckson, Karl (editor). *Aesthetes and Decadents of the 1890's*. New York: Vintage Books, 1966.

Bewley, Marius. "Hart Crane's Last Poem," *Accent*, XIX (Spring 1959), 75–85.

Blackmur, R. P. *Form and Value in Modern Poetry*. Garden City: Anchor Books, 1957.

Bogan, Louise. *Achievement in American Poetry 1900–1950*. Chicago: Henry Regnery Company, 1951.

Brower, Reuben. *The Fields of Light: An Experiment in Critical Reading*. New York: Galaxy Books, 1962.

Cambon, Glauco. *The Inclusive Flame*. Bloomington: Indiana University Press, 1963.

Clark, David R. "Hart Crane's Technique," *Texas Studies in Language and Literature*, V (Autumn 1963), 389–97.

Coffman, Stanley K., Jr. "Symbolism in *The Bridge*," *PMLA*, LXV (March 1951), 65–77.

Cowley, Malcolm. *Exile's Return*. New York: Compass Books, 1956.

Cummings, E. E. *i, Six Nonlectures.* Cambridge, Mass.: Harvard University Press, 1953.

Davie, Donald. *Articulate Energy: An Enquiry into the Syntax of English Poetry.* New York: Harcourt, Brace and Company, 1955.

—— *Ezra Pound, Poet as Sculptor.* New York: Oxford University Press, 1965.

—— *Purity of Diction in English Verse.* London: Chatto & Windus, 1952.

Dahlberg, Edward. "A Review of Hart Crane's *Letters,*" *The New York Review of Books* (January 20, 1966).

Dembo, L. S. "Hart Crane's Early Poetry," *The University of Kansas City Review,* XXVII (March 1961), 181–87.

—— *Hart Crane's Sanskrit Charge: A Study of the Bridge.* Ithaca: Cornell University Press, 1960.

Eliot, T. S. *The Complete Poems and Plays 1909–1950.* New York: Harcourt, Brace and Company.

—— *The Sacred Wood.* London: Methuen & Company, 1920.

—— *Selected Essays.* New York: Harcourt, Brace and Company, 1932.

Emerson, Ralph Waldo. *The Complete Essays and Other Writings of Ralph Waldo Emerson.* Edited by Brooks Atkinson. New York: Modern Library, 1950.

Empson, William. *The Structure of Complex Words.* Norfolk, Conn.: New Directions, n.d.

Frank, Waldo. *Our America.* New York: Boni and Liveright, 1919.

Frye, Northrop. *Anatomy of Criticism.* Princeton: Princeton University Press, 1957.

Fussell, Paul, Jr. *Poetic Meter and Poetic Form.* New York: Random House, 1965.

Gregory, Horace, and Marya Zaturenska. *A History of American Poetry, 1900–1940.* New York: Harcourt, Brace and Company, 1946.

Gross, Harvey. *Sound and Form in Modern Poetry.* Ann Arbor: University of Michigan Press, 1964.

Hartman, Geoffrey. *Wordsworth's Poetry 1787–1814*. New Haven: Yale University Press, 1964.

Hazo, Samuel. *Hart Crane: An Introduction and Interpretation*. New York: Barnes and Noble, 1963.

Herman, Barbara. "The Language of Hart Crane," *The Sewanee Review*, LVIII (Winter 1950), 52–67.

Hoffman, Frederick J. *The Twenties*. New York: The Viking Press, 1955.

Honig, Edwin. "American Poetry and the Rationalist Critic," *The Virginia Quarterly Review*, XXXVI (Summer 1960), 416–29.

Horton, Philip. *Hart Crane: The Life of an American Poet*. New York: Compass Books, 1957. Includes as Appendices Crane's essay "General Aims and Theories" and a letter to Harriet Monroe about "At Melville's Tomb."

Hough, Graham. *Image and Experience*. Lincoln: University of Nebraska Press, 1960.

Hulme, T. E. *Speculations*. Edited by Herbert Read. New York: Harcourt, Brace and Company, n.d.

Joyce, James. *Ulysses*. New York: Viking Press, 1961.

"Kenyon Review Symposium on Metrics," *The Kenyon Review*, XVIII (Summer 1956).

Kermode, Frank. *Romantic Image*. 2nd edition revised. London: Routledge and Kegan Paul, 1961.

Langer, Susanne. *Feeling and Form: A Theory of Art*. New York: Charles Scribner's Sons, 1953.

—— *Philosophy in a New Key*. New York: Mentor Books, 1951.

Larrabee, Ankey. "The Symbol of the Sea in Crane's 'Voyages'," *Accent*, III (Winter 1943), 117–19.

Lewis, C. S. *Studies in Words*. Cambridge: Cambridge University Press, 1960.

Lewis, R. W. B. "Hart Crane and the Clown Tradition," *The Massachusetts Review*, IV (Summer 1963), 745–67.

—— "Hart Crane's Visionary Lyrics," *The Massachusetts Review*, VII, 2 (Spring 1966).

Lowell, Robert. "The Art of Poetry: An Interview with Robert Lowell," *The Paris Review,* XXV (Spring 1961).

Marlowe, Christopher. *Five Plays.* Edited by Havelock Ellis. New York: Hill and Wang, Inc., 1956.

Martey, Herbert. "Hart Crane's 'The Broken Tower'," *The University of Kansas City Review,* XVIII (Spring 1952), 199–205.

Melville, Herman. *Moby Dick.* Indianapolis: Bobbs-Merrill, 1964.

Miles, Josephine. *Eras and Modes in English Poetry.* Berkeley and Los Angeles: University of California Press. 2nd edition revised and enlarged, 1964.

Miller, James E., Jr., Karl Shapiro and Bernice Slote. *Start With the Sun: Studies in Cosmic Poetry.* Lincoln: University of Nebraska Press, 1960.

Morris, H. C. "Crane's 'Voyages' as a Single Poem," *Accent,* XIV (Autumn 1954), 291–99.

Perry, Robert L. *The Shared Vision of Waldo Frank and Hart Crane.* University of Nebraska Studies, XXXIII. Lincoln: 1966.

Pound, Ezra. *The Selected Poems of Ezra Pound.* New York: New Directions Paperbook, 1957.

—— *The Literary Essays of Ezra Pound.* Edited by T. S. Eliot. Norfolk: New Directions, 1954.

Quinn, Sister M. Bernetta. *The Metamorphic Tradition in Modern Poetry.* New Brunswick: Rutgers University Press, 1955.

Quinn, Vincent. *Hart Crane.* New York: Twayne, 1963.

Ransom, John Crowe. *The World's Body.* New York: Charles Scribner's Sons, 1938.

Richards, I. A. *Principles of Literary Criticism.* New York: Harcourt, Brace and Company, 1928.

Rosenberg, Harold. *The Tradition of the New.* New York: Horizon Press Inc., 1959.

Rosenthal, M. L. *The Modern Poets: A Critical Introduction.* New York: Oxford University Press, 1960.

Rowe, H. D. *Hart Crane: A Bibliography.* Denver: Swallow, 1955.

Saintsbury, George. *A History of English Prosody from the Twelfth*

Century to the Present Day. 3 vols. New York: The Macmillan Company, 1906–1910.

Santayana, George. *Three Philosophical Poets.* Garden City: Anchor Books, 1953.

Schoonmaker, Frank. *Encyclopedia of Wine.* New York: Hastings House, 1965.

Sebeok, Thomas (editor). *Style in Language.* New York: John Wiley & Sons, 1960.

Shockley, Martin S. "Hart Crane's 'Lachrymae Christi'," *The University of Kansas City Review,* XVI (Autumn 1949), 31–36.

Simpson, Louis. "Dead Horses and Live Issues," *The Nation,* CCIV, 17 (April 24, 1967).

Spears, Monroe K. *Hart Crane.* University of Minnesota Pamphlets on American Writers, 47, Minneapolis: University of Minnesota Press, 1965.

Stevens, Wallace. *Opus Posthumous.* New York: Knopf, 1957.

Stewart, George R., Jr., *The Technique of English Verse.* New York: Henry Holt and Co., 1930.

Tate, Allen. *Collected Essays.* Denver: Swallow, 1959.

Taupin, Rene. *L'Influence du Symbolisme Francais sur la Poesie Amaricaine.* Paris: Librairie Ancienne Honore Champion, 1929.

Taylor, Frajan. "Keats and Crane: An Airy Citadel," *Accent,* VII (Autumn 1947), 34–40.

Thompson, John. *The Founding of English Metre.* New York: Columbia University Press, 1961.

Trachtenberg, Alan. *Brooklyn Bridge, Fact and Symbol.* New York: Oxford University Press, 1965.

Unterecker, John. "The Architecture of *The Bridge,*" *Wisconsin Studies in Contemporary Literature,* III (Spring-Summer 1962), 5–20.

Valery, Paul. *The Art of Poetry.* Translated by Denise Folliot. Bollingen Series, XLV–7. New York: Pantheon Books, 1958.

Van Doren, Mark. *Introduction to Poetry.* New York: William Sloane Associates, 1950.

Waggoner, Hyatt Howe. *The Heel of Elohim: Science and Values in Modern American Poetry*. Norman: University of Oklahoma Press, 1950.

Weber, Brom. *Hart Crane: A Biographical and Critical Study*. New York: Bodley Press, 1948.

Webster, John. *The Complete Works of John Webster*. Edited by F. L. Lucas. New York: Oxford University Press, 1937.

Williams, William Carlos. *The Autobiography of William Carlos Williams*. New York: Random House, 1951.

Wimsatt, W. K. Jr. *The Verbal Icon: Studies in the Meaning of Poetry*. Lexington, Ky.: University of Kentucky Press, 1954.

—— and Monroe Beardsley. "The Concept of Meter: An Exercise in Abstraction," *PMLA*, LXXIV (1959), 585–98.

Winters, Yvor. *In Defense of Reason*. New York: Swallow and Morrow, 1947.

Wordsworth, William. *Selected Poetry*. Edited by Mark Van Doren. New York: Random House, 1950.

Yeats, William Butler. *The Autobiography of William Butler Yeats*. Garden City: Anchor Books, 1958.

—— *The Collected Poems of William Butler Yeats*. New York: The Macmillan Company, 1956.

—— *Essays and Introductions*. New York: The Macmillan Company, 1961.

Index

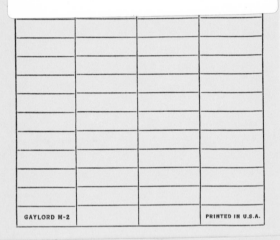